The Internet of Educational Things

Muralidhar Kurni • Srinivasa K. G.

The Internet of Educational Things

Enhancing Students' Engagement and Learning Performance

Springer

Muralidhar Kurni
Department of Computer Science
and Engineering
Anantha Lakshmi Institute of Technology
and Sciences
Anantapuramu, Andhra Pradesh, India

Srinivasa K. G.
Department of Data Science
and Artificial Intelligence
International Institute of Information
Technology
Naya Raipur, Chhattisgarh, India

ISBN 978-3-031-67386-3 ISBN 978-3-031-67387-0 (eBook)
https://doi.org/10.1007/978-3-031-67387-0

This Springer imprint is published by the registered company Springer Nature Switzerland AG
The registered company address is: Gewerbestrasse 11, 6330 Cham, Switzerland

Preface

Integrating technology is changing and revolutionizing traditional teaching methods and learning experiences in the ever-evolving field of education. *The Internet of Educational Things: Enhancing Students' Engagement and Learning Performance* delves into the transformative power of the Internet of Things (IoT) in reshaping educational settings. This book aims to inspire by offering an insight into how IoT contributes to creating learning environments that are not just interactive, adaptive, and data-focused but also futuristic. It serves as a beacon of knowledge for students, teachers, scholars, researchers, and professionals in the future of education. By exploring applications and theoretical frameworks of IoT in education, this book strives to connect technology with teaching practices by providing innovative tips and strategies to enhance student engagement and academic success.

The book's content is designed to be practical and applicable. It covers developing IoT-enabled classrooms, implementing intelligent tutoring systems, and integrating online labs and remote experiments. Each chapter is enriched with real-world examples and case studies highlighting the benefits and challenges of incorporating IoT in educational setups. Moreover, it addresses critical issues such as data privacy, cybersecurity concerns, and ethical considerations, providing a comprehensive understanding of the implications of IoT in education. The ultimate aim is to equip educators, policymakers, and tech innovators with the knowledge and resources to establish secure IoT-driven educational environments. This book is a call to action, encouraging creativity and promoting a collaborative effort in reshaping education for the digital era.

Organization of the Book

Chapter 1 delves into how IoT revolutionizes adaptable, efficient learning environments by incorporating tools such as sensors and smart projectors. It improves school management, data monitoring, and individualized assistance while tackling issues related to privacy, security, and implementation challenges.

Chapter 2 presents Smart Learning Environments (SLEs) powered by IoT technology, highlighting the importance of connectivity, data analysis, and automation in customizing learning experiences. It also emphasizes enhancing security measures, sustainability practices, and decision-making processes through real-world illustrations.

Chapter 3 showcases the shift from traditional classrooms to IoT-enabled smart classrooms that prioritize personalized learning journeys, heightened student engagement levels, real-time supervision capabilities, and strategies to address concerns regarding security, privacy protection, and implementation hurdles.

Chapter 4 explores IoT's influence on education through IoT-driven hardware solutions like smart classrooms, software platforms such as Learning Management Systems (LMS), and educational applications. The focus is on cybersecurity measures and the integration of cutting-edge technologies, like Artificial Intelligence (AI) and Augmented/Virtual Reality (AR/VR).

Chapter 5 delves into how IoT and network infrastructure improve learning experiences, personalized learning, and assessment methods in Smart Education. It also addresses the challenges related to connectivity, scalability, and security.

Chapter 6 explores the integration of Intelligent Tutoring Systems (ITS), Augmented Reality (AR), Virtual Reality (VR), and IoT in education to enrich personalized learning, student engagement, and adaptive instruction. It includes case studies and future trends in this area.

Chapter 7 examines the development of online laboratories improved by IoT technology. It emphasizes accessibility, affordability, real-time data collection, and practical implementation strategies through real-world examples.

Chapter 8 discusses IoT influences remote learning data analysis practices and upcoming trends. The focus is on creating inclusive, globally connected learning environments while addressing challenges related to data security, integration issues, and accessibility.

Chapter 9 investigates using IoT-enabled experiments and assessments for remote learning, especially in STEM fields. It focuses on hands-on learning, assessment techniques, practical illustrations, and upcoming trends in education using IoT technology.

Chapter 10 explores how IoT-powered gamification transforms learning experiences by emphasizing real-time data analysis, personalized learning paths, and practical hurdles. It also delves into future directions and strategies for incorporating this approach into the curriculum.

Chapter 11 delves into the use of IoT technology in educational environments, focusing on implementing security best practices, real-world applications, and future trends. It provides insights into planning strategies, risk assessment procedures, and maintaining secure IoT systems within classroom settings.

Chapter 12 delves into how IoT technologies enhance students' critical thinking abilities by promoting problem-solving skills, decision-making processes, and collaborative learning. It underscores the importance of data analysis, real-time feedback mechanisms, and ethical considerations within an educational context.

Chapter 13 explores the dimensions of employing IoT technologies in education, including issues related to privacy protection, data security measures, obtaining informed consent from stakeholders, and ensuring accountability. It recommends enhancing the deployment of IoT solutions while upholding ethical standards in educational settings.

Appendix A focuses on how simulation contributes to hands-on learning and improving skills. It delves into ways of incorporating simulations utilizing IoT advancements and presents a real-life example of applying IoT technology to enhance participation and comprehension in high school physics teaching.

Appendix B delves into the concept of digital twins within education, discussing how they are utilized in learning settings, virtual laboratories, and campus administration. A case study from Monash University showcases their influence on learning outcomes.

Key Features of the Book

- The book delves deeply into how IoT is used in various educational environments.
- It discusses ways to protect data and ensure the security of IoT systems.
- The focus is developing interactive, adaptable, and data-centred learning spaces.
- It also emphasizes incorporating AI, AR, VR, and digital twins in IoT education.
- Moreover, the book offers practical tips for incorporating IoT into educational scenarios.

Anantapuramu, Andhra Pradesh, India — Muralidhar Kurni
Naya Raipur, Chhattisgarh, India — Srinivasa K. G.

Acknowledgments

Muralidhar would like to thank his mother P. Sanjeevamma, friends Dr. Mujeeb Shaik Mohammed, Thanooj, and K. Somasena Reddy, and his students K. Shahir Basha and K. Anusha for their wholehearted support in completing this book.

Srinivasa would like to thank Dr. Pradeep K. Sinha, Vice Chancellor and Director, IIIT Naya Raipur, for his kind encouragement for publishing this book. He also would like to thank all IIIT Naya Raipur faculty members for their wholehearted support in publishing this book.

Contents

Chapter 1
IoT for Education

Abstract The rise of the Internet of Things (IoT) is changing various industries, and education is one area that is benefiting greatly. IoT, which connects devices and systems, is improving homes and healthcare and transforming modern education. This chapter explores how IoT can create a technology-focused learning environment that's more adaptable, efficient, and tailored to needs. Educational institutions can establish an ecosystem that promotes communication and collaboration by incorporating tools like sensors, smart projectors, and wearable technology. The chapter looks at how IoT can gather real-time data on student performance, enabling personalized support and optimizing resource allocation through smart campus management. It points out the difficulties in education without IoT, such as outdated teaching materials, lack of student engagement in class, and resource management. On the other hand, integrating IoT into education brings benefits like enhanced school administration efficiency, data tracking capabilities, and global connectivity. Moreover, the chapter explores IoT technologies used in education—including RFID systems, sensors, smart gadgets, and cloud computing—and their practical applications. It provides examples of real-world implementations across educational levels to demonstrate the advantages of smart classrooms, distance learning solutions, and data-informed decision-making. The chapter also discusses the difficulties of incorporating IoT in education, including worries about privacy and security, financial implications, infrastructure preparedness, and the necessity of training staff. Finally, this chapter offers suggestions for merging IoT into educational environments, highlighting the significance of gradual rollouts, professional growth initiatives, and embracing universal design concepts. By integrating IoT technology, educational institutions can establish a cutting-edge learning atmosphere that equips students for the future while prioritizing inclusivity and ethical standards.

Keywords Internet of Things (IoT) · Technology-focused learning · Smart campus management · Personalized support · Data tracking capabilities · Smart classrooms · Privacy and security

M. Kurni, Srinivasa K. G., *The Internet of Educational Things*,
https://doi.org/10.1007/978-3-031-67387-0_1

1.1 Introduction to IoT in Education

The advent of the Internet of Things (IoT), a network of interconnected devices and systems, is revolutionizing various sectors. IoT is not just limited to smart homes or advanced healthcare; its potential is rooted in modern education. As learning environments worldwide lean towards technology-driven solutions, understanding how IoT in education revolutionizes learning becomes essential. This network of smart devices promises to enhance the quality of learning and revolutionize traditional teaching by making methods more responsive, efficient, and personalized (Aucott, 2023; Thomas, 2022; Cohen, 2020). Let us explore how IoT sets the stage for a brighter, more interconnected future in education.

What Is IoT? The Internet of Things (IoT) is a game-changing concept that allows physical devices to connect to the Internet, enabling them to gather and exchange data (Aucott, 2023; IBM, 2022; AWS, 2022; Cisco Systems, 2022; Oracle, 2023). These devices can range in education from sensors and wearable technology to displays and interconnected infrastructure. By harnessing the potential of IoT, educational institutions can establish an ecosystem that fosters smooth communication and collaboration (Aucott, 2023).

In education, IoT devices encompass a range of tools such as smart projectors, interactive whiteboards, temperature sensors, attendance trackers, and even wearable gadgets that monitor students' physical activity or level of engagement. The information generated by these devices can be analyzed to gain insights into student behavior and learning patterns and the overall effectiveness of educational processes (Aucott, 2023).

The Role of IoT in Education The use of IoT in education enhances the learning experience. One crucial aspect is the ability to collect real-time data on how students perform and engage with their studies. For instance, smart devices can monitor how students interact with educational materials, identify areas where they need help, and provide personalized interventions to address their learning needs (Arduino Education, 2024).

Furthermore, IoT enables the development of smart campuses, where interconnected systems optimize resource usage, energy efficiency, and security. IoT technologies streamline administrative processes, from lighting and climate control to automated attendance tracking, freeing educators to focus more on teaching than manual tasks (Intuz, 2023).

Education Without IoT Integrating the Internet of Things (IoT) in the education industry is an advancement. Exploring the obstacles the education sector encounters without integration is essential to grasp its importance fully.

Without the presence of IoT (see Fig. 1.1), the field of education faces difficulties and obstacles (Macharla, 2020):

Fig. 1.1 Education without IoT

- ***Outdated Curriculum:*** Numerous educational institutions follow curricula that overlook elements necessary for the future in our fast-changing technological world. Apart from the subjects, allocating time and resources to students' essential skills, including creativity, logical thinking, problem-solving abilities, ethical understanding, and other fundamental prerequisites, is crucial for thriving in a competitive global environment. Neglecting the integration of these skills can result in students being equipped to meet the evolving demands of the job market.
- ***Standardized exams:*** While standardized tests are designed to evaluate students' abilities and knowledge, they often fail to capture their capabilities. Focusing on these exams can create stress and a fear of not performing while neglecting essential skills like creativity and problem-solving. As a result, these tests may not assess students' overall learning journey.
- ***Low Classroom Engagement:*** Outdated teaching techniques impact students' focus and engagement, making it difficult for teachers to keep up with trends and tailor their instruction. Successful teaching goes beyond delivering information; it involves using approaches that capture students' attention and enhance their learning experiences.

While these observations may not apply to every situation, they have often encountered challenges. As technology advances, we have seen progress in teaching methods, allowing for communication between students and teachers. This progress promotes a learning experience. Integrating the Internet of Things (IoT) expands learning beyond textbooks, allowing students to gain knowledge and develop skills. IoT assists in monitoring classrooms efficiently and offers vital support for individuals with disabilities.

Education with IoT The inclusion of Internet of Things (IoT) technology has brought about a fast-forward age of intelligence in educational environments, revolutionizing classrooms and libraries into smart learning spaces.

Integrating IoT into education (see Fig. 1.2) has benefits (Macharla, 2020).

Fig. 1.2 Education with IoT

- ***Improved School Management Efficiency:*** The Internet of Things (IoT) provides a secure alternative to fashioned paperwork, making supply management and fund distribution more efficient. It creates a decision-making system that involves students, teachers, parents, and other stakeholders, leading to enhancements in educational facilities.
- ***Real-time Data Collection:*** The Internet of Things (IoT) allows for handling data volumes, enabling various applications such as tracking safety and monitoring progress. It also provides insights into teachers' areas of expertise. This capability enhances the testing and grading system while promoting methods to enhance classroom involvement.
- ***Improved Resource Management:*** Technology reduces operational and storage expenses while improving efficiency. It offers monitoring tools for tracking energy consumption, power usage, and water utilization in institutions that promote sustainability and resource efficiency.
- ***Global Interconnection:*** The Internet of Things (IoT) makes it easier for teachers to create and maintain teaching practices. It allows them to share resources, exchange ideas, and enhance their teaching methods on a large scale. This interconnectedness promotes collaboration and continuous improvement in the field of education.

IoT Can Solve Problems in the Education Industry Incorporating the Internet of Things (IoT) into education offers a potent solution to the industry's challenges before IoT became prevalent. These challenges included outdated teaching methods, a lack of feedback, and limited access to learning materials. With the introduction of IoT, everything changed (Soni, 2023).

- ***Outdated Teaching Methods:*** In the past, education heavily relied on traditional teaching approaches that followed a one-size-fits-all model. However, IoT revolutionizes this by enabling adaptive learning experiences. Teachers can customize their methods based on real-time student progress data, ensuring an effective and engaging journey.

- ***Lack of Immediate Feedback:*** Waiting for assessments and grades to assess student performance was a limitation in the traditional education system. IoT bridges this gap by providing real-time feedback. With connected devices and sensors, educators can monitor student progress in time, allowing for timely interventions and adjustments in teaching methods to address individual needs.
- ***Limited Access to Learning Resources:*** IoT transforms the accessibility of learning resources. Previously, students were restricted to resources within the confines of their school or library. With the Internet of Things (IoT), the digital world offers an expansive knowledge landscape. Students can access a wealth of information through cloud-based platforms, online repositories, and interconnected devices without being limited by geography or resource constraints.
- ***Inefficient resource management:*** One challenge IoT helps overcome is inefficient resource management. Tasks like attendance tracking, inventory management, and energy consumption optimization used to be labor-intensive. However, with IoT, these processes are automated. RFID technology seamlessly tracks attendance, smart devices manage inventory, and sensors optimize building energy usage. This not only saves time but also reduces operational costs.
- ***Limited Interactivity:*** Another traditional classroom limitation that IoT addresses is limited interactivity. By leveraging technologies, classrooms become dynamic spaces where real-time collaboration is the norm. Interactive whiteboards, connected devices, and virtual discussions break physical classroom barriers and create a more engaging and participatory learning environment.

IoT in education catalyzes overcoming longstanding education industry challenges. It brings efficiency, personalization, and real-time insights to the forefront of education. The problems that once hindered progress are now seen as opportunities for innovation and growth.

Technologies Used for Integrating IoT in Education The education sector has witnessed the integration of the Internet of Things (IoT) with sophisticated technologies. These technologies work together to create an intelligent ecosystem that enhances the learning experience (Macharla, 2020).

- ***RFID Technology:*** Radio Frequency Identification (RFID) is an educational IoT technology. It utilizes RFID tags to track and manage various aspects, including student attendance. Using RFID-enabled student cards automates attendance tracking, saving teaching time while ensuring accurate attendance data.
- ***Sensors and Actuators:*** Sensors capture real-time data within educational environments. They can monitor environmental conditions, track resource usage, and assess student engagement. Actuators enable actions based on the collected data, leading to a dynamic and adaptive learning environment.
- ***Smart Devices:*** The widespread use of tablets, laptops, and interactive whiteboards has transformed traditional classrooms into smart classrooms. These

devices facilitate real-time collaboration, interactive learning experiences, and personalized content delivery.

- ***Cloud Computing:*** Cloud computing plays a vital role in education, providing an easily accessible platform for storing, processing, and analyzing data. This technology allows educators and students to access learning materials from anywhere, creating a collaborative and flexible learning environment.
- ***Machine Learning (ML) and Artificial Intelligence (AI):*** ML and AI play vital roles in analyzing the amounts of data generated by IoT devices. These advanced technologies enable the development of adaptive learning platforms that customize educational content according to each student's needs. This personalized approach enhances the effectiveness of learning experiences.
- ***Connectivity Protocols:*** Various connectivity protocols, such as Wi-Fi, Bluetooth, and Zigbee, facilitate IoT device communication. These protocols ensure that IoT devices can exchange data and insights, creating an interconnected educational ecosystem.
- ***Data Analytics:*** Using advanced analytics tools, educators can harness the data from IoT devices to gain valuable insights into student performance, learning patterns, and resource utilization. This data-driven approach enhances decision-making processes and facilitates improvement in teaching methodologies.

The technologies supporting IoT in education create an infrastructure beyond connectivity. Integrating RFID technology, sensors, smart devices, cloud computing, machine learning algorithms, connectivity protocols, and data analytics work to establish an interactive educational setting that aims to improve the learning experience for students and educators.

Benefits of IoT in Education Smart classrooms with Internet of Things (IoT) devices enhance the learning environment by creating interactive spaces. Students are encouraged to collaborate and actively participate in their education through interactive displays, connected tablets, and other technologies (Intuz, 2023). Figure 1.3 highlights the benefits of IoT in education.

- ***Data-driven Decision-Making:*** One of the benefits of IoT in education is data-driven decision-making. The abundance of data collected from IoT devices enables educators and administrators to make evidence-based decisions. This includes identifying areas for curriculum improvement and assessing the effectiveness of teaching methods. By leveraging data analytics, educational strategies can be shaped effectively.
- ***Efficient Campus Management:*** Efficiency in campus management is another advantage IoT brings. Automated systems for maintenance, security, and energy usage contribute to cost reduction and a more sustainable and environmentally conscious educational ecosystem.
- ***Accessibility and Inclusivity:*** IoT technologies can be tailored to meet learning needs, promoting accessibility and inclusivity in education. For example, smart devices with accessibility features benefit students with disabilities, ensuring that education remains accessible to all.

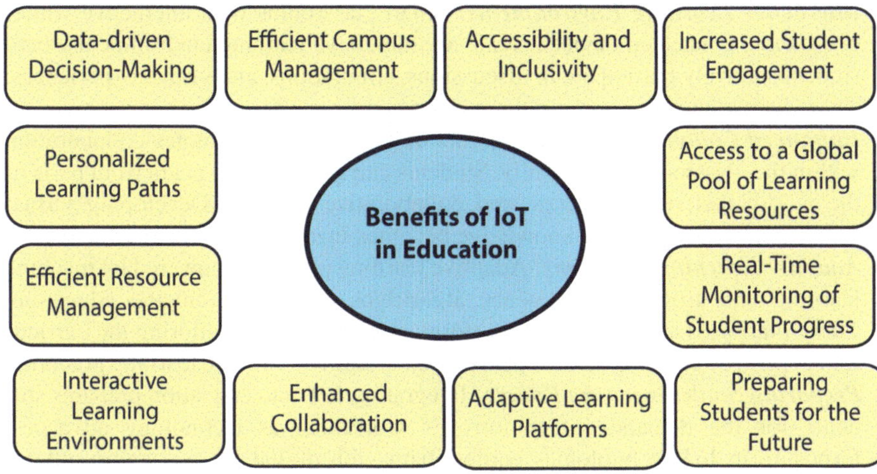

Fig. 1.3 Benefits of IoT in education

- ***Increased Student Engagement:*** IoT enhances student engagement by transforming classrooms into interactive spaces. Smart devices, interactive whiteboards, and real-time collaboration tools capture students' attention and encourage participation, leading to a learning experience beyond traditional teaching methods' limitations.
- ***Personalized Learning Paths:*** With the advent of IoT, traditional one-size-fits-all educational approaches are becoming outdated. By leveraging data collected from sensors and smart devices, educators can gain insights into individual learning styles, preferences, and progress. This wealth of information empowers them to customize learning paths for each student, ensuring their education is tailored to their unique needs.
- ***Efficient Resource Management:*** IoT benefits resource management in educational institutions. From automated attendance tracking using RFID technology to energy management in buildings, this technology streamlines operations and saves time and costs. As a result, educators can dedicate more time to teaching than administrative tasks.
- ***Real-Time Monitoring of Student Progress:*** The days of waiting for test results to assess student performance are gone. Thanks to IoTs' real-time monitoring capabilities through connected devices and sensors, educators can instantly track individual achievements and challenges. This allows for interventions and adjustments in teaching strategies based on student progress.
- ***Access to a Global Pool of Learning Resources:*** Cloud-based platforms and online repositories provide students with access to an array of learning resources beyond the traditional confines of libraries. Whether eBooks, multimedia content, or collaborative tools, IoT ensures that educational materials are readily available, breaking down geographical barriers.

- ***Interactive Learning Environments:*** Smart classrooms with interactive whiteboards and connected devices create an immersive learning environment where students actively participate in discussions, simulations, and virtual experiences. These hands-on activities help them grasp concepts effectively.
- ***Enhanced Collaboration:*** The Internet of Things (IoT) promotes collaboration within the classroom and globally. Students can connect with peers from parts of the world, fostering exchange and collaborative projects. Developing virtual teamwork skills alongside knowledge becomes invaluable.
- ***Adaptive Learning Platforms:*** Adaptive learning platforms powered by machine learning and artificial intelligence algorithms are revolutionizing education. These platforms analyze student performance data in time, tailoring the curriculum to provide challenge and support for each student's unique learning potential.
- ***Preparing Students for the Future:*** Integrating IoT into education prepares students for the demands of tomorrow's workforce as technology advances. Exposure to IoT technologies equips them with digital literacy and problem-solving skills that are increasingly crucial in our tech-driven world.

1.2 IoT Devices and Technologies

IoT devices and technologies have grown in education, improving effectiveness, automation, and data-informed decision-making. Let us explore some elements of IoT devices and technologies (Kumar et al., 2019; Meylani, 2024)

Sensors and Actuators

Definition and Functionality Internet of Things (IoT) devices often rely on sensors and actuators to collect and respond to data in education. Sensors, such as measuring temperature, detecting motion, or gauging light levels, gather information from the surroundings. On the other hand, actuators take action based on the received data. In an educational setting, these components collaborate to create responsive learning environments.

Applications in Education

- ***Smart Lighting and Climate Control:*** Sensors can adjust lighting and climate conditions based on occupancy levels to create comfortable classrooms while efficiently conserving energy.
- ***Attendance Tracking:*** Motion sensors combined with facial recognition technology can automate attendance tracking processes, alleviating burdens for educators.

- ***Interactive Learning Tools:*** Actuators can be integrated into interactive displays, enabling students to interact with educational content.

Wearable Devices

Wearables in Education Wearable devices like smartwatches and fitness trackers offer possibilities for enhancing the educational experience. These devices can track students' physical activity, monitor their health metrics, and even provide feedback on their level of involvement.

Educational Applications

- ***Health and Wellness:*** Wearables can promote student well-being by encouraging physical activity and monitoring stress levels, contributing to a holistic approach to education.
- ***Real-Time Feedback:*** Providing feedback on student engagement and participation can inform teaching strategies, enabling educators to adapt their methods for optimal learning outcomes.

Smart Classrooms

Definition and Components Smart classrooms are designed to create a collaborative learning environment by integrating IoT devices and technologies. These include interactive displays, connected projectors, and communication tools facilitating information sharing.

Benefits for Education

- ***Enhanced Collaboration:*** Smart classrooms promote collaboration through interactive displays, allowing students to share content in time and work together to solve problems.
- ***Personalized Learning:*** IoT in smart classrooms enables personalized learning experiences tailored to individual learning styles and preferences.

Data Analytics and Machine Learning

Leveraging Data in Education Data collected from IoT devices in education holds value when adequately analyzed. Using data analytics tools alongside machine learning algorithms can gain valuable insights regarding student performance and learning patterns. Recommendations for improvements can be offered.

Applications and Considerations

- ***Predictive Analytics:*** Machine learning algorithms can predict student success rates and identify areas where students may need additional support, enabling timely interventions.
- ***Adaptive Learning Platforms:*** Personalized learning platforms leverage machine learning techniques to adapt content delivery methods and teaching strategies based on each student's progress.

1.3 IoT Applications in Education

The Internet of Things (IoT) can revolutionize education by introducing solutions that enhance the learning experience, improve efficiency, and create opportunities for educators and students. Here are several ways in which IoT can be applied in education (Intuz, 2023; Appsierra, 2023).

Smart Campus Management

Definition and Components A smart campus utilizes IoT technologies to optimize educational institution management. This involves integrating sensors, connected devices, and data analytics to improve resource allocation, streamline processes, and enhance campus operations' efficiency.

Applications and Benefits

- ***Energy Management:*** Smart campuses can effectively monitor and manage energy usage in time, reducing costs and contributing to sustainability initiatives.
- ***Facility Maintenance:*** Sensors that detect issues can be utilized to take proactive maintenance measures to minimize disruptions to campus activities.

- ***Space Utilization:*** Data on occupancy and space utilization aid in optimizing classroom scheduling and ensuring facility utilization.

Personalized Learning

Customizing Education with IoT Personalized learning involves tailoring experiences based on individual student needs, preferences, and learning styles. IoT plays a vital role in collecting and analyzing data to create adaptive learning environments.

Applications and Impacts

- ***Adaptive Content Delivery:*** IoT devices track students' progress and adjust learning materials in time. This allows for content that matches each student's pace and level of understanding.
- ***Gamification and Engagement:*** Learning platforms incorporating gamification leverage IoT data to create interactive and captivating educational experiences that encourage active participation.

Remote Learning and Virtual Labs

Enabling Education from a Distance The emergence of IoT has impacted learning by offering tools and technologies that bridge the physical gap between students and educators.

Applications and Innovations

- ***Virtual Laboratories:*** IoT can help create virtual labs, enabling students to conduct experiments and simulations remotely.
- ***Collaborative Tools:*** Connected devices facilitate real-time collaboration, making remote learning experiences more interactive and engaging.

Campus Safety and Security

Enhancing Safety Measures on Campus IoT enhances campus safety by providing real-time monitoring, surveillance, and emergency response systems.

Applications and Technologies

- ***Surveillance and Monitoring:*** Smart cameras and sensors enhance campus security by monitoring key areas for unusual activities.
- ***Emergency Alert Systems:*** IoT-based alert systems instantly notify individuals in emergencies, ensuring a prompt and well-coordinated response.

Education Accessibility

Creating Inclusive Learning Environments Internet of Things (IoT) technologies can be customized to establish inclusive learning environments that cater to the needs of students with requirements.

Practical Applications and Considerations

- ***Assisting Students with Disabilities:*** Tailored IoT devices support students with disabilities, promoting an inclusive educational experience.
- ***Analyzing Accessibility:*** Data analytics help identify areas for enhancement of accessibility, ensuring that educational resources are accessible to all students.

1.4 Examples of IoT Implementations at Various Levels of Education

The following are some examples of IoT implementations at various levels of education (Dewhirst, 2021; Cogniteq, 2023).

IoT Implementation in K-12 Education

Smart Classrooms and Personalized Learning IoT has brought about a revolutionary transformation in traditional classrooms within K12 education. For example, schools have started integrating smart boards and connected devices to create interactive learning spaces. These technologies enable teachers to customize lessons based on real-time data, adjusting the pace and content to meet each student's needs. As a result, student engagement and performance are improved, and a dynamic learning environment has increased.

Remote Learning Solutions IoT played a vital role in ensuring educational continuity during the transition to remote learning. A school can provide students with IoT-enabled devices in a region by collaborating with telecom providers to ensure uninterrupted internet connectivity and seamless remote learning experiences. Teachers can utilize remote labs and collaborative tools to conduct lessons successfully. The success of this implementation demonstrates how the adaptability of IoT can address unforeseen challenges.

IoT in Higher Education Institutions

Campus Management and Sustainability Higher education institutions can leverage IoT for campus management and sustainability practices by deploying sensors across campus buildings to optimize energy usage, reduce costs, and minimize impact.

Furthermore, implementing IoT-based maintenance systems has been instrumental in reducing equipment downtime and ensuring the functioning of academic operations. This initiative's success highlights IoT's potential to transform traditional education campuses into intelligent and sustainable environments.

Data-Driven Decision-Making A university can leverage IoT to enhance its processes in data-driven decision-making. By incorporating IoT devices in laboratories and lecture halls, the university can gather data on equipment usage, student attendance, and facility utilization. Analyzing this data offers valuable insights that enable administrators to optimize resource allocation, improve teaching methodologies, and enhance students' academic experiences.

Success Stories and Best Practices

Inclusive Learning Environments Success stories and best practices have been related to implementing IoT technologies to create inclusive learning environments. Schools and universities worldwide have customized devices to cater to students with diverse needs, fostering an environment where every learner can thrive. These success stories underscore the significance of considering inclusivity when designing and implementing IoT solutions in education.

Collaborative Learning Platforms Educational institutions have recognized the importance of collaborative skills by adopting learning platforms driven by IoT. These platforms facilitate real-time communication, file sharing, and group activities that foster a sense of community among students. To fully harness the advantages of these tools, it is crucial to prioritize user interfaces, maintain secure data transmission, and provide continuous training for educators.

1.5 Challenges and Considerations

Although the education sector gains advantages from implementing IoT, there are challenges to consider. We outline some considerations for integrating IoT into education (Oliynyk, 2024; IoT MAG, 2024).

Privacy and Security Concerns

Risks to Data Privacy One hurdle in incorporating IoT in education is compromising student and staff data. Since information like attendance records, learning patterns, and personal details are collected, institutions must prioritize data encryption, secure storage practices, and compliance with data protection regulations. Addressing these concerns is vital for maintaining trust among stakeholders and ensuring ethical data usage.

Cybersecurity Threats The interconnected nature of IoT devices introduces vulnerabilities that malicious actors may exploit. Educational institutions must implement cybersecurity measures such as firewalls, intrusion detection systems, and regular security audits. Moreover, educating users about cybersecurity practices is essential for preventing access and data breaches.

Cost and Infrastructure

Initial Investment While long-term benefits are associated with adopting IoT in education, one significant challenge is the investment required. Installing IoT devices, ensuring network connectivity, and training staff all demand substantial financial resources. Institutions must evaluate their limitations and create a well-planned approach to manage costs effectively.

Infrastructure Readiness The success of IoT heavily relies on having a scalable infrastructure, including high-speed Internet, sufficient bandwidth, and compatible devices. Educational institutions may face difficulties providing IoT experience in areas without adequate infrastructure. Collaborating with governments, telecom providers, and technology partners is crucial to address these infrastructure limitations.

Integration with Existing Systems

Compatibility Issues Many educational institutions already have systems and technologies that may not seamlessly integrate with IoT devices. To avoid disruptions to operations and maximize the benefits of implementation, it is essential to ensure compatibility and interoperability between new IoT solutions and established systems.

Staff Training and Acceptance Successful IoT integration in education requires a skilled workforce capable of using and maintaining these technologies. Comprehensive training programs for educators and administrative staff are vital. Additionally, fostering a culture of acceptance and adaptability is necessary to overcome resistance to change and ensure the adoption of IoT solutions.

Ethical Considerations

Bias in Data Analytics Data generated by IoT devices can inadvertently perpetuate biases if not handled carefully. Machine learning algorithms, for instance, can reflect existing biases in data. Educational institutions must recognize and minimize biases in data analytics to ensure that all students are treated fairly and receive equal opportunities.

Digital Divide One particular concern is the potential for a digital divide to be exacerbated by adopting IoT (Internet of Things) technology in education. This could create a situation where some students can access technologies while others do not. To tackle this issue, institutions should develop strategies, such as providing devices to underserved communities and ensuring everyone can access digital resources.

1.6 Future Innovations

This section will explore the trends and advancements shaping education technology. We will specifically focus on how 5G technology is vital in connecting Internet of Things (IoT) devices for education. We will also explore how edge computing affects processing and privacy in the context of education. Additionally, we will discuss how IoT can be integrated with augmented and virtual reality (AR/VR) to enhance the learning experience. The following sections will provide recommendations for implementing IoT in education and address regulatory and ethical considerations. Offer additional resources for further exploration. By keeping up with these developments, educational institutions can embrace innovation to create an advanced learning environment.

The Impact of 5G on IoT in Education Here, we delve into the influence of 5G technology on education about the Internet of Things (IoT). In particular, we explore the advancements in connectivity and explore uses such as virtual laboratories and augmented reality (Chandran, 2023; Eklavvya, 2023).

Enhanced Connectivity The widespread adoption of 5G technology is set to transform IoT in education. With the speed and reduced latency of 5G networks, device connectivity becomes more seamless. This means data transfer happens quicker, facilitating real-time collaboration and providing user experiences in virtual labs and augmented reality.

Accessible for All 5 G's coverage and enhanced connectivity capabilities are crucial in bridging the digital divide within education. Educational institutions in underserved areas can leverage 5G networks to ensure students can access quality educational resources that foster an inclusive learning environment.

Edge Computing Role in Education Here, we will explore how Edge Computing revolutionizes education technology (ASUSTeK Computer Inc., 2023; Bonderud, 2021).

Localized Data Processing Edge computing involves processing data to where it originates rather than depending solely on centralized cloud servers. In the context of education, IoT devices can process and analyze data locally, reducing delay and improving responsiveness in real-time scenarios. This is particularly advantageous for applications requiring instant feedback, such as adaptive learning platforms.

Privacy and Security Considerations Another benefit of edge computing is that it addresses privacy and security concerns by minimizing the need to transmit data over distances. Localized processing ensures that crucial information remains within the institution's network, reducing the chances of data breaches and unauthorized access.

IoT and Augmented/Virtual Reality This section explores integrating IoT technology with augmented and virtual reality (AR/VR) in education (Yashika, 2023; Telnet Nigeria Limited, 2023).

Enhancing Learning Experiences with Immersion Integrating IoT with augmented reality (AR) and virtual reality (VR) offers possibilities for creating immersive learning experiences. Smart devices can collaborate with AR and VR applications to provide contextual information, simulations, and hands-on learning opportunities, enhancing the educational journey.

Learning Through Simulations IoT-powered AR and VR applications enable learners to use simulation-based learning scenarios. For instance, aspiring medical professionals can practice surgical procedures virtually, improving their skills in a safe setting. This trend has the potential to revolutionize practical training across fields.

1.7 Recommendations for Incorporating IoT in Education

In this section, we present suggestions to ensure the integration of IoT in education. To begin with, it is essential to conduct an assessment of needs and implement the process in phases. Additionally, we emphasize the significance of training staff members to establish data policies, foster expertise in analytics, and engage stakeholders collaboratively. Furthermore, we highlight the importance of considering accessibility and universal design principles. Moving forward, we delve into ethical aspects that educational institutions should consider. When implementing solutions, it is crucial to prioritize privacy, security, and inclusivity.

Developing a Plan for IoT Implementation This section offers guidance to institutions on integrating IoT into their educational systems.

Assessing Needs Before introducing IoT in education, educational institutions should conduct an assessment to identify challenges, areas that need improvement, and goals that can be addressed through IoT adoption. This step ensures that the integration aligns with the institution's objectives.

Phased Implementations Institutions should consider implementing IoT in phases, considering its complexity and potential costs. Starting with pilot projects in departments or classrooms allows for assessing feasibility, gathering feedback, and making adjustments before expanding its implementation throughout the institution.

Training and Development for Staff This section emphasizes the significance of training staff members. We advocate implementing professional development programs and fostering a continuous learning culture. These initiatives aim to equip educators with IoT (Internet of Things) skills and enable them to adapt to the ever-changing technological landscape. The ultimate goal is to facilitate the integration of IoT technology into education.

Professional Development Programs Investing in comprehensive professional development programs is crucial to empower educators and staff with the necessary skills to utilize IoT technologies effectively. These programs should cover the usage of IoT devices, data analysis tools, and best practices for integrating IoT into teaching methods.

Cultivating a Culture of Continuous Learning Encouraging ongoing training opportunities and fostering a continuous learning culture is essential as technology advances rapidly within education settings. Educators must have the knowledge and skills to adapt to IoT applications in education while maximizing its benefits.

Managing and Analyzing Data This section delves into managing and analyzing education data driven by the Internet of Things (IoT). We emphasize the significance of having ethical data policies and expertise in data analytics to effectively handle the complexities involved in collecting, storing, and utilizing student and staff data while ensuring compliance with data protection regulations.

Communicating Data Policies Establish data policies that effectively convey how student and staff data will be collected, stored, and utilized. Comply with data protection regulations and prioritize the privacy and security of information.

Developing Expertise in Analytics Cultivate expertise in data analytics to derive insights from the amount of data generated by IoT devices. This may involve hiring data analysts, collaborating with external experts, or training existing staff members to enhance their data analysis skills.

Collaboration and Engaging Stakeholders This section highlights the importance of collaboration and involving stakeholders in integrating IoT for education. It emphasizes the need for departments to work together and engage with the learning community to create an inclusive approach.

Promoting Collaboration Across Departments Foster collaboration among departments within the institution as IoT implementation often involves stakeholders such as IT departments, educators, administrators, and facilities management teams. Establish channels of communication to ensure an integrated approach.

Engaging the Educational Community Engage with an educational community, including students, parents, and local communities, in decision-making processes related to IoT implementation projects. Seek feedback to address concerns. Ensure that the adoption aligns with all stakeholders' values and expectations.

Accessibility for All Students This section focuses on making IoT integration in education accessible and inclusive. The emphasis is placed on adopting Universal Design Principles and Digital Literacy Programs to guarantee access for all students and encourage digital behavior.

Embracing Universal Design Principles Implement IoT applications using universal design principles to guarantee accessibility for students with diverse learning needs. Consider aspects such as ease of use, adaptability, and versatility to accommodate various abilities.

Digital Literacy Programs Implementing initiatives that focus on equipping students with technology skills is essential. These programs should cover topics such as using IoT devices, critically evaluating digital content, and promoting responsible and ethical behavior in the online world.

1.8 Regulatory and Ethical Considerations

In the evolving realm of technology, incorporating Internet of Things (IoT) technologies brings forth various prospects and obstacles. Educational institutions face the task of embracing IoT while considering ethical factors. This segment delves into ensuring compliance with data protection regulations, safeguarding student privacy, promoting inclusivity, and nurturing a sense of digital citizenship.

Compliance with Data Protection Regulations This section stresses the importance of following data protection regulations, such as GDPR and FERPA (New America, 2023; eTech Consultancy, 2017), in the field of educational technology and the integration of IoT. It highlights the importance of being transparent, obtaining consent, and implementing strong security measures to protect the privacy of students and staff.

General Data Protection Regulation (GDPR) Educational institutions incorporating IoT technologies must adhere to data protection regulations like GDPR. Data practices must obtain informed consent when necessary and establish security measures to safeguard the privacy of students and staff.

Family Educational Rights and Privacy Act (FERPA) In the United States, it is crucial to comply with FERPA regulations. FERPA governs the disclosure of student records. Requires institutions to protect sensitive information appropriately. When implementing IoT solutions, institutions should ensure that data collection and storage align with FERPA guidelines.

Student Privacy This section highlights the significance of protecting students' privacy when implementing IoT in educational settings (El-Haggar et al., 2023; Wambua, 2024).

Anonymization and De-identification Implementing techniques that anonymize and de-identify data is essential to safeguard student privacy. The goal is to collect and store information to prevent students from being identified, thus reducing the risk of privacy breaches.

Consent and Transparency Obtaining informed consent from students and their parents or guardians regarding data collection and use through IoT devices is crucial in maintaining ethical practices in education technology initiatives. Transparent communication about the purpose, scope, and implications of data collection builds trust among stakeholders.

Inclusivity and Accessibility This section focuses on the role of creating inclusive solutions that take into account diversity, explicitly addressing the requirements of students with disabilities (Suri, 2024; Inclusive education: Teaching students with disability, 2020).

Designing for Diversity When introducing IoT in education settings, it is essential to prioritize inclusivity in device design and applications. Let us ensure that IoT solutions in education consider the needs of students, including those with disabilities, and are accessible and usable by everyone.

Equity in Access To ensure fairness and equal access, it is essential to address equity concerns and implement strategies that provide opportunities for all students to access IoT devices, connectivity, and educational resources. This should be done regardless of their socio-background.

Digital Citizenship Education This section suggests including ethics in the curriculum, promoting responsible conduct, privacy awareness, critical thinking skills, and cybersecurity knowledge among students and staff. The aim is to address risks related to IoT devices (Dhirani et al., 2023; Berkeley Extension, 2020).

Incorporating Digital Ethics Incorporating digital citizenship education into the curriculum is crucial. It helps instill principles in students, fostering an understanding of behavior, respect for privacy, and critical thinking about the impact of technology use.

Cybersecurity Awareness Promoting cybersecurity awareness among students and staff is also essential. This helps mitigate risks associated with IoT devices. Educating users about practices like creating passwords, recognizing phishing attempts, and reporting suspicious activities is essential.

1.9 Conclusion

The use of the Internet of Things (IoT) in education is changing the way students learn. IoT improves education by connecting devices, enhancing communication, collecting real-time data, and customizing learning experiences. Some challenges to overcome include ensuring privacy and security, preparing infrastructure, managing costs, and providing staff training. Protecting data and maintaining cybersecurity is crucial for building trust and safeguarding information. Effective planning, collaboration, and inclusivity are key to implementing IoT. The future of IoT in education holds promise with advancements like 5G and edge computing. Combining reality

(AR/VR) with IoT will offer engaging and interactive learning opportunities. Strategic planning, gradual implementation steps, and ongoing assessment are essential to unlocking the potential of IoT. Educators must receive training to utilize IoT technologies effectively. Encouraging a culture of continuous learning and innovation will help educational institutions adapt to changes in the field. In summary, IoT is revolutionizing education by making it more effective, personalized, and inclusive. By tackling challenges head-on while embracing possibilities, educational institutions can create an interconnected future for students. Prioritizing ethics considerations, data security measures, and fairness will ensure that everyone in the educational community benefits from IoT integration into the educational community.

References

Appsierra. (2023). *9 IoT applications in Education*. Appsierra. https://www.appsierra.com/blog/9-iot-in-education

Arduino Education. (2024). *The role of the IoT in education*. Arduino Education. https://www.arduino.cc/education/the-role-of-the-iot-in-education

ASUSTeK Computer Inc. (2023). *Learning on the edge: How edge computing could benefit classrooms*. ASUSTeK Computer Inc. https://www.asus.com/resourcecenter/zhsqjg5hjly6rfer/learning-on-the-edge-how-edge-computing-could-benefit-classrooms#:~:text=Edgecomputingsupportssmootherand,dataprocessingandlowlatencies

Aucott, J. (2023). *The future of learning: IoT in education*. Haptic Networks. https://www.haptic-networks.com/education/iot-in-education/

AWS. (2022). *What is IoT (Internet of Things)?* AWS. https://aws.amazon.com/what-is/iot/

Berkeley Extension. (2020). Cybersecurity in education: What teachers, parents and students should know. . https://bootcamp.berkeley.edu/blog/cybersecurity-in-education-what-teachers-parents-and-students-should-know/

Bonderud, D. (2021). What is edge computing, and how can it be leveraged for higher Ed? *EdTech Magazine*, 1–6. https://edtechmagazine.com/higher/article/2021/11/what-edge-computing-and-how-can-it-be-leveraged-higher-ed-perfcon

Chandran, R. (2023). *5G impact in Education system*. LinkedIn. https://www.linkedin.com/pulse/5g-impact-education-system-ramya-chandran-pbjec/

Cisco Systems, I. (2022). *What is IoT (Internet of Things)?* Cisco Systems, Inc. https://www.cisco.com/c/en/us/solutions/internet-of-things/what-is-iot.html#~iot-management

Cogniteq. (2023). *Implementing IoT in education: Applications and benefits*. Cogniteq. https://www.cogniteq.com/blog/implementing-iot-education-benefits-challenges-use-cases

Cohen, H. (2020). *An introduction to IoT applications in education*. IoT For All. https://www.iotforall.com/introduction-iot-applications-in-education

Dewhirst, D. (2021). *The internet of things in K-12*. Kajeet, Inc. https://www.kajeet.com/en/blog/the-internet-of-things-in-k-12

Dhirani, L. L., Mukhtiar, N., Chowdhry, B. S., & Newe, T. (2023). Ethical dilemmas and privacy issues in emerging technologies: A review. *Sensors, 23*(1151), 1–18.

Eklavvya. (2023). *The impact of 5G on the education technology landscape*. Eklavvya. https://www.eklavvya.com/blog/5g-in-education/

El-Haggar, N., Amouri, L., Alsumayt, A., Alghamedy, F. H., & Aljameel, S. S. (2023). The effectiveness and privacy preservation of IoT on ubiquitous learning: Modern learning paradigm to enhance higher education. *Applied Sciences, 13*(9003), 1–21.

eTech Consultancy. (2017). *What is CESG, GDPR, HIPAA, FERPA & PCI?* ETech Consultancy. https://etflconsultancy.wordpress.com/2017/11/03/what-is-gdpr-hipaa-ferpa-pci/

IBM. (2022). *What is the Internet of Things (IoT)?* IBM. https://www.ibm.com/topics/internet-of-things

Inclusive education: Teaching students with disability. (2020). AITSL. https://www.aitsl.edu.au/research/spotlights/inclusive-education-teaching-students-with-disability

Intuz. (2023). *IoT in the education industry: Embracing the new way of learning*. LinkedIn. https://www.linkedin.com/pulse/iot-education-industry-embracing-new-way-learning-intuz-1f/

IoT MAG. (2024). *Step-by-step guide to implementing IoT in education in 2024*. IOTMAG. https://www.iotmag.de/iot-in-education/

Kumar, S., Tiwari, P., & Zymbler, M. (2019). Internet of Things is a revolutionary approach for future technology enhancement: A review. *Journal of Big Data, 6*(111), 1–21. https://doi.org/10.1186/s40537-019-0268-2

Macharla, M. (2020). *IoT in the education sector*. IoTEDU. https://iot4beginners.com/iot-in-the-education-sector/

Meylani, R. (2024, February). Transforming Education with the internet of things: A journey into smarter learning environments. *International Journal of Research in Education and Science*, 161–178. https://doi.org/10.46328/ijres.3362

New America. (2023). *Privacy considerations in higher education online learning: Applicable Laws*. New America. https://www.newamerica.org/oti/reports/privacy-considerations-higher-education-online-learning/applicable-laws/

Oliynyk, K. (2024). *IoT technology in education [Full Manual for The2024]*. WebbyLab. https://webbylab.com/blog/impact-of-iot-technology-on-education/#:~:text=Safetyofstudents%2Cteachers%2Candclassrooms&text=Bytheway%2Csuchsystems,theinfrastructureofeducationalinstitutions

Oracle. (2023). *What is IoT?* Oracle. https://www.oracle.com/in/internet-of-things/what-is-iot/

Soni, A. (2023). *IoT in education industry [complete guide 2023]*. Auxano Global Services. https://www.auxanoglobalservices.com/iot-in-education-industry/#gref

Suri, A. (2024). *Beyond barriers: A collective approach to inclusive education*. LinkedIn. https://www.linkedin.com/pulse/beyond-barriers-collective-approach-inclusive-education-anoop-suri-o9xbf/

Telnet Nigeria Limited. (2023). *Transforming education with virtual and augmented reality: Creating immersive learning experiences*. LinkedIn. https://www.linkedin.com/pulse/title-transforming-education-virtual-augmented-reality-creating-ha5nf/

Thomas, M. (2022). *IoT in education: 10 connected classroom examples*. Built In. https://builtin.com/articles/iot-education-examples

Wambua, R. N. (2024). Internet of things security and privacy in higher education institutions in developing countries. *Research Journal of Education, Teaching and Curriculum Studies, 2*(1), 1–7.

Yashika. (2023). *AR and VR in education: Preparing students for an IoT-driven future*. Medium. https://medium.com/@nisha0309/ar-and-vr-in-education-preparing-students-for-an-iot-driven-future-cf646ad9dfc9#:~:text=IoTisallaboutreal,environment%2Chealthcare%2Candmore

Chapter 2
IoT for Smart Learning Environment

Abstract This chapter introduces Smart Learning Environments (SLEs). Highlights the role of the Internet of Things (IoT) in contemporary education. SLEs are systems that leverage technology to prioritize interaction, customization, and insights based on data. The chapter delves into how it influences connectivity, data analysis, automation, and tailored learning experiences. It examines established models and frameworks for IoT-driven education, focusing on organized implementation methods. Real-world examples showcase how IoT can revolutionize security measures, personalize learning experiences, facilitate remote laboratories, promote sustainability efforts, and aid in data-informed decision-making in education.

Keywords Smart Learning Environments (SLEs) · Internet of Things (IoT) · Connectivity · Data analysis · Automation · Tailored learning experiences · Data-informed decision-making

2.1 What Is a Smart Learning Environment?

In the changing field of education, traditional learning settings are being replaced by an approach called Smart Learning Environments. These modern setups utilize cutting-edge technologies to establish interactive and adaptable spaces that enrich the learning journey. A Smart Learning Environment goes beyond a physical classroom; it integrates physical spaces, digital tools, and data-driven insights to promote a comprehensive approach to education.

Defining Smart Learning Environments A Smart Learning Environment, also known as an SLE, is an educational system that technologically enhances the learning process for both students and educators. These environments are specifically designed to create an efficient and personalized learning experience (HundrED, 2019; Hwang, 2014; Temdee, 2020). Key features of a Smart Learning Environment include (UNESCO, 2022; Uskov et al., 2018):

M. Kurni, Srinivasa K. G., *The Internet of Educational Things*,
https://doi.org/10.1007/978-3-031-67387-0_2

- ***Interactivity:*** Smart Learning Environments encourage student participation and engagement through digital tools, interactive whiteboards, and collaborative platforms, which enable real-time communication and feedback.
- ***Personalization:*** SLEs are customized to meet learners' needs and preferences. They adapt to each student's learning style, pace, and abilities by providing personalized content and challenges.
- ***Data-driven Insights:*** One of the defining characteristics of SLEs is their use of data analytics. These environments gather information about student performance, behavior, and preferences to help educators make informed decisions and adjustments.
- ***Accessibility:*** SLEs prioritize inclusion by ensuring all students have access to resources regardless of their diverse needs or abilities. This includes incorporating adaptive technologies and assistive tools for students with disabilities.
- ***Integration of Technology:*** Smart Learning Environments combine technologies such as the Internet of Things (IoT), virtual reality, artificial intelligence, and more. These technologies work harmoniously to provide a cutting-edge and uninterrupted learning experience.

The Shift from Traditional to Smart Learning Environments Traditional classrooms have long been the place for education. However, they often need more flexibility, interaction, and personalization than Smart Learning Environments offer. In a traditional classroom, teaching is usually a one-size-fits-all approach, and the teacher sets the pace of instruction. On the other hand, Smart Learning Environments empower students to take charge of their learning and give educators insights to enhance their teaching methods (Singh & Hassan, 2017).

The emergence of IoT technology has transformed traditional classrooms into Smart Learning Environments. IoT enables real-time data collection and automates various tasks by connecting physical objects and devices to the internet, creating an engaging and adaptable educational environment (Sapale & Banerjee, 2023).

2.2 The Role of IoT in Creating a Smart Learning Environment

The Internet of Things (IoT) is affecting industries, including education. Regarding Smart Learning Environments, IoT is vital in establishing interconnected and data-oriented educational spaces. This section delves into the influence of IoT on education and its pivotal role in shaping Smart Learning Environments.

IoT in Education: A Game Changer The Internet of Things (IoT) refers to a network of interconnected objects, devices, and sensors capable of gathering and exchanging data. IoT is vital in integrating smart devices and sensors into the learning environment in education. This integration enhances the educational experience (Meylani, 2024; Fernández-Batanero et al., 2023).

- ***Improved Connectivity:*** Within a Smart Learning Environment, IoT devices are interconnected through networks, allowing for seamless communication between different devices, systems, teachers, students, and administrators. This connectivity fosters collaboration, real-time data sharing, and efficient communication.
- ***Data Collection and Analysis:*** IoT sensors and devices can collect extensive data, including student engagement levels, behavior patterns, and performance metrics. By analyzing this data thoroughly, valuable insights about how students learn can be gained. It also helps identify areas for improvement and informs instructional decisions.
- ***Automation and Efficiency:*** IoT enables the automation of tasks such as tracking attendance records or controlling room temperature. It also aids in resource allocation. By automating these tasks through IoT technology in education settings, educators gain time to focus on meaningful interactions with their students.
- ***Personalization:*** IoT-powered smart learning environments can adapt to students' needs and preferences. This personalized approach ensures that each student receives an educational experience tailored to them.
- ***Relevance to the Real World:*** IoT connects education, real-world applications, and industries. Students can engage with IoT devices and data that simulate real-life situations, equipping them with the skills for careers in fields where IoT plays a vital role.

Key Components of IoT in Smart Learning Environments To effectively integrate IoT into a Smart Learning Environment, some components play a crucial role (Mehar, 2023; Khan, 2020):

- ***Sensors and Devices:*** These physical components gather data from the surroundings, such as temperature sensors, motion detectors, RFID tags, and wearable devices.
- ***Connectivity Solutions:*** IoT devices use network connectivity to transmit data seamlessly. Wireless technologies such as Wi-Fi, Bluetooth, and LoRaWAN are commonly used.
- ***Data Processing and Storage:*** Collected data must be processed, analyzed, and stored. Cloud computing, edge computing, and data analytics platforms play a key role in managing the data generated by IoT.
- ***User Interfaces:*** User interfaces in web or mobile applications allow educators, students, and administrators to access and interact with the valuable insights derived from IoT-generated data.

Integrating IoT into education represents a shift in creating Smart Learning Environments. It empowers educators and students with insights driven by data analysis while enabling automation, personalization, and connectivity previously impossible in traditional educational settings.

Existing Models for IoT-Based Teaching and Learning In the evolving landscape of education, the integration of IoT has led to the creation and implementation of models and approaches aimed at enhancing teaching and learning experiences.

These models exemplify how IoT can be utilized in educational settings (Ghashim & Arshad, 2023; Alia et al., 2017; Petrović et al., 2021).

- ***Flipped Classroom Model:*** The Flipped Classroom model stands out as a pioneering approach that has successfully integrated IoT into teaching and learning practices. Under this model, traditional teaching methods are reimagined. Students are often introduced to concepts and materials outside the classroom through resources such as videos or e-books, allowing them to learn at their own pace and review material. Classroom time is then dedicated to discussions, problem-solving, and hands-on activities.

  IoT plays a vital role within the Flipped Classroom model by providing students access to resources, online assessments, and real-time data. For instance, IoT-enabled platforms can track students' progress and comprehension as they engage with class materials, offering educators valuable insights into areas where additional support might be required.
- ***Smart Campus Model:*** With IoT contributions, Smart Campuses have emerged as technologically advanced educational institutions that leverage connectivity for enhanced educational experiences. In a Smart Campus, the strategic deployment of IoT sensors and devices aims to improve safety, security, and resource management. For instance, security cameras and access control systems based on IoT can ensure the well-being of students and staff, while energy management systems optimize resource usage.

  Furthermore, Smart Campuses often utilize IoT to enhance students' experiences. For example, interactive whiteboards in classrooms, connected devices, and personalized learning platforms offer a highly immersive and engaging educational experience.
- ***Adaptive Learning Model:*** One approach that is gaining popularity is Adaptive Learning. It tailors content and methods to cater to each student's needs and learning pace. IoT plays a vital role in collecting and analyzing the data for Adaptive Learning. Using IoT sensors, student engagement can be monitored, progress can be made, and individual learning styles can be recorded. All are contributing to customized learning pathways.

  In an Adaptive Learning environment, IoT devices provide real-time feedback to students and educators. This enables adjustments to materials and methods as needed. Such dynamic personalization fosters better comprehension of course content while improving retention rates.
- ***Augmented and Virtual Reality (AR/VR):*** IoT technology has also opened doors for integrating Augmented Reality (AR) and Virtual Reality (VR) into learning. In this model, using IoT sensors enables the creation of immersive learning experiences. For instance, students can utilize AR/VR headsets and IoT-connected objects to explore historical sites, conduct virtual science experiments, or engage in realistic simulations.

  These technologies make learning interactive and captivating, providing educators valuable insights into how students engage with virtual content. IoT data on a student's gaze movements and interactions can be captured, which helps refine and enhance the AR/VR learning experience.

- ***Gamified Learning Model:*** Another effective model is Gamified Learning. This approach applies gaming principles to the learning process. With the integration of IoT, gamified learning can be further enhanced by tracking students' progress and performance in games and simulations. Gamified learning platforms often motivate students using leaderboards, rewards systems, and challenges.

  IoT devices collect data on students' gaming behavior and performance, offering educators insights into which aspects of the game effectively convey concepts. This valuable information can then be used to create engaging educational games.

These existing models demonstrate how versatile IoT is in education. They illustrate how technology seamlessly integrates into practices to create personalized, data-driven learning experiences.

Different Frameworks for Applying IoT in Smart Education Various educational models and frameworks have emerged (shown in Fig. 2.1) to demonstrate how IoT technology can be effectively incorporated into teaching and learning processes. These models provide educators and institutions with insights into integrating IoT into the educational setting. Let us explore a few of these models (Kendon & Anselmo, 2024; Pedraza, 2017; HeyHi, 2023).

- ***The SAMR Model:*** The SAMR (Substitution, Augmentation, Modification, Redefinition) model is a framework that evaluates the impact of technology on teaching and learning. It categorizes technology integration into four levels:
  - *Substitution:* Technology serves as a substitute for traditional learning methods.
  - *Augmentation:* Technology provides enhancements and additional features to traditional methods.

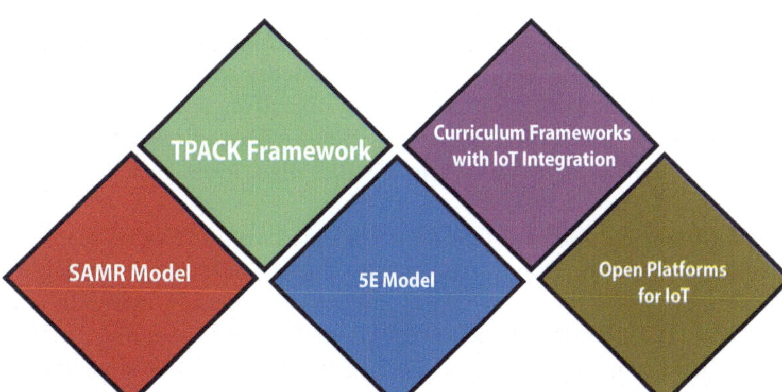

Fig. 2.1 Different frameworks for applying IoT in Smart Education

- *Modification:* Technology enables the redesign of the learning experience.
- *Redefinition:* Technology leads to the creation of learning experiences that were previously unimaginable.

IoT can be integrated at each level of the SAMR model. For instance, at the "Modification" level, IoT may enable real-time projects involving data collection from IoT sensors and devices, transforming the learning experience. At the "Redefinition" level, IoT can facilitate modern forms of education, like remote labs or immersive virtual field trips.

- ***TPACK Framework:*** The framework of Technological Pedagogical Content Knowledge (TPACK) focuses on the intersection of three types of knowledge, namely:

  - Technological knowledge (TK)
  - Pedagogical knowledge (PK), and
  - Content knowledge (CK)

  TPACK helps educators understand how to incorporate technology into their teaching practices. When educators implement IoT in education using the TPACK framework, they consider how their technological knowledge aligns with their content knowledge. For instance, teachers can identify IoT devices and tools that enhance their ability to teach subjects while effectively engaging students.
- ***The 5E Model:*** The 5E model is a framework that follows the phases of Engage, Explore, Explain, Elaborate, and Evaluate. While it is particularly beneficial, its principles can be applied broadly to science education.

  IoT can be integrated into the 5E phases to create a data-rich learning experience. For example, during the "Engage" phase, IoT sensors can collect data related to a phenomenon to pique students' interest. In the "Explore" phase, students actively interact with devices to gather data, and during the "Explain" phase, they analyze the collected information. The "Elaborate" phase allows for exploration and experimentation facilitated by IoT devices. In the "Evaluate" phase, educators can assess the data and insights generated by students using IoT.
- ***Curriculum Frameworks with IoT Integration:*** Some educational institutions have created curriculum frameworks that explicitly incorporate IoT into their courses. These frameworks outline learning objectives and outcomes related to IoT, providing guidelines for selecting technologies and resources. They offer educators an approach to designing courses that leverage IoT for learning experiences.
- ***Open Platforms for IoT:*** Certain organizations have developed platforms and ecosystems tailored to institutions' needs. These platforms provide plug-and-play solutions, IoT devices, and tools educators can easily integrate into their teaching practices. They streamline the process of implementing IoT in classrooms while also offering a community of educators and additional resources.

These frameworks are resources for educators and institutions aiming to incorporate IoT into Smart Education. Whether assessing technologies' potential through the

SAMR model, considering the intersection of knowledge areas with TPACK following the 5E model, designing curriculum frameworks enhanced by IoT, or utilizing open platforms for IoT integration, these frameworks offer structured approaches to harnessing IoT's power for more engaging, data-driven, personalized learning experiences.

2.3 Frameworks for Applying IoT in Smart Education

Educational institutions and educators can employ various frameworks and models (as shown in Fig. 2.2) to harness the potential of the Internet of Things (IoT) in Smart Education.

These frameworks offer a structured approach to integrating IoT into education, resulting in immersive, data-driven, and personalized learning experiences. Here are some diverse frameworks for implementing IoT in Smart Education (Kristina Hollis, 2014; coi.athabascau.ca, 2014; ELM Learning, 2014; Structural Learning, 2023; Burgstahler, 2023):

- ***The TEC-VARIETY Model:*** Developed by Curtis Bonk and Elaine Khoo, the TEC-VARIETY model is a framework that focuses on creating online learning environments. While initially designed for online education, this model's principles can also be adapted to face-to-face learning environments enhanced by IoT. The acronym TEC-VARIETY represents:
  - T: Tone/Climate- Establishing a supportive and motivating learning atmosphere.
  - E: Encouragement- Provide feedback and assistance to learners.
  - C: Curiosity- Cultivating curiosity through engaging activities and content.
  - V: Variety- Offer an array of learning resources and experiences.
  - A: Autonomy- Encouraging self-directed learning.

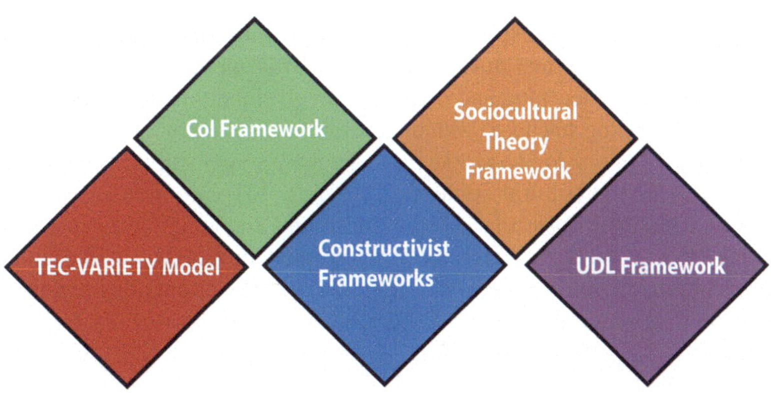

Fig. 2.2 Frameworks for Applying IoT in Smart Education

– R: Relevance- Ensure the learning experience is relevant to learners.
– I: Interactive- Promoting interactions among learners and with the content.
– E: Engagement- Keep learners engaged through various activities.
– T: Tension- Introducing manageable challenges to maintain interest.
– Y: Yield- Ensuring the learning experience results in valuable outcomes.

IoT plays a significant role in incorporating the TEC-VARIETY model by introducing challenges that maintain interest and ensure valuable learning outcomes. One way IoT contributes is by providing real-time data for learning, allowing learners to engage with connected devices that offer a variety of resources and activities. This connection to real-world applications makes learning more relevant.

- ***The Community of Inquiry (CoI) Framework:*** Another framework called the Community of Inquiry (CoI), developed by Garrison, Anderson, and Archer, focuses on creating a community of learners actively engaged in inquiry. It emphasizes three elements:

  – *Cognitive Presence* refers to how learners construct meaning through sustained communication and reflection.
  – *Social Presence* involves projecting oneself as a real person within the learner community.
  – *Teaching Presence* encompasses the design, facilitation, and direction of experiences.

  IoT can enhance the CoI framework in many ways. First, it provides data that supports cognitive presence during learning activities. Second, collaborative IoT-based activities promote increased social presence among learners. Third, educators can leverage IoTs' data-driven insights to improve their teaching presence and make decisions in education settings, thereby supporting teaching presence.
- ***Constructivist Frameworks:*** Constructivist Frameworks emphasize the role of learners in constructing their understanding. Several IoT applications align with these principles by allowing students to engage in learning, actively experiment with real-world data, and collaboratively build knowledge.

  For instance, labs and experiments enabled with IoT allow students to collect sensor data, analyze it, and draw conclusions. This approach aligns with principles that emphasize learning and the active involvement of learners in constructing knowledge using IoT as a valuable tool.
- ***Sociocultural Theory Framework:*** Lev Vygotsky's Sociocultural Theory framework highlights the cultural context of learning. IoT can facilitate learning by connecting learners, fostering collaboration, and encouraging discussions. For example, IoT-enabled projects can promote student teamwork to tackle real-world problems. Online platforms integrated with functionalities can also provide social learning experiences where students can share and discuss data and insights.

- ***The Universal Design for Learning (UDL) Framework:*** The Universal Design for Learning (UDL) framework aims to create inclusive and accessible learning environments. By leveraging IoT technology, UDL can be enhanced through personalized learning experiences. For example, Internet of Things (IoT) sensors can personalize content based on individual learning requirements. Additionally, IoT-connected devices can support students with disabilities, ensuring inclusive and accessible learning experiences for all.

These frameworks offer educators and educational institutions a range of strategies to incorporate IoT into Smart Education. By integrating IoT initiatives within these frameworks, educators can establish impactful and inclusive learning environments that cater to the diverse needs of learners and equip them with the necessary skills for navigating the challenges of the modern era.

2.4 Examples and Practical Instances

Examples and practical instances of integrating IoT into education offer insights into how this technology impacts teaching learning and the overall educational experience. These instances and success stories shed light on how IoT is applied in Smart Learning Environments (SLEs) and how they benefit students, educators, and institutions. Here are a few illustrative cases.

- ***Enhancing Campus Security:*** Many educational institutions have adopted IoT technology to bolster campus security. For instance, a university can implement a network of security cameras, access control systems, and sensor-based alert systems. This integration enables time monitoring and threat detection, ensuring the safety of students and staff. Additionally, it facilitates the allocation of resources by directing security personnel to areas with increased activity or potential issues. The outcome will be a more secure campus environment.
- ***Personalized Learning Platforms:*** IoT technology has made personalized learning platforms possible. For example, a K-12 school district can implement a system with IoT sensors and devices to track student progress and engagement. These devices collect data on individual learning patterns, which the platform then uses to customize content according to each student's needs. The outcomes will be impressive when the students display motivation, better understanding, and improved academic performance.
- ***Remote Labs and Virtual Field Trips:*** The Internet of Things (IoT) has made it possible to create remote laboratories and virtual field trips offering authentic experiences within the classroom. A rural high school may face challenges in providing science experiments due to the lack of resources. To overcome this hurdle, they can incorporate IoT technology to provide access to remote lab equipment and virtual field trips. Students can control lab equipment and interact with environments through the internet. This enables them to conduct experi-

ments and explore places they would not have had access to, greatly enhancing their learning experiences.

- ***Energy Efficiency and Sustainability:*** Campuses can use IoT technology to promote sustainability and energy efficiency. For example, a college campus can integrate IoT-connected sensors into its lighting, heating, and cooling systems. These sensors adjust resource usage based on occupancy levels and environmental conditions, saving energy. This will reduce costs and serve as an educational tool for teaching students about sustainable practices and environmental conservation.
- ***Data-driven decision-making:*** Many higher education institutions embrace data-driven decision-making through IoT. Educators and administrators gather classroom information on usage, student attendance, and course engagement. By analyzing this data, they can make informed choices to enhance course delivery and allocate resources effectively. Based on data analysis, this approach will result in improved outcomes and more streamlined operations.

These examples and practical instances vividly showcase the transformative applications of IoT in education. They illustrate how IoT technology can bolster security measures, personalize learning experiences, broaden access to resources, promote sustainability efforts, and facilitate decision-making based on data insights. These practical instances provide inspiration and guidance for educational institutions seeking to leverage the potential of IoT in their own Smart Learning Environments.

2.5 Conclusion

This chapter has highlighted how Smart Learning Environments (SLEs) empowered by the Internet of Things (IoT) change education in many ways. By incorporating cutting-edge technologies, SLEs provide personalized, data-driven learning experiences beyond classroom settings. The chapter emphasizes the role of SLEs in promoting engagement, customization, and data-driven decision-making through IoT. It presents models and practical examples demonstrating how IoT enhances teaching and learning methods from flipped classrooms to eco campuses. Moreover, it underscores the importance of structured frameworks for integrating IoT, offering guidance on implementation strategies. By embracing IoT technology, educational institutions can improve security measures, tailor learning experiences to individuals' needs, support sustainability efforts, and make decisions based on data analysis. Integrating IoT into SLEs opens avenues for innovation and advancement as education progresses. Exploring and harnessing the potential of IoT will enable educators and institutions to create transformative learning environments that empower students for success in today's digital age.

References

Alia, M., Bilala, H. S. M., Razzaq, M. A., Khan, J., Lee, S., Idris, M., Aazam, M., Choi, T., Han, S. C., & Kang, B. H. (2017). IoTFLiP: IoT-based flipped learning platform for medical education. *Digital Communications and Networks, 3*(3), 188–194. https://doi.org/10.1016/j.dcan.2017.03.002

Burgstahler, S. (2023). *Universal design: Process, principles, and applications*. University of Washington. https://www.washington.edu/doit/universal-design-process-principles-and-applications#:~:text=Universaldesignforlearning(UDL,on after-the-fact

coi.athabascau.ca. (2014). *CoI framework*. Coi.Athabascau.Ca. https://coi.athabascau.ca/coi-model/

ELM Learning. (2014). *Constructivist learning theory*. ELM Learning. https://elmlearning.com/hub/learning-theories/constructivism/

Fernández-Batanero, J. M., Montenegro-Rueda, M., Fernández-Cerero, J., & Menéses, E. L. (2023). Adoption of the Internet of Things in higher education: Opportunities and challenges. *Interactive Technology and Smart Education, 21*, 292–307. https://doi.org/10.1108/ITSE-01-2023-0025

Ghashim, I. A., & Arshad, M. (2023). Internet of Things (IoT)-based teaching and learning: Modern trends and open challenges. *Sustainability, 15*(21), 1–21. https://doi.org/10.3390/su152115656

HeyHi. (2023). *Comparison of TPACK Vs SAMR model: Which one is better?* HeyHi. https://blog.heyhi.sg/comparison-of-tpack-vs-samr-model-which-one-is-better/

HundrED. (2019). *Smart learning environments*. HundrED. https://hundred.org/en/innovations/smart-learning-environments#location

Hwang, G. (2014). Definition, framework and research issues of smart learning environments – A context-aware ubiquitous learning perspective. *Smart Learning Environments, 1*(4), 1–14. https://doi.org/10.1186/s40561-014-0004-5

Kendon, T., & Anselmo, L. (2024). *SAMR and TPACK: Two models to help with integrating technology into your courses*. University of Calgary. https://taylorinstitute.ucalgary.ca/resources/SAMR-TPACK

Khan, Y. (2020). *Components of an IoT ecosystem*. G2.Com, Inc. https://learn.g2.com/iot-ecosystem

Kristina Hollis. (2014). *A new 21st century pedagogical model*. Kristina Hollis. https://kristinahollis.wordpress.com/tag/tec-variety/

Mehar, A. (2023). *The major components of IoT explained*. AlmaBetter. https://www.almabetter.com/bytes/articles/components-of-iot

Meylani, R. (2024). Transforming education with the Internet of Things: A journey into smarter learning environments. *International Journal of Research in Education and Science (IJRES), 10*(1), 161–178. https://doi.org/10.46328/ijres.3362

Pedraza. (2017). *Frameworks for educational technology integration and innovation*. Medium. https://medium.com/@pezucation/frameworks-for-educational-technology-integration-and-innovation-b69823bce37b

Petrović, L., Stojanović, D., Živojinović, L., & Đurđević, B. (2021). IoT game-based learning model in education. *International Conference on E-Business Technologies, 3*, 271–275.

Sapale, S., & Banerjee, S. (2023). Empowering education: Exploring the impact of IoT in smart learning environments. *International Journal of Advance Innovations, Thoughts & Ideas, 12*(5), 1–6. https://doi.org/10.4172/2277-1891.1000231

Singh, A. D., & Hassan, M. (2017). *In pursuit of smart learning environments for the 21 st century* (Issue 12).

Structural Learning. (2023). *Sociocultural theory*. Cambridge, UK. https://www.structural-learning.com/post/sociocultural-theory

Temdee, P. (2020). Smart learning environment: Paradigm shift for online learning. In *Multi agent systems – Strategies and applications* (pp. 1–14). https://doi.org/10.5772/intechopen.85787

UNESCO. (2022). *Analytical report on the global innovations and monitoring of the status of smart education*. https://unesdoc.unesco.org/ark:/48223/pf0000383676

Uskov, V. L., Bakken, J. P., Howlett, R. J., & Jain, L. C. (2018). *Smart universities – Concepts, systems, and technologies* (Vol. 70). Springer.

Chapter 3
IoT-Based Smart Classroom

Abstract This chapter explores IoT-enabled smart classrooms, highlighting their capacity to transform traditional educational practices. Split into two segments, the initial portion introduces the concept of IoT-based classrooms. Underscores their importance in catering to the changing needs of contemporary learners. It covers incorporating technology in classrooms, resulting in tailored learning experiences, increased engagement, and real-time supervision. The latter part delves deeper into the structure of smart classrooms, concentrating on sensor networks, communication standards, and cloud-based systems. It examines the devices and sensors in IoT-driven classrooms, emphasizing their contribution to creating interactive and immersive learning environments. Additionally, this chapter touches upon security and privacy concerns, examples from real-world scenarios, obstacles faced, and prospects for IoT-powered smart classrooms. By adopting a multidimensional approach, this chapter offers insights into how IoT technology can revolutionize the future of education by cultivating inclusive, engaging, and personalized learning settings for students in the digital era.

Keywords Internet of Things (IoT) · IoT-enabled smart classrooms · Traditional educational practices · Tailored learning experiences · Sensor networks · Interactive learning environments · Security and privacy concerns · Personalized learning settings

3.1 Introduction

With today's rapid technological progress and digital evolution, the Internet of Things (IoT) has become a game-changing idea with wide implications in different industries, including education. The convergence of IoT and education has brought about the "IoT-Based Smart Classroom." This chapter delves into the incorporation of IoT technology within classrooms, showcasing its immense potential to transform the methods we use for teaching and learning.

M. Kurni, Srinivasa K. G., *The Internet of Educational Things*,
https://doi.org/10.1007/978-3-031-67387-0_3

The Need for Smart Classrooms in the Modern Education System The traditional way of teaching, where the teacher stands at the front and lectures students, is no longer the most effective method. Nowadays, students, often referred to as "digital natives," grow up in a world filled with technology. They expect their education to reflect this reality. They are used for instant access to information, personalized learning experiences, and interactivity (Das, 2020).

Smart classrooms based on Internet of Things (IoT) technology cater to students' and educators' changing needs and expectations by utilizing technology to create efficient learning environments. These classrooms have sensors, smart devices, and connectivity solutions, allowing real-time data collection, analysis, and adaptation according to each student's requirements (Venkatesh et al., 2022). This approach encourages active learning, collaboration, and creativity, all skills for success in the twenty-first-century workforce.

Benefits and Advantages of IoT-Based Smart Classrooms The integration of Internet of Things (IoT) technology in education offers the following benefits (as shown in Fig. 3.1) (Rajput, 2019; Riseapps, 2021; IoTDunia, 2020).

- ***Personalized Learning:*** IoT enables real-time data collection on students' progress, allowing for tailored learning paths. This means that each student's strengths and weaknesses can be identified, leading to customized curriculum adjustments that meet their needs.

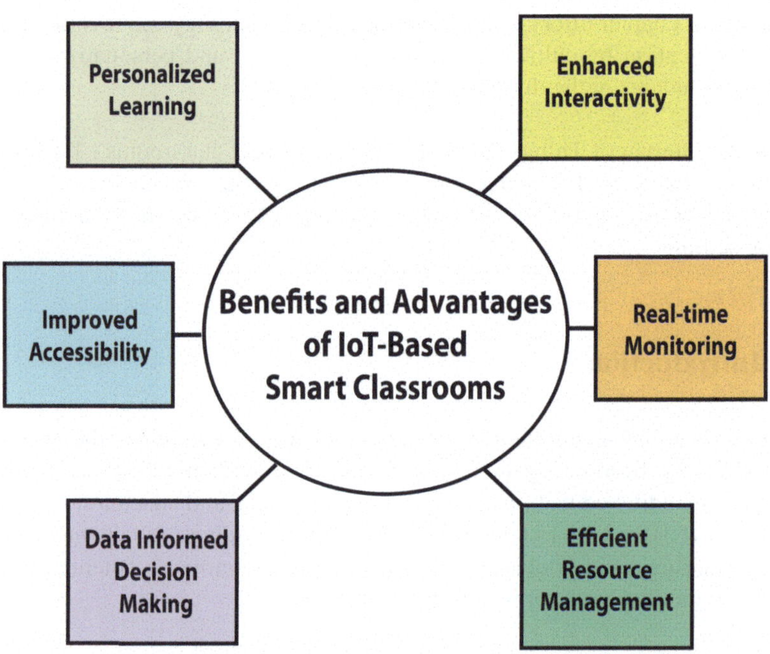

Fig. 3.1 Benefits & advantages of IoT-based smart classrooms

- ***Enhanced Interactivity:*** IoT devices and smart boards promote interaction within the classroom. Students can actively engage through digital tools, while teachers can receive feedback on comprehension and participation levels.
- ***Real-time Monitoring:*** Educators can monitor students' attendance, behavior, and engagement. This information helps identify and address any issues resulting in a learning environment.
- ***Efficient Resource Management:*** IoT facilitates optimizing resource utilization from energy-efficient lighting and climate control to smart scheduling and space management. This leads to the efficient use of resources within educational institutions.
- ***Improved Accessibility:*** IoT technology provides inclusive options for students with disabilities, ensuring that education is accessible to all learners.
- ***Data Informed Decision Making:*** Schools and universities can make decisions using data analytics. This data-driven approach enhances administrative efficiency and improves educational quality.

3.2 The Architecture of IoT-Based Smart Classroom

In this section, we will delve into the structure of a smart classroom based on IoT technology. This structure is the basis for developing an intelligent and adaptable learning environment. It incorporates sensors, devices, and network infrastructure to gather and analyze data, ultimately improving the educational experience (Burunkaya & Duraklar, 2022; Yaganoglu et al., 2023; Dai et al., 2023).

Sensor Networks and Their Role Sensor networks are vital in creating smart classrooms based on the Internet of Things (IoT). These networks comprise a wide range of strategically placed sensors throughout the learning space, capturing various types of data. Here are some examples;

- ***Environmental Sensors:*** These sensors monitor classroom temperature, humidity, air quality, and lighting conditions, ensuring a comfortable and conducive learning environment.
- ***Occupancy Sensors:*** By detecting student presence, occupancy sensors enable features like lighting control and energy efficiency.
- ***Motion Sensors:*** Motion sensors track student movement and engagement within the classroom, providing insights into the dynamics of the learning environment.
- ***RFID Sensors:*** Radio frequency identification (RFID) sensors monitor the movement and usage of educational resources such as books and equipment.
- ***Smartboards and Interactive Displays:*** Equipped with touch and pen sensors, interactive whiteboards and displays facilitate engaging digital interactions and real-time feedback.

These interconnected sensors continuously collect data, which is then transmitted to a central system for analysis and decision-making.

Communication Protocols and Data Transmission Effective communication is crucial for the functioning of IoT-based smart classrooms. Various protocols and technologies are employed to facilitate this communication;

- ***Wi-Fi:*** Wi-Fi connectivity is widely available in classrooms and is the primary means for IoT devices to connect to the Internet and communicate with each other.
- ***Bluetooth:*** Bluetooth technology establishes short-range connections between smartphones, tablets, and wearable technology.
- ***Zigbee:*** Zigbee is a communication protocol specifically designed for low-power and low-data-rate connections between IoT devices in smart classrooms.
- ***LoRaWAN:*** Smart classrooms use Long Range Wide Area Network (LoRaWAN) technology to enable long-range, low-power communication to connect sensors and devices across a wide area.
- ***Ethernet:*** In some scenarios, ethernet cables directly connect IoT devices to the school area network (LAN).

These communication protocols facilitate data exchange between devices and the central system, often in the cloud.

Cloud-Based Systems for Data Storage and Processing The data collected from the sensor network and IoT devices in a smart classroom is sent to cloud-based systems for storage and processing. These systems offer benefits such as:

- ***Scalability:*** The cloud infrastructure can easily handle the increasing amount of data generated in the classroom.
- ***Accessibility:*** Authorized users, such as educators and administrators, can access data and insights as long as they have an internet connection.
- ***Real-time Processing:*** Cloud systems can process data instantly, allowing for feedback and adjustments in the classroom environment.
- ***Data Security:*** Cloud providers usually have security measures to safeguard educational data.
- ***Integration with Analytics Tools:*** Data stored in the cloud can be seamlessly combined with analytics software to gain insights into student performance and classroom behavior.

The IoT-based smart classroom architecture, including sensor networks, communication protocols, and cloud-based systems, forms the foundation of a technologically advanced educational environment. This infrastructure enables data collection, analysis, and utilization to create a responsive classroom that meets the needs of educators and students.

3.3 IoT Devices and Sensors

This section will explore the devices and sensors essential for making an IoT-powered smart classroom. These devices act as the classroom senses, collecting data and enabling various applications to improve the learning experience.

Types of IoT Devices Used in Smart Classrooms In classrooms, IoT devices consist of various technologies and tools to support educators and students. Some used IoT devices in classrooms include (Schoolnet India, 2022);

- ***Interactive Whiteboards:*** These advanced whiteboards, with touch and pen sensors, transform traditional chalkboards into interactive digital surfaces. They offer real-time writing, drawing, and interactive lessons that promote student engagement and collaboration.
- ***Tablets and Laptops:*** Many students bring their tablets or laptops to class, which can seamlessly integrate into the classroom environment. These devices allow access to content, interactive exercises, and collaborative tools.
- ***Wearable Technology:*** Students can utilize wearable devices like smartwatches and fitness trackers to monitor their physical activity, track attendance, and gather health-related data.
- ***Smart Projectors:*** With high-definition displays and interactive capabilities, smart projectors add an engaging element by projecting lessons, presentations, and educational content in a captivating manner.
- ***Smart Lighting Systems:*** IoT-enabled lighting systems are equipped with sensors that automatically adjust lighting levels based on natural light availability, occupancy, and energy efficiency in the classroom. These systems enhance the classroom experience while also promoting energy conservation.
- ***Environmental sensors:*** These IoT devices contribute significantly to creating a learning environment by leveraging cutting-edge technology to benefit educators and students. Environmental sensors monitor temperature, humidity, and air quality to create a comfortable and conducive learning environment.
- ***Student response systems:*** Student response systems enable students to answer questions and provide feedback, encouraging active participation and facilitating instant assessment.
- ***RFID technology:*** RFID technology utilizes tags and readers to track the movement of educational resources such as textbooks, preventing misplacement and assisting with inventory management.

Sensor Technologies for Monitoring and Data Collection The effectiveness of IoT devices in a classroom relies on the types of sensors incorporated into these devices. Sensors play a significant role in collecting data that informs decision-making and actions within the classroom. Some standard sensor technologies used include (Arrow Electronics, 2021):

- ***Motion Sensors:*** These sensors detect movement within the classroom. They can track student activity, engagement, and behavior, providing insights into the class dynamics.
- ***Proximity Sensors:*** Proximity sensors determine the distance between objects, making them helpful in tracking attendance or creating interactive experiences when students approach devices.
- ***Light Sensors:*** Light sensors adjust lighting levels based on natural light conditions, promoting energy efficiency and creating a comfortable learning environment.
- ***Temperature Sensors:*** Temperature sensors monitor the classroom's ambient temperature, ensuring it remains within an optimal range for effective learning.
- ***Air Quality Sensors:*** Air Quality Sensors measure air quality factors such as carbon dioxide (CO2) levels, humidity, and particulate matter. They contribute to maintaining a healthy classroom environment.
- ***Touch and Pressure Sensors:*** Interactive whiteboards, touch screens, and devices with touch capabilities incorporate these sensors. They detect touch and pressure to enable interactive input.
- ***Biometric Sensors:*** Biometric sensors have applications in the educational setting, such as student identification, enhancement of security measures, and even monitoring of physiological data in certain instances.

Integrating IoT devices and sensors fosters an environment with rich data in smart classrooms, enabling valuable insights into student behavior, engagement levels, and overall classroom conditions.

Integration with Existing Classroom Infrastructure One benefit of smart classrooms based on IoT is their seamless integration with existing classroom infrastructure. This integration helps minimize disruptions and allows educators to maximize their resources effectively. Many IoT devices and sensors can be easily incorporated into an established classroom without renovations.

Furthermore, teachers and administrators have the flexibility to introduce solutions gradually, ensuring a transition towards an IoT-based smart classroom model. This adaptability makes IoT technology accessible and practical for institutions. The IoT devices and sensors in classrooms play a vital role in collecting critical data and facilitating personalized learning, interactivity, and real-time data analysis (Rathor, 2024; Ollivachreis, 2024).

3.4 Data Analytics and Visualization

This section explores the role of data analytics and visualization in an IoT-based smart classroom. The information gathered from IoT devices and sensors is converted into actionable insights, creating a learning environment tailored, immersive, and driven by data.

Data Collection and Processing Smart classrooms that utilize Internet of Things (IoT) technology are filled with data. Various sensors, devices, and other sources continuously gather information about student behavior, classroom conditions, and resource usage. Analyzing and visualizing this data begins with its collection.

In a classroom setting, the data sources include (Kaur & Bhatia, 2022):

- ***Student Devices:*** Devices used by students include tablets, laptops, and wearable technology.
- ***Sensor Networks:*** Motion sensors, environmental sensors, and more.
- ***Smartboards and Interactive Displays:*** Data collected from interactive whiteboards.
- ***Student Response Systems:*** Capturing student feedback and responses.
- ***RFID Sensors:*** Gathering data on resource utilization and tracking purposes.
- ***Smart Lighting and Environmental Controls:*** Insights into energy usage patterns and classroom conditions.

All the collected data is then transmitted to a central system to be processed and analyzed. Cloud-based solutions are often utilized to handle the volume of data generated.

Real-Time Monitoring and Analytics One benefit of incorporating IoT technology into classrooms is the ability to monitor and analyze in real-time. Educators and administrators can access up-to-date information about classroom activities, such as student engagement and resource usage. Real-time analytics allow immediate responses to issues, creating effective teaching and learning opportunities.

Some important aspects of real-time monitoring and analysis include (Lumen Learning, 2023; Explorance, 2023):

- ***Student Engagement:*** Tracking how students interact with devices and smartboards to gauge their level of engagement.
- ***Attendance Tracking:*** Automatically tracking attendance using motion and proximity sensors.
- ***Interactive Feedback:*** Getting feedback from students on questions and exercises in time.
- ***Resource Utilization:*** Monitoring the movement and usage of educational resources through RFID sensors.
- ***Environmental Conditions:*** Monitor temperature, air quality, and lighting to ensure a comfortable learning environment.

By utilizing these features of IoT, smart classrooms enable educators to understand what is happening in real time, leading to more effective teaching methods.

Visualization Tools and Dashboards Visualization tools and dashboards are crucial to understanding and making sense of the data collected and analyzed. These tools provide easy-to-understand and interpret information, enabling educators and administrators to make well-informed decisions.

There are visualization techniques and tools that are often used (Gerela et al., 2022; Wandr, 2023):

- ***Dashboards:*** These customizable dashboards give an overall view of classroom data, including attendance, engagement levels, and environmental conditions.
- ***Graphs and Charts:*** Data is frequently visualized using bar charts, line graphs, or pie charts to showcase trends and patterns.
- ***Heatmaps:*** Heatmaps can illustrate student activity levels and engagement across different classroom areas.
- ***Alerts and Notifications:*** Automated alerts can notify educators about important events such as low attendance or high CO_2 levels.
- ***Predictive Analytics:*** Predictive models can forecast student performance and suggest interventions.

Visualization tools allow educators to interpret data and proactively improve the classroom experience.

Benefits of Data Analytics and Visualization Integrating data analytics and visualization into a smart classroom based on the Internet of Things (IoT) brings advantages (Liston et al., 2022):

- ***Personalized Learning:*** We can use data analytics to identify each student's needs and tailor the content accordingly.
- ***Enhanced Engagement:*** Real-time engagement data empowers educators to adapt their teaching methods to keep students actively involved.
- ***Optimal Resource Allocation:*** Monitoring resource utilization enables us to allocate educational materials and ensure they are used effectively and efficiently.
- ***Informed Decision Making:*** Insights derived from data-driven analysis provide valuable support for educators and administrators when making informed decisions.
- ***Continuous Improvement:*** Analyzing classroom data allows for enhancements to the learning environment.

Challenges and Considerations While using data analytics and visualization in a classroom has benefits, some challenges must be considered. These include ensuring data privacy and security, providing training and support, and avoiding information overload. Striking a balance between data-based decisions and respecting privacy is crucial in creating a smart classroom.

To sum up, data analytics and visualization are vital in an IoT-based classroom. They allow educators and administrators to utilize data's potential for learning and continuous improvement fully. With real-time monitoring and visual representations of data, educators can make decisions that create a dynamic and responsive learning environment.

3.5 Enhanced Learning Experiences

This section will explore how smart classrooms based on IoT revolutionize the traditional learning environment, providing students and educators with improved learning experiences. Incorporating IoT technology allows for interactive, adaptable, and engaging opportunities that empower teachers and learners.

Adaptive Learning and Personalized Content Delivery One advantage of smart classrooms powered by IoT is the ability to offer customized and personalized learning experiences. This level of customization is made possible by collecting and analyzing data within the classroom. Adaptive learning can be implemented in various ways (Lake, 2023; Morze et al., 2021):

- ***Personalized Content:*** IoT systems can tailor content to students' learning preferences, performance, and progress. This ensures that every student receives materials and exercises best suited to their needs.
- ***Progress Monitoring:*** Educators can track individual student progress in time, identifying areas where students may require additional support and adjusting their teaching methods accordingly.
- ***Adaptive Assessments:*** IoT systems can help generate adaptive assessments. These assessments adjust their difficulty level based on a student's performance, ensuring appropriate challenge.
- ***Immediate Feedback:*** Students receive instant feedback on their assignments, quizzes, and exercises. This allows them to reflect on their performance and make improvements.

In summary, smart classrooms enabled by IoT provide features that enhance the learning experience by offering personalized content, monitoring progress, generating adaptive assessments, and providing instant feedback to students.

Interactive and Immersive Experiences IoT devices and sensors play a vital role in classrooms, promoting interactivity and creating immersive learning experiences (Sapale & Banerjee, 2023; Campbell, 2024). Here are some key components:

- ***Interactive Whiteboards:*** Educators can utilize whiteboards and displays to draw, write, and manipulate content on a digital surface. This allows students to actively engage with the material, solve problems, and participate hands-on.
- ***Smart Projectors:*** Introducing smart projectors into classrooms can transform the learning space into an interactive digital environment. These projectors can display content, simulations, and multimedia materials to enhance the learning experience.
- ***Student Response Systems:*** With student response systems, students can provide real-time responses to questions, quizzes, and surveys. Immediate feedback encourages participation and helps deepen students' understanding of the subject.
- ***Virtual and Augmented Reality (VR/AR):*** IoT integration enables using VR/AR technology in classrooms. Students can explore virtual environments and interact with digital objects to better understand complex subjects.

- ***Gamification:*** Leveraging IoT data allows gamification techniques that turn lessons and exercises into enjoyable activities. By incorporating elements into the learning process through gamification, students are motivated to participate while gaining knowledge.

These technologies foster student engagement by making learning more interactive and enjoyable.

Gamification and IoT in Education Gamification can be a game changer in smart classrooms that utilize IoT technology. It involves incorporating game elements and principles into the learning process to make it more exciting and enjoyable (ANTT Robotics Ltd, 2024; Costa, 2023). By leveraging the data collected by IoT devices and sensors, educators can create engaging learning experiences that offer benefits:

- ***Recognizing Achievements:*** Students can earn points, badges, or other rewards when they complete tasks and show mastery of a subject.
- ***Encouraging Healthy Competition:*** Friendly competition among students can motivate them to excel and actively participate in classroom activities.
- ***Providing Instant Feedback:*** Gamified activities often provide immediate feedback, allowing students to track their progress and make improvements.
- ***Cultivating Collaboration:*** Gamification fosters collaboration, which is an essential skill for success in today's world.

By combining IoT technology with gamification strategies, smart classrooms become interactive environments that keep students engaged and motivated to learn.

3.6 Security and Privacy

In this section, we will delve into the factors concerning security and privacy in smart classrooms based on the Internet of Things (IoT). While these classrooms offer advantages, they also present challenges in protecting sensitive information and maintaining the privacy of students and teachers alike.

Data Security Considerations Ensuring data security in IoT-based smart classrooms is of utmost importance. To achieve this, educational institutions and technology providers must implement security measures (Hearon et al., 2021; Trend Micro, 2021; Balbix, 2024). Here are some key steps to consider.

- ***Data Encryption:*** Encrypting all data transmitted between IoT devices and cloud-based systems is crucial to safeguard against interception.
- ***Access Control:*** Strict access controls should be in place to ensure that authorized personnel can access and modify the data.
- ***Regular Software Updates:*** Keeping devices and software up to date helps address any security vulnerabilities that may arise.

- ***Intrusion Detection Systems (IDS):*** Implementing IDS can monitor the network for suspicious activities and promptly alert administrators about potential security breaches.
- ***Secure APIs:*** Communication through Application Programming Interfaces (APIs) should be secured to prevent unauthorized access.
- ***Physical Security:*** Restricting access to IoT devices and servers is essential in preventing tampering or theft incidents.
- ***Incident Response Plan:*** A defined incident response plan enables action to address security breaches and minimize their impact.
- ***User Training:*** Educators and students should receive training on data security best practices to help them avoid inadvertent data exposure.

By implementing these measures, educational institutions can significantly enhance data protection in IoT-driven smart classrooms.

Privacy Concerns and Compliance with Regulations In smart classrooms that utilize IoT technology, a vast amount of student information is gathered, including student interactions, attendance records, and academic performance. However, this raises privacy concerns that must be addressed (Hearon et al., 2021). To ensure privacy, some measures and considerations should be taken into account:

- ***Consent:*** Educational institutions must obtain consent from students and their guardians before collecting and processing data.
- ***Anonymization:*** Whenever possible, data should be stripped of any information to protect individuals' identities.
- ***Compliance:*** Schools must comply with data protection regulations, such as the Family Educational Rights and Privacy Act (FERPA) in the United States or the General Data Protection Regulation (GDPR) in the European Union.
- ***Transparency:*** It is crucial to maintain transparency with students, parents, and educators regarding what types of data are collected, how they are utilized, and who has access to them.
- ***Data Retention:*** Institutions should establish policies outlining how long data will be stored and when it will be deleted.
- ***Data Ownership:*** Determining ownership rights over the collected data is essential, especially involving third-party technology providers.
- ***Audit Trails:*** Maintaining audit trails can help track the usage and access of student information.

By implementing these measures and considerations, we can ensure privacy protection for students while leveraging the benefits of IoT-based classrooms.

Best Practices for Ensuring the Safety of IoT-Based Smart Classrooms To address security and privacy concerns, educators and administrators can take these steps:

- ***Assessing Risks:*** Evaluate potential vulnerabilities related to security and privacy.

- ***Creating Security Policies:*** Developing and implementing security policies and guidelines for IoT-based smart classrooms.
- ***Evaluating Third-Party Vendors:*** Carefully assess third-party technology providers to ensure they adhere to security and privacy standards.
- ***Minimizing Data Collection:*** Only gather data necessary for educational purposes while limiting the collection of sensitive information.
- ***Conducting Audits:*** Audit security measures and privacy protocols to identify weaknesses or areas for improvement.
- ***Establishing an Incident Response Plan:*** Set up a defined action plan to address possible data breaches.
- ***Promoting cybersecurity education initiatives:*** Raising awareness among educators and students about the importance of cybersecurity practices.
- ***Collaborate with IT experts:*** Work closely with IT and security experts to stay informed about emerging threats and industry best practices.

While IoT-based smart classrooms provide advancements in education, it is crucial to prioritize protecting collected data by implementing robust security measures, complying with privacy regulations, and following established best practices. The effective blending of security and privacy measures is essential in establishing a favorable learning atmosphere for students and educators.

3.7 Case Studies

This section will examine real-life examples of smart classroom integration using IoT technology in educational environments. These case studies showcase how IoT revolutionizes students' learning and benefits learners, teachers, and educational institutions.

Case Study 1: Smart Classroom Initiative at XYZ University

Overview XYZ University, an education institution, embarked on an extensive initiative known as the Smart Classroom Initiative to enhance its students' learning experience. This initiative equipped classrooms with cutting-edge IoT devices and sensors, creating a data-driven educational environment.

Implementation

- XYZ University incorporated whiteboards, smart projectors, and IoT sensors into classrooms.

- Environmental sensors were utilized to monitor temperature, humidity, and lighting levels, ensuring a comfortable and conducive learning atmosphere.
- RFID technology was employed to track the movement of resources, optimizing their availability while reducing the risk of loss.
- Real-time data analytics tools were implemented to process and visualize data, providing insights into student engagement levels and classroom conditions.

Impact

- Student engagement grew due to the interactive whiteboards and real-time feedback encouraging active participation.
- Educators gained insights into classroom dynamics, enabling them to make teaching adjustments.
- Resource utilization improved significantly as there was decreased loss or misplacement of educational materials, leading to cost savings.
- The initiative received positive feedback from students and faculty members, solidifying its position as an exemplary model for IoT-based smart classrooms in higher education.

Case Study 2: Smart Elementary School in Cityville

Summary An elementary school in Cityville has transformed its classrooms into learning spaces using IoT technology. The goal is to create an engaging environment for young students.

Implementation

- The school has installed interactive whiteboards and provided tablet devices for students.
- IoT sensors have been deployed to monitor classroom conditions such as temperature, lighting, and air quality.
- Student response systems are being used to provide instant feedback and assessments.
- Gamification elements have been incorporated into lessons to encourage participation and healthy competition.

Impact

- Introducing smart classrooms has increased student engagement, making the learning experience more enjoyable for learners.

- Educators have observed improved student attendance rates and a deeper understanding of the subject.
- The use of gamification elements has motivated students to participate actively in lessons.
- This innovative educational model implemented by the school has gained recognition, serving as an example of IoT-based learning in education.

Case Study 3: IoT-Powered High School Learning Labs

Summary A school can introduce Learning Labs powered by IoT as a trial program to provide students with a more personalized and adaptable learning environment.

Implementation

- The Learning Labs can incorporate IoT devices such as smart displays and wearable technology.
- Lessons can be customized based on real-time data to meet the needs of students using content delivery systems.
- Motion and proximity sensors can track student movements, allowing attendance tracking and adaptive lighting control.
- The school can use real-time data analytics to evaluate student performance and engagement.

Impact

- The tailored lessons based on individual learning preferences and progress can improve student achievement.
- An increase both in attendance and engagement can be observed by the school, leading to higher truancy rates.
- Educators were able to adjust their teaching methods, resulting in effective instruction.
- The pilot program's success will prompt the expansion of IoT-based learning labs into high schools within the district.

These examples showcase how IoT-based smart classrooms can transform educational settings. Whether education institutions, elementary schools, or high schools, integrating devices, sensors, and data analytics enhances the learning experience. It actively engages students while providing support for educators in delivering instruction. These impressive implementations demonstrate how IoT technology is transforming the future of education, creating interactive and adaptable learning environments that captivate and engage students.

3.8 Challenges and Future Directions

In this section, we will discuss the difficulties encountered in smart classrooms based on IoT (Internet of Things) technology and also delve into the future advancements of this innovative educational technology.

Challenges While smart classrooms that utilize IoT technology offer advantages, they also encounter challenges that must be addressed for successful implementation.

- ***Cost and Infrastructure:*** Implementing IoT technology requires an initial investment for educational institutions, which can pose financial difficulties. Moreover, older facilities might need infrastructure upgrades to support IoT devices and sensors.
- ***Security and Privacy:*** Safeguarding classroom-sensitive data is important. However, dealing with data security privacy concerns and complying with regulations can be challenging.
- ***Training and Adoption:*** Educators may require training to incorporate IoT technology into their teaching practices. Overcoming resistance to change and adoption barriers can impede the integration process.
- ***Maintenance and Support:*** Maintenance and support are necessary for IoT devices and sensors. Ensuring their reliability and functionality presents challenges.
- ***Interoperability:*** As the IoT ecosystem evolves, ensuring compatibility between IoT devices and systems from different manufacturers remains an ongoing challenge.

Future Directions Despite the challenges, smart classrooms based on IoT offer the potential for the future of education. There are directions for further development and implementation of this technology, including:

- ***Expanding the IoT ecosystem:*** With a broader range of devices and sensors becoming available, the IoT ecosystem can expect to grow even more. This expansion will unlock possibilities for creating interconnected smart classrooms.
- ***Integrating Artificial Intelligence (AI):*** Combining AI with IoT can enrich learning experiences. AI-powered adaptive learning systems have the potential to deliver tailored content and assessments.
- ***Embracing 5G Connectivity:*** The deployment of 5G networks will increase connectivity to IoT devices in smart classrooms, enabling real-time data transmission and creating more immersive educational experiences.
- ***Harnessing Augmented Reality (AR) and Virtual Reality (VR):*** Integrating IoT with AR and VR technologies allows us to build immersive and interactive learning environments. This approach can make complex subjects more accessible and engaging for students.

- ***Supporting Teachers with Augmented Technology:*** Leveraging IoT technology offers educators real-time support, including automated attendance tracking, early warning systems for at-risk students and analytics to optimize teaching strategies.
- ***Inclusive Education:*** Utilizing IoT technology has the potential to establish inclusive learning environments, guaranteeing that students with disabilities are equipped with the necessary tools and resources for their academic success.
- ***Ongoing Research and Development:*** Continuous research and development efforts are crucial to tackling existing challenges and exploring new possibilities for implementing IoT in education. Collaboration between institutions, educators, and technology providers will drive innovation forward.
- ***Student-Focused Approach:*** The future vision for smart classrooms should prioritize the students' learning journey. By collecting and analyzing data on students' unique needs, preferences, and performance, educators can design learning experiences tailored to each student.

The obstacles IoT-powered smart classrooms face are matched by the opportunities they bring to revolutionize education. As technology advances further and more educational institutions embrace IoT-based models, these challenges can be overcome, paving the way for smart classrooms to become the norm. The future of IoT-based smart classrooms promises a more interactive, adaptable, and personalized learning experience that will shape the next generation of successful learners in this digital age.

3.9 Conclusion

IoT technology in classrooms signifies educational progress, offering numerous advantages for students, teachers, and educational institutions. By utilizing smart classrooms based on IoT, educators can customize learning experiences, boost interaction, and monitor student advancement in time. These classrooms' structure, consisting of sensor networks, communication protocols, and cloud systems, establishes a base for creating immersive learning environments. Key devices and sensors play a vital role in encouraging student participation and optimizing the use of resources. Nevertheless, like any advancement, IoT-based classrooms present challenges, especially related to expenses, security issues, and privacy concerns. Overcoming these obstacles involves planning, robust security measures, and adherence to privacy laws. Real-world examples illustrate technology integration in educational settings by highlighting its concrete benefits, enhancing student engagement levels, elevating learning outcomes quality, and refining resource management. Looking ahead to the future of classrooms powered by IoT holds potential for advancements and growth. Expanding the network scope by incorporating AI and AR/VR technologies, embracing 5G connectivity, and providing educators with technology support are just some avenues worth exploring. To sum up, smart classrooms powered by IoT signify a change in education, providing a flexible and adaptive learning setting designed to meet the requirements of learners. By adopting this innovation and tackling related obstacles, educational institutions can discover possibilities for promoting inclusive, engaging, and customized learning encounters that enable students to excel in the digital era.

References

ANTT Robotics Ltd. (2024). *Revolutionizing education with IoT and gamification in math and science the power of gamification in math*. LinkedIn. https://www.linkedin.com/pulse/revolutionizing-education-iot-gamification-math-science-ovcvc/

Arrow Electronics, I. (2021). *Sensor technology: How they work & their applications*. Arrow Electronics, Inc. https://www.arrow.com/en/research-and-events/articles/sensor-technologies

Balbix. (2024). *IoT security challenges and problems*. Balbix. https://www.balbix.com/insights/addressing-iot-security-challenges/

Burunkaya, M., & Duraklar, K. (2022). Design and implementation of an IoT-based smart classroom incubator. *Applied Sciences, 12*(4), 1–18.

Campbell, R. (2024). *How the IoT classroom transforms the learning experience for students and teachers*. Richard Campbell. https://richardccampbell.com/the-iot-classroom/

Costa, R. L. (2023). *Building a gamified IoT learning platform: Empowering students through engagement*. LinkedIn. https://www.linkedin.com/pulse/building-gamified-iot-learning-platform-empowering-students-costa/

Dai, Z., Zhang, Q., Zhao, L., Zhu, X., & Zhou, D. (2023). Cloud-edge computing technology-based internet of things system for smart classroom environment. *International Journal of Emerging Technologies in Learning, 18*(08), 79–96.

Das, S. (2020). Smart classroom-an innovative concept of modern education. *International Journal of English Learning and Teaching Skills, 2*(3), 1–18. https://doi.org/10.15864/ijelts.2312

Explorance. (2023). *7 reasons why students need technology in the classroom*. Explorance. https://explorance.com/blog/7-reasons-students-need-technology-classroom/

Gerela, P., Mishra, P. N., & Vipat, R. (2022). Study on data visualization: It's importance in education sector. *International Journal of Health Sciences, 6*(May), 6298–6305.

Hearon, K. O., Mckee, M., Hossain, N., & Canbaz, M. A. (2021, July 1–9). *IoT privacy and security in teaching institutions: Inside the classroom and beyond*. American Association of Engineering Education. https://doi.org/10.18260/1-2%2D%2D37407

IoTDunia. (2020). *How is IoT changing today's school and classroom to Smart?* IoTDunia. https://iotdunia.com/smart-school-and-smart-classroom-with-iot/

Kaur, A., & Bhatia, M. (2022). Education sciences a survey of smart classroom literature. *Education Sciences, 12*(86), 1–30.

Lake, K. (2023). *How to implement adaptive learning in your organization*. ELearning Industry. https://elearningindustry.com/how-to-implement-adaptive-learning-in-your-organization

Liston, M., Morrin, A. M., Furlong, T., & Griffin, L. (2022, August). Integrating data science and the internet of things into science, technology, engineering, arts, and mathematics education through the use of new and emerging technologies. *Frontiers in Education, 7*, 1–21. https://doi.org/10.3389/feduc.2022.757866

Lumen Learning. (2023). *Benefits of technology in the classroom*. Lumen Learning. https://lumenlearning.com/technology-in-the-classroom/

Morze, N., Varchenko-trotsenko, L., Terletska, T., & Smyrnova-trybulska, E. (2021). *Implementation of adaptive learning at higher education institutions by means of Moodle LMS* (pp. 1–13). Journal of Physics. https://doi.org/10.1088/1742-6596/1840/1/012062

Ollivachreis. (2024). *IoT revolutionizing education from smart classrooms to personalized Learning*. Medium. https://medium.com/@oliviachris5567/iot-revolutionizing-education-from-smart-classrooms-to-personalized-learning-522ad42f1be0

Rajput, M. (2019). *Use of IoT in the education sector and why it's a good idea*. IoT For All. https://www.iotforall.com/smart-classroom-technology

Rathor, S. (2024). *The Internet of Things: Revolutionizing how we play and learn*. ELearning Industry. https://elearningindustry.com/iot-internet-of-things-trends-2020

Riseapps. (2021). *IoT in education: Benefits, opportunities, and examples*. LinkedIn. https://www.linkedin.com/pulse/iot-education-benefits-opportunities-examples-riseapps/

Sapale, S., & Banerjee, S. (2023). Empowering education: Exploring the impact of IoT in smart Learning environments. *International Journal of Advance Innovations, Thoughts & Ideas, 12*(5), 1–6. https://doi.org/10.4172/2277-1891.1000231

Schoolnet India. (2022). *Smart classroom: The future of learning with IoT integration*. Schoolnet India. https://www.schoolnetindia.com/blog/what-is-a-smart-classroom/

Trend Micro. (2021). *IoT security issues, threats, and defenses*. Trend Micro. https://www.trendmicro.com/vinfo/us/security/news/internet-of-things/iot-security-101-threats-issues-and-defenses

Venkatesh, C., Jayakrishna, D., & Sivayamini, L. (2022). Design of smart classroom in educational institutes for smart and a sustainable campus based on Internet of Things. In *Modern approaches in machine learning & cognitive science: A walkthrough* (pp. 1–29), Springer.

Wandr. (2023). *Data visualization in education*. Wandr. https://www.wandr.studio/blog/data-visualization-in-education

Yaganoglu, M., Bozkurt, F., Günay, F. B., Kul, S., Şimşek, E., Öztürk, G., & Karaman, S. (2023). Design and validation of IoT based smart classroom. *Multimedia Tools and Applications, 83*(22), 10–22.

Chapter 4
IoT-Based Educational Software and Hardware Systems

Abstract This chapter delves into the impact of incorporating Internet of Things (IoT) technology in education. It highlights the significance of developing and utilizing IoT-based software and hardware systems to enhance learning experiences. The discussion begins by exploring how IoT can transform education, making it more interactive, practical, and tailored to needs. The chapter further explores IoT-driven educational hardware systems, such as smart classroom setups, and various IoT devices used in education, such as interactive smart boards, environmental sensors, and wearable gadgets. Real-life examples demonstrate how IoT is practically applied in educational settings, from creating smart campuses to integrating wearables into physical education activities. Furthermore, it delves into IoT-powered educational software systems like learning management platforms (LMS), educational apps, and data analytics tools that showcase how integrating IoT can improve functionalities, support personalized learning paths, and facilitate dynamic content delivery. Cybersecurity in IoT-based education is emphasized through discussions on safeguarding data privacy, addressing device security vulnerabilities, and strengthening network protection measures. Recommendations on securing devices within environments and insights on adhering to privacy regulations through relevant case studies and practical instances are outlined. In addition, the chapter delves into trends and advancements in IoT for education, such as emerging technologies like 5G connectivity, edge computing, AI, AR, VR, and blockchain. It also discusses the expected integration of IoT platforms for learning, enhanced accessibility, and ethical concerns. The chapter emphasizes the significance of AI in IoT-driven education by focusing on learning experiences, predictive analytics, intelligent content suggestions, and sophisticated assessment methods. In summary, this chapter offers educators, administrators, and policymakers insights into how IoT could transform education and guides them on implementation strategies and security measures to consider and prospects in the educational field.

Keywords Internet of Things (IoT) technology · Learning experiences · Educational hardware systems · Educational software systems · Cybersecurity · Trends and advancements · Artificial intelligence (AI)

M. Kurni, Srinivasa K. G., *The Internet of Educational Things*,
https://doi.org/10.1007/978-3-031-67387-0_4

4.1 Introduction

Integrating Internet of Things (IoT) technology in specific sectors has brought about significant transformations. One area that has particularly shown promise and potential for IoT is education. By leveraging IoT technology, we can reshape the education landscape, making learning more engaging, efficient, and personalized. This chapter explores the intersection between IoT and education, focusing on how educational software and hardware systems are developed and implemented and their impact.

The digital era has completely revolutionized how we access information and gain knowledge. With the widespread use of smartphones, tablets, and internet connectivity options, learners of all ages now have access to vast information and resources within arm's reach. However, the educational sector has yet to tap into IoT's potential to enhance the learning experience.

This chapter examines the vital components of IoT in education, namely software and hardware systems, and how crucial they are in modern education.

4.2 IoT-Based Educational Hardware System

Integrating Internet of Things (IoT) technologies has transformed education, introducing interactive learning environments. In this section, we will delve into the range of hardware systems based on IoT. These systems aim to enhance the physical learning space and revolutionize student interaction with educational content.

Smart Classroom Infrastructure Various devices and technologies aim to improve the physical learning environment in education. One important aspect is developing classroom infrastructure, incorporating IoT devices and technology to create interactive and dynamic learning spaces (Q-NEX Technology, 2024).

- ***Interactive Smart Boards and Displays:*** Interactive smart boards or displays are a significant classroom feature. These interactive surfaces allow teachers to project lessons, diagrams, and multimedia content, facilitating student engagement. Moreover, these boards support touch, pen, or gesture-based interactions, encouraging collaborative learning experiences.
- ***Environmental Monitoring and Control:*** Smart classrooms can be equipped with IoT sensors that monitor and control the classroom environment. These sensors can adjust lighting, temperature, and ventilation to provide a comfortable and conducive learning environment. Additionally, they can detect occupancy levels to help conserve energy when the classroom is unoccupied.

- ***IoT-enabled Student Devices:*** Many educational institutions provide students with IoT-enabled devices, like tablets, laptops, or wearable technologies. These devices are designed to connect to the school network, allowing students to engage in interactive lessons, access learning resources, and collaborate with their classmates.

IoT Devices for Education IoT devices designed for education purposes extend their benefits beyond classrooms. These devices aim to enrich the learning experience inside and outside the classroom (Kumar, 2023).

- ***Wearable Technologies:*** Smartwatches or fitness trackers have educational uses. They assist students in monitoring their physical activity, managing their well-being, and even receiving updates about their academic progress. Wearable devices can also be utilized in educational games and activities.
- ***Educational Robotics:*** Robots powered by IoT technology are increasingly employed in educational settings to teach coding, problem-solving, and critical thinking skills. Students can program these robots to perform various tasks, fostering creativity and promoting STEM (Science, Technology, Engineering, and Mathematics) education.
- ***IoT Sensors in Laboratories:*** IoT sensors are deployed in science and engineering laboratories to collect and analyze data. These sensors can measure temperature, pressure, humidity, and other parameters, enabling students to gain hands-on experience conducting experiments and gathering data.

Case Studies and Examples To gain a grasp of how IoT-based educational hardware systems are implemented in practice, let us examine a few case studies and examples;

- ***Smart Campus Infrastructure:*** Universities and schools worldwide invest in smart campus infrastructure. For instance, the University of California, Los Angeles (UCLA) has utilized IoT technology to create smart classrooms, optimize energy consumption, and equip students with IoT-enabled devices for enhanced learning experiences.
- ***Wearables in Physical Education:*** Some educational institutions have introduced wearable devices for physical education classes. These wearables keep track of students' physical activity levels, motivating them to stay active and adopt healthy lifestyles. The E-Textiles Lab at North Carolina State University has developed wearables designed explicitly for this purpose.
- ***Robotic Learning:*** Various robotics platforms, such as LEGO Mindstorms, have gained popularity in schools as tools for teaching robotics and programming concepts. Students can program robots to accomplish tasks, fostering an understanding of technology and problem-solving abilities.

4.3 IoT-Based Educational Software Systems

In this section, let us focus on the influence of software systems based on the Internet of Things (IoT). These systems, such as Learning Management Systems (LMS), educational applications, and data analytics tools, revolutionize learning. They provide interactivity, customization options, and valuable insights driven by data.

Learning Management Systems (LMS) Learning Management Systems (LMS) are vital in modern education as they are the foundation of digital learning environments. They offer a comprehensive platform for educators, students, and administrators to manage and deliver educational content. IoT technology integration has revolutionized LMS, making them more interactive and data-driven (Narasimhan, 2023).

- ***Real-time Progress Tracking:*** LMSs empowered by IoT can monitor student progress in real-time. This includes monitoring student engagement, assessment results, and attendance. Educators can access this information to gain insights into student performance and adjust their teaching methods accordingly.
- ***Personalized Learning Paths:*** LMS uses data analytics to create personalized student learning paths. By analyzing a student's performance and preferences, the system can suggest resources, assignments, or activities that cater to their needs. This personalized approach greatly enhances the learning experience.
- ***Interactive Content:*** With IoT integration, LMS can provide interactive content and activities. For instance, online quizzes can adapt based on a student's proficiency level, while virtual labs offer hands-on experiments with real-time data collection.
- ***Communication and Collaboration:*** IoT-driven LMS often incorporate features that facilitate improved user communication and collaboration. Students can participate in real-time discussions, collaborate on group assignments, and stay informed about course updates and reminders.

Educational Apps and Platforms In addition to learning management systems (LMS), educational apps and platforms have become a part of IoT-based educational software systems. These apps serve specific learning purposes and can be accessed on smartphones, tablets, and computers (Intuz, 2023; Pappas et al., 2022; Yashika, 2023).

- ***Mobile Learning Apps:*** Leveraging IoT connectivity, mobile learning apps offer students convenient access to educational content. They often include quizzes, flashcards, and video lectures. These apps are great for reinforcing classroom learning and self-paced study.
- ***Gamified Learning Platforms:*** Education has embraced gamification with the help of IoT technology. Gamified platforms incorporate game design elements to make learning more engaging and enjoyable. Students can earn points, badges, or rewards as they complete tasks.

- ***Virtual Reality (VR) & Augmented Reality (AR):*** The development of VR and AR applications for education is closely linked to IoT advancements. These technologies provide immersive experiences that allow students to explore virtual environments and interact with 3D models. For instance, medical students can use AR to visualize complex anatomical structures.

Data Analytics and Personalized Learning The core of software systems based on IoT revolves around data analytics. IoT generates a wealth of data to enrich learning (Jagdale, 2023).

- ***Insights from Data:*** Data analytics can offer educators insights into student performance, engagement, and learning preferences. By analyzing this data, educators can pinpoint areas where students might encounter difficulties and provide targeted assistance.
- ***Predicting the Future:*** Predictive analytics utilizes past data to predict future outcomes. Predictive analytics can help identify students at risk of falling or dropping out, allowing educators to intervene and offer additional support.
- ***Customized Learning Systems:*** Educational software systems powered by IoT can employ adaptive learning algorithms. These systems adapt the difficulty level and pace of content based on each student's progress, ensuring that the learning experience is neither easy nor challenging.

Case Studies and Examples Let us examine some real-life case studies and examples to demonstrate how IoT-based educational software systems are implemented.

- ***Edmodo:*** Edmodo is an educational platform incorporating features to establish a collaborative and interactive learning environment. It offers teachers and students tools for communicating, submitting assignments, and tracking timely progress.
- ***Duolingo:*** Duolingo is a language learning application that utilizes gamification to engage users. It utilizes IoT technology to monitor user progress and provide personalized lessons. Students can learn at their own pace while receiving immediate feedback on their performance.
- ***Labster:*** Labster is a virtual laboratory platform used in science education. It leverages IoT technology to provide lab simulations where students can conduct experiments and gather data virtually.

4.4 IoT Security in Education

In the age of education powered by the Internet of Things (IoT), ensuring security becomes a priority. As educational institutions adopt IoT to enhance learning experiences, they encounter security hurdles that require thoughtful attention and robust solutions.

IoT Security Challenges As educational institutions continue to adopt IoT technology to enhance learning experiences, they must also address various security challenges that accompany it (Hearon et al., 2021; Oliynyk, 2023). IoT security is a multifaceted concern in educational settings where specific considerations arise.

- ***Safeguarding Data Privacy:*** Protecting student and faculty data is essential. Educational institutions handle academic information, making them appealing targets for cyberattacks. Stringent regulations like the Family Educational Rights and Privacy Act (FERPA) in the United States impose requirements on how this data should be handled and safeguarded.
- ***Addressing Device Vulnerabilities:*** Properly securing IoT devices is crucial as they can be exploited. Many IoT devices lack built-in security features, and manufacturers may not prioritize security measures. This vulnerability can potentially compromise data integrity and device functionality.
- ***Enhancing Network Security:*** Since IoT devices connect to an institution's network, ensuring proper security is vital. A compromised device could be an entry point for attackers seeking access to data or network resources.

Best Practices for Securing IoT in Education To address the security challenges of using IoT devices in education, following specific guidelines and implementing security measures are essential (Sander, 2024; Amos, 2023). Figure 4.1 showcases recommendations for enhancing security in educational settings, offering valuable tips on protecting school environments from possible security risks.

- ***Device Management:*** Keep a comprehensive record of all IoT devices connected to the network and ensure they are regularly updated with the latest security patches and firmware. Review and remove any devices that are no longer needed or in use regularly.
- ***Access Control:*** Establish access controls to ensure authorized individuals can access and manage IoT devices. This can be achieved through implementing role-based access control and authentication protocols.
- ***Encryption:*** Utilize encryption techniques to safeguard data while it is transmitted and stored. Encryption adds a layer of protection even if a device becomes compromised by preventing access to sensitive information.
- ***Network Segmentation:*** Divide the network into segments or sections, isolating IoT devices from critical systems. In a security breach, this segmentation helps limit its impact and prevents attackers from moving through the network.
- ***Security Awareness:*** Educate staff members and students on best practices for IoT security and increase awareness about risks associated with these devices, such as using weak passwords or sharing personal information.
- ***Security Audits and Penetration Testing:*** Conduct regular penetration tests to identify IoT infrastructure vulnerabilities. This allows for detecting weaknesses before malicious actors can exploit them, which can assist in resolving problems before they are exploited by individuals with intent.

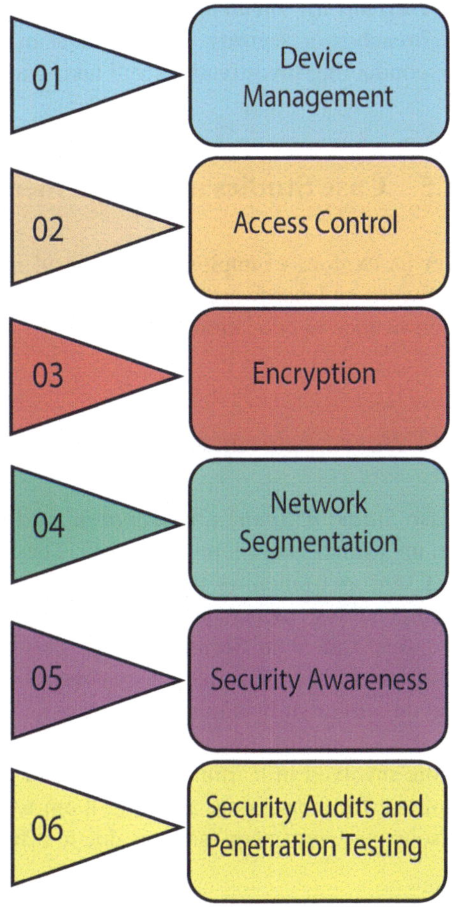

Fig. 4.1 Best practices for securing IoT in Education

Privacy Concerns and Compliance Ensuring data privacy is extremely important in the field of education. Educational institutions must comply with regulations (Ashbel, 2020; Bisht, 2023). Here are some recommended steps.

- ***Familiarity with Data Protection Laws:*** Understanding and adhering to data protection laws, such as FERPA in the United States or GDPR in Europe, is essential. Make sure your data privacy policies align with these laws.
- ***Be transparent and obtain consent:*** Communicate your policies on collecting and using data from students and staff members. Obtaining consent for data collection and processing is essential, allowing individuals to exercise their rights regarding their information.
- ***Establish Data Retention Policies:*** Implement policies that ensure you do not retain data longer than necessary. This helps minimize the risk of privacy breaches and unauthorized access.

- ***Develop an Incident Response Plan:*** Create a plan for addressing any data breaches or security incidents that may occur. This includes notifying parties conducting investigations and taking appropriate actions to resolve the issue.

4.5 Case Studies and Implementations

Let us explore examples of successful implementation of IoT-based educational software and hardware systems to truly grasp IoT's implications and real-world significance in education.

IoT-Based Education in K-12

Case Study: A Smart Classroom in an Elementary School IoT devices can help set up a smart classroom in a school. These devices include interactive smartboards, IoT sensors to monitor the environment, and tablets for students. This smart classroom enables teachers to create engaging lessons with interactive content and display real-time data. Students can actively participate in quizzes and group activities using the tablets. The IoT sensors ensure the classroom maintains an optimal learning environment by adjusting lighting and temperature.

Implementing this technology increases student engagement as they become more involved in learning. Teachers can identify struggling students through real-time performance data, allowing them to provide timely support. The school will also experience energy savings due to efficient classroom management.

Higher Education and IoT

Case Study: IoT on a University Campus A university campus can incorporate IoT technology into its facilities and classrooms. It can install IoT sensors to monitor classroom occupancy, energy consumption, and security. Moreover, the campus provides students and faculty members with IoT-enabled devices like smart student ID cards and wearable technologies. These devices allow students to access course materials, track attendance, and receive notifications regarding events and deadlines.

The IoT system can also include a Learning Management System (LMS) seamlessly integrated with the campus infrastructure. The LMS can offer personalized learning paths for students while educators utilize real-time data to adapt their teaching methods accordingly. The system's predictive analytics capabilities are instrumental in identifying students facing challenges and enabling interventions.

Lifelong Learning and Professional Development

Case Study: IoT in a Professional Development Program A program for professional development and lifelong learning can incorporate IoT technology to enhance the learning experience of adult learners. The participants have IoT devices to monitor their physical activity, stress levels, and sleep patterns. This valuable data can then be integrated into the educational platform to promote a work-life balance and effective stress management.

Furthermore, the program can utilize IoT-enabled remote learning platforms, allowing adult learners to access course materials and participate actively in classrooms. By receiving real-time feedback from the wearable devices and the learning platform, individuals can make informed decisions regarding their professional development journey and overall well-being.

Success Stories and Lessons Learned While incorporating IoT in education has advantages, the case studies also provide lessons and success stories.

- ***Personalization:*** IoT enhances student engagement by offering feedback and personalized learning experiences in time. Educators can observe increased motivation and active participation among students.
- ***Data-driven decision-making:*** Real-time data analytics empower educators to make decisions regarding student support and curriculum adjustments. This proves advantageous for identifying struggling students and providing timely intervention.
- ***Resource Optimization:*** Implementing IoT often leads to resource savings by managing classrooms and campuses, including reduced energy consumption.
- ***Privacy and Security:*** Institutions must prioritize addressing privacy and security concerns surrounding implementation. Compliance with data protection regulations is crucial in safeguarding information.

4.6 Future Trends and Innovations

The Internet of Things (IoT) in education is an evolving area. It is crucial to anticipate and adjust to the latest developments and advancements. This section will delve into the future of IoT in education and the emerging technologies expected to impact it.

Emerging Technologies in IoT for Education As we progress in education, incorporating advanced technologies into the Internet of Things (IoT) can transform our learning. These state-of-the-art technologies present opportunities to improve connectivity, enable data analysis, and offer immersive learning experiences. Let us explore some emerging technologies in IoT that can revolutionize education,

- ***5G Connectivity:*** Introducing 5G networks promises more reliable internet connectivity. This advancement will enable communication and data exchange among IoT devices, enhancing remote learning and supporting real-time immersive experiences in classrooms and virtual environments.
- ***Edge computing:*** Edge computing, which involves processing data closer to its source, reduces latency and improves the speed at which IoT devices can respond to commands. This technology is essential for delivering real-time analytics and supporting applications in education.
- ***Artificial Intelligence (AI):*** AI has the potential to revolutionize education by providing analytics and personalized learning experiences. By analyzing data from IoT devices, AI algorithms can customize learning materials, assessment methods, and support strategies to meet each student's needs.
- ***Augmented Reality (AR) and Virtual Reality (VR):*** AR/VR technologies are increasingly prevalent in education. They offer interactive experiences that allow students to explore virtual environments, conduct experiments, and engage in simulations, greatly enhancing their understanding of subjects.
- ***Blockchain:*** Blockchain technology offers a way to store educational credentials, certificates, and records. This groundbreaking advancement aims to create a system ensuring accomplishments' integrity and transparency. Its primary purpose is to simplify the process of students sharing their credentials with employers and educational institutions, guaranteeing that they are genuine and unaltered.

Predictions for the Future As the Internet of Things (IoT) continues to shape the field of education, here are some predictions for what the future holds.

- ***Ubiquitous IoT Integration:*** IoT devices and sensors will be integrated into all aspects of education, from classrooms to administrative processes. These tools will provide data and insights that can enhance decision-making.
- ***Lifelong Learning Platforms:*** IoT will support lifelong learning by offering individuals of all ages access to educational and professional development opportunities that cater to their needs and preferences.
- ***Improved Accessibility:*** IoT will help make education more accessible to students in underserved areas. Remote learning will be possible in places with limited connectivity.
- ***Ethical Considerations:*** As IoT gathers increasing student data, addressing privacy and data usage concerns becomes crucial. Educational institutions must establish policies and practices that safeguard students' privacy.

The Role of Artificial Intelligence in IoT Education The potential of combining IoT and artificial intelligence for education is highly promising. AI can leverage the vast amount of data generated by IoT devices, offering valuable insights for educators and students (Stemrobo Technologies, 2023). Here are some key areas where AI will play a vital role in IoT-based education.

- ***Personalized Learning:*** AI algorithms will utilize IoT device data to customize learning materials and activities according to each student's needs. This personalization approach will cater to various learning styles, speeds, and preferences.

- ***Predictive Analytics:*** AI can identify students at risk of falling or dropping out, providing timely intervention and support. Additionally, AI can predict areas where students might struggle and recommend resources accordingly.
- ***Intelligent Content Recommendations:*** Based on a student's learning history and progress, AI will provide content recommendations that encourage self-directed learning while aligning with individual interests and goals.
- ***Smart Assessment:*** AI-powered assessment tools will offer real-time feedback on student performance. They can efficiently grade assignments and exams, reducing educators' workload while providing students insights into their progress.

Keeping up with the latest advancements and utilizing technology to enhance learning experiences is crucial in this changing environment.

4.7 Conclusion

In summary, incorporating Internet of Things (IoT) technology in education marks a paradigm shift in teaching and learning. This chapter has explored the opportunities and challenges of using IoT-based software and hardware systems. It highlights the potential for creating classrooms and personalized learning paths through IoT-driven learning management systems, offering educators tools to build engaging learning environments. However, it also emphasizes the need to address concerns around data privacy, device security, and ethical implications to safeguard educational ecosystems. The future of IoT in education holds promise for innovation and transformation, with technologies like artificial intelligence, augmented reality, and blockchain set to enhance learning experiences and accessibility. By embracing these advancements while prioritizing security and privacy considerations, educational institutions can leverage IoT's potential to unlock opportunities and shape a more inclusive, adaptive, and impactful educational landscape.

References

Amos, Z. (2023). *How to improve IoT security in the classroom*. HackerNoon. https://hackernoon.com/how-to-improve-iot-security-in-the-classroom

Ashbel, A. (2020). *A beginner's guide to data privacy laws and compliance in the education industry*. NetApp, Inc. https://bluexp.netapp.com/blog/ccs-blg-data-privacy-laws-and-compliance-in-the-education-industry

Bisht, A. (2023). *7 tips to ensure security and data privacy in school management solutions*. Schoolcues Blog. https://www.schoolcues.com/blog/7-tips-to-ensure-security-and-data-privacy-in-school-management-solutions/

Hearon, K. O., Mckee, M., Hossain, N., & Canbaz, M. A. (2021, July 1–9). *IoT privacy and security in teaching institutions: Inside the classroom and beyond*. American Association of Engineering Education. https://doi.org/10.18260/1-2%2D%2D37407

Intuz. (2023). *IoT in the education industry: Embracing the new way of learning*. LinkedIn. https://www.linkedin.com/pulse/iot-education-industry-embracing-new-way-learning-intuz-1f/

Jagdale, S. (2023). *Leveraging IoT technology for a smarter education system*. IoT Times. https://iot.eetimes.com/is-the-future-of-iot-batteryless/

Kumar, A. (2023). *IoT in education: A future of smart and sustainable learning*. LinkedIn. https://www.linkedin.com/pulse/iot-education-future-smart-sustainable-learning-ankit-kumar/

Narasimhan, S. (2023). *Why integrating IoT technology into your LMS is the future of learning*. HurixDigital. https://www.hurix.com/why-integrating-iot-technology-into-your-lms-is-the-future-of-learning/

Oliynyk, K. (2023). *IoT technology in education*. WebbyLab. https://webbylab.com/blog/impact-of-iot-technology-on-education/#:~:text=PrivacyandSecurityConcerns,soonarenotexcluded

Pappas, G., Siegel, J., Vogiatzakis, I. N., & Politopoulos, K. (2022, June). Gamification and the internet of things in education. In *Handbook of intelligent techniques in educational process* (pp. 317–339). Springer International Publishing. https://doi.org/10.1007/978-3-031-04662-9

Q-NEX Technology. (2024). *How to build your smart classroom: A step-y-step guide*. Q-NEX Technology.. https://qnextech.com/blog/how-to-build-your-smart-classroom-a-step-by-step-guide/

Sander, C. (2024). *IoT threats in schools: Best practices for mitigating dangers*. The Fast Mode. https://www.thefastmode.com/expert-opinion/35132-iot-threats-in-schools-best-practices-for-mitigating-dangers

Stemrobo Technologies. (2023). *AI and IoT labs: Transforming schools into innovation hubs*. Stemrobo Technologies. https://www.stemrobo.com/ai-and-iot-labs-in-schools-ai-and-iot-in-education/

Yashika. (2023). *AR and VR in education: Preparing students for an IoT-driven future*. Medium. https://medium.com/@nisha0309/ar-and-vr-in-education-preparing-students-for-an-iot-driven-future-cf646ad9dfc9

Chapter 5
IoT and Network Infrastructure for Smart Education

Abstract This chapter delves into Smart Education and its connection with IoT (Internet of Things) technology and network infrastructure. It introduces Smart Education and discusses how it changes traditional learning methods, highlighting IoT's role in shaping modern educational environments. The chapter also discusses the advantages of smart education, such as improved learning experiences, personalized learning, accessibility, efficiency, and better assessment techniques. It examines aspects of smart education, such as learning management systems (LMS), e-learning tools, and data analytics. Moreover, it emphasizes the importance of network infrastructure in enabling smart education by focusing on elements like connectivity, scalability, data transfer, and security. The challenges in setting up network infrastructure for smart education and considerations for managing data and security within the IoT and network infrastructure environment are discussed. Real-life examples demonstrate how IoT technology and network infrastructure are transforming education in institutions. Additionally, the chapter explores incorporating IoT devices with network infrastructure while addressing challenges like reliability, scalability, compatibility, and security concerns. Exciting new developments and advancements in smart education like AI, AR/VR, 5G connectivity, and blockchain are being explored alongside predictions for the future of education. The obstacles and factors in integrating network infrastructure into educational settings are also being examined. These include issues like bridging connectivity gaps, ensuring accessibility, providing training, safeguarding data privacy, considering financial aspects, promoting literacy, enhancing cybersecurity measures, adapting to change effectively, and pondering ethical implications. This examination sheds light on how IoT and network infrastructure could revolutionize education while highlighting the challenges that must be addressed for smart education initiatives' implementation and long-term sustainability.

Keywords Smart Education · Internet of Things (IoT) technology · Network infrastructure · Learning management systems (LMS) · Data Analytics · Connectivity · Security

M. Kurni, Srinivasa K. G., *The Internet of Educational Things*,
https://doi.org/10.1007/978-3-031-67387-0_5

5.1 Introduction

Over the years, there has been a significant shift in education due to technological advancements and the vast expansion of the Internet. Digitally enhanced approaches replace conventional teaching and learning methods, collectively called "Smart Education" (Demir, 2021). In this chapter, we will introduce the concept of smart education and delve into how the Internet of Things (IoT) and network infrastructure play a vital role in shaping the future of learning.

The Digital Transformation of Education Gone are the days when education relied on chalkboards, textbooks, and standardized tests. The digital revolution in education has completely changed how knowledge is shared, spread, and absorbed. Digital technology has made education more accessible, interactive, and tailored to needs. Smart education is leading this transformation by leveraging technology to improve learning and create efficient educational settings (Dua, 2018)

Role of IoT in Smart Education The Internet of Things concept, known as IoT, refers to a network that connects devices, sensors, and objects to allow for data collection and exchange. It is important to note that IoT goes beyond applications or smart homes; it has also made its way into the field of education. In educational settings, IoT devices play a vital role in collecting valuable data, monitoring in real-time, and connecting different elements within the learning environment. This enables educators to make decisions based on data, tailor learning experiences according to needs, and optimize resource allocation effectively (Terzieva et al., 2022)

5.2 Smart Education: Concepts and Benefits

Smart Education is a learning method that utilizes technology and creative techniques to enhance the educational process, making it more efficient and captivating. In this section, we will delve into the fundamental concepts of smart education and its numerous advantages to students, teachers, and educational institutions.

Defining Smart Education Smart education encompasses various strategies and technologies to enhance the quality of education. It goes beyond traditional classroom teaching and learning methods, taking a holistic approach by integrating digital tools, utilizing data-driven decision-making, and providing personalized learning experiences. At its essence, smart education utilizes technology to improve every aspect of the educational journey, including content delivery and assessment (Demir, 2021)

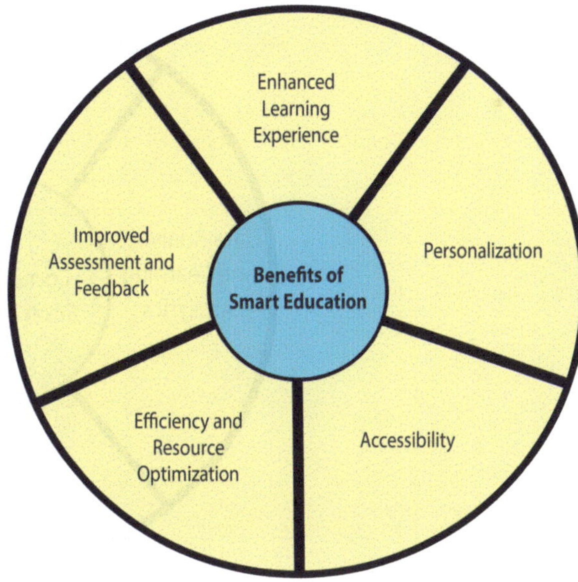

Fig. 5.1 Benefits of smart education

Benefits of Smart Education Implementing smart education brings a range of advantages (as shown in Fig. 5.1) for everyone involved (Best Education Sikar, 2024; Bach, 2015):

- ***Enhanced Learning Experience:*** Smart education incorporates engaging multimedia content, interactive simulations, and online resources to make learning more exciting and dynamic. Students can access information and collaborate with peers to expand their knowledge base.
- ***Personalization:*** Smart education utilizes data and analytics to customize educational content based on students' needs and preferences. Adaptive learning systems can identify areas where students may struggle and provide targeted support.
- ***Accessibility:*** Smart education breaks down physical barriers, making education accessible to remote areas and underserved populations. Students can learn independently by following flexible schedules accommodating different learning styles and requirements.
- ***Efficiency and Resource Optimization:*** Data-driven insights can help educational institutions make informed decisions about resource allocation and curriculum development. Automation processes and digital resources alleviate administrative burdens, enabling educators to focus on teaching.
- ***Improved Assessment and Feedback:*** Smart education platforms offer sophisticated assessment tools that facilitate real-time evaluation of student progress. Students can receive prompt feedback, enabling them to monitor their progress and make improvements.

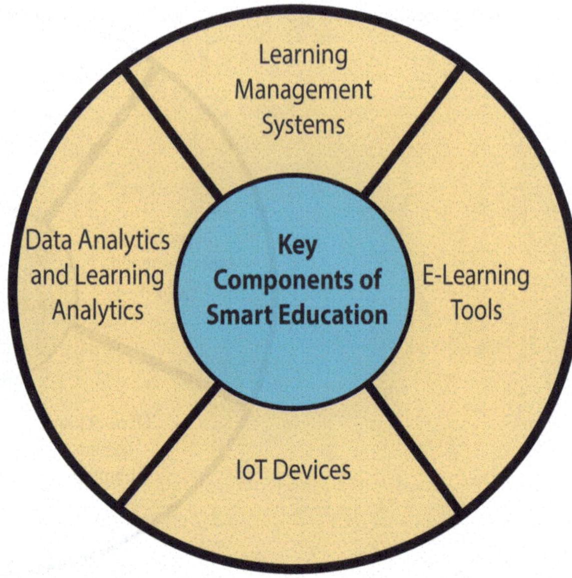

Fig. 5.2 Key components of smart education

Key Components of Smart Education Smart education is a multifaceted concept encompassing various essential elements (as shown in Fig. 5.2) (Demir, 2021; UNESCO, 2011; Jiang et al., 2022).

- ***Learning Management Systems (LMS):*** LMS platforms make creating, managing, and delivering digital content easier. They also enable collaboration, assessment, and progress tracking.
- ***E-learning tools:*** E-learning tools include many resources, such as online courses, interactive modules, and virtual labs. These tools allow students to learn at their own pace.
- ***Data Analytics and Learning Analytics:*** Data analytics involves collecting and analyzing data from various sources, including student performance and engagement. Learning analytics uses data to enhance the learning experience, identify students who need extra support, and tailor content accordingly.
- ***IoT Devices:*** IoT devices play a vital role in smart education by providing real-time data from classrooms, labs, and campuses. They contribute to improved resource management and personalized learning experiences.

5.3 Network Infrastructure for Smart Education

Network infrastructure is the foundation of any technological transformation, including smart education. In this section, we will delve into network infrastructure's role in facilitating and maintaining the revolution in education.

Importance of Robust Network Infrastructure In smart education, having a robust and reliable network infrastructure is crucial as it is the cornerstone that connects all the system components (Alexa, 2021). The significance of a network infrastructure in education can be summarized as follows.

- ***Connectivity:*** The network facilitates communication between devices, sensors, students, teachers, and the digital materials they interact with.
- ***Accessibility:*** A reliable network ensures that educational content and resources are readily accessible to students regardless of location or device.
- ***Scalability:*** As educational institutions expand and incorporate digital tools, the network infrastructure needs to scale up to meet increasing demands for bandwidth and connectivity.
- ***Data Transmission:*** The network is responsible for transmitting data from IoT devices and other sources to data centers for analysis. This allows educators to gather insights and make informed decisions.
- ***Security:*** Maintaining a secure network infrastructure is essential in safeguarding student data and upholding the integrity of digital learning resources.

Types of Network Technologies Smart education relies on a set of technologies to support its network infrastructure (Demir, 2021), including:

- ***Wired Networks:*** Educational institutions rely on ethernet and fiber optic cables to establish reliable connections, vital in computer labs and other fixed devices.
- ***Wireless Networks:*** Wi-Fi networks are ubiquitous in educational settings, offering flexibility and mobility for both students and educators. In areas like lecture halls and libraries, high-density Wi-Fi is essential.
- ***Edge Computing:*** Edge computing involves processing data closer to its source, reducing latency, and improving real-time data analysis. This approach is relevant for IoT applications in education.

Challenges in Network Infrastructure for Smart Education Implementing and maintaining a network infrastructure for smart education presents its obstacles (Buzzapp, 2024):

- ***Bandwidth and Capacity:*** The growing utilization of digital resources and IoT devices demands substantial bandwidth. Educational institutions must ensure they possess the capacity to support digital initiatives.
- ***Network Security:*** Safeguarding sensitive student data and ensuring network security are significant concerns. Institutions must implement security measures to protect their networks.
- ***Redundancy:*** Network downtime can disrupt classes and administrative processes. Therefore, redundancy and backup systems are crucial to ensure reliability.
- ***Budget Constraints:*** Developing and maintaining a robust network infrastructure can be expensive. Educational institutions must allocate resources carefully to ensure the infrastructure meets their needs within limitations.

- ***Accessibility and Inclusivity:*** Ensuring equal access to the network for all students is vital. Educational institutions must address issues related to accessibility and inclusivity, thereby preventing any disparities in learning opportunities.

5.4 Data Management and Security

Data management and security are essential in an IoT and network infrastructure ecosystem. This section will explore the obstacles and factors to consider regarding managing and protecting data about IoT devices and network infrastructure within education.

Data Collection and Analysis One of the advantages of incorporating IoT devices in education is the abundance of data they generate. This data encompasses aspects such as students' interactions with resources and the conditions within the classroom. The collection and analysis of this data bring forth several benefits (Cambridge Spark, 2023):

- ***Personalization:*** By leveraging this data, educators can personalize learning experiences by tailoring content to meet each student's needs.
- ***Assessment:*** Real-time analysis allows educators to assess student progress, identify areas where students may require support, and provide assistance.
- ***Resource Management:*** Data can also be utilized to make informed decisions regarding resource allocation, ensuring that educational materials are distributed effectively.

These advantages highlight how IoT devices significantly enhance education by enabling personalized learning experiences, facilitating assessment procedures, and optimizing resource management.

Data Privacy and Security Concerns While data collection has benefits, it is crucial to address the privacy and security concerns that come with it (AI and the LinkedIn Community, 2024a; Deetya Education, 2023).

- ***Protecting Student Privacy:*** Safeguarding student data confidentiality is essential. Educational institutions must adhere to data protection regulations. Ensure that sensitive information remains secure.
- ***Ensuring Data Security:*** Protecting data from unauthorized access and potential breaches is vital. Implementing cybersecurity measures becomes essential to safeguard educational networks and their valuable data.
- ***Complying with Regulations:*** Educational institutions must comply with data protection laws like the Family Educational Rights and Privacy Act (FERPA) in the United States or the General Data Protection Regulation (GDPR) in the European Union.

- ***Data Retention Considerations:*** Determining how long data should be retained, who should have access to it, and establishing protocols for disposing of it when no longer necessary require careful attention.

Compliance with Education Regulations Educational institutions must comply with national laws to avoid complications and maintain the public's trust. These regulations vary depending on the region and cover data privacy and accessibility.

Moreover, data breaches and privacy violations can have significant consequences in terms of penalties and damage to reputation. Therefore, having a robust framework for managing and securing data is vital.

Educational institutions must take a multifaceted data management and security approach, including solutions and administrative measures. This may involve implementing encryption and access controls, conducting security audits, providing staff training, and establishing data collection, use, and storage policies.

Effectively managing and securing data in a smart education environment is crucial not for safeguarding the privacy and security of student information but for fostering trust among stakeholders within the educational community.

5.5 Case Studies

This section will delve into real-life scenarios that showcase network infrastructure utilization in the education sector. These instances demonstrate how these technologies are revolutionizing conventional educational spaces and turning them into intelligent and data-oriented environments.

Smart Campus at XYZ University

Background XYZ University set out to create a smart and interconnected campus. It aimed to enhance the learning experience, simplify processes, and improve resource management.

Applications of the Internet of Things (IoT)

- ***Connected Classrooms:*** They can deploy IoT sensors to monitor classroom occupancy and environmental conditions, helping to optimize energy usage and ensure an ideal learning environment.
- ***Smart Libraries:*** They can track library resources in real-time using smart shelves and RFID tags, improving resource management and accessibility.
- ***Student Engagement:*** Wearable devices can be introduced to promote student activity and collaboration. These devices offer gamified learning experiences.

Benefits Achieved

- ***Energy Savings:*** Implementing IoT sensors will reduce energy consumption, which saves the university money on energy expenses.
- ***Resource Optimization:*** Smart libraries enhance resource availability and streamline book checkouts, benefiting students and staff.
- ***Enhanced Learning Experience:*** Using gamified learning experiences and real-time classroom data improves student engagement and success rates.

Adaptive Learning at ABC School District

Background The ABC School District serves students from kindergarten to K-12 grade and has a student population faced with the challenge of accommodating different learning speeds among students. They can implement adaptive learning solutions to personalize education to tackle this issue.

IoT Applications

- ***Adaptive Learning Platforms:*** Student progress and behavior can be tracked using IoT devices and software, enabling customized learning materials and pacing based on needs.
- ***Data-Driven Interventions:*** Real-time data analysis can be utilized to identify students who are struggling academically, triggering targeted interventions designed to support them.

Benefits

- ***Improved Student Outcomes:*** Implementing adaptive learning will enhance performance, particularly among students who had previously faced difficulties in their studies.
- ***Enhanced Teacher Effectiveness:*** Educators receive insights based on data analysis, allowing them to tailor their teaching methods according to each student's needs.
- ***Equity in Education:*** Adaptive learning is vital in bridging achievement gaps and ensuring equal access to a quality education.

Secure Distance Learning at DEF School System

Background DEF School System prioritized data privacy and security to ensure a transition in response to a need for distance learning during a public health crisis.

Various IoT Applications Can Be Utilized to Address These Concerns

- ***Secure Video Conferencing:*** IoT-enabled platforms facilitate secure communication between students and educators during video conferences.
- ***Data Encryption:*** All data transmitted during distance learning can be encrypted to safeguard student privacy.
- ***Access Controls:*** Stringent measures can be implemented to control access to sensitive data, preventing unauthorized individuals from gaining entry.

The Benefits of These Measures Will Be Significant

- ***Continuous Education:*** The DEF School System will ensure uninterrupted access to quality education throughout the crisis.
- ***Data Privacy:*** By prioritizing security and privacy, student and educator data remain protected against risks associated with learning.
- ***Trust and Confidence:*** Stakeholders such as parents and teachers will have the utmost confidence in the security and privacy of the remote learning tools employed.

These real-life examples exemplify how IoT technology and network infrastructure have revolutionized education from university campuses to K-12 school districts. The practical implementation of these technologies has demonstrated their ability to enhance the learning experience, optimize resource allocation, and maintain data security within educational environments.

5.6 IoT and Network Infrastructure Integration

The effective use of IoT in education heavily depends on how IoT devices are integrated with a robust network infrastructure. In this section, we will explore the details of this integration process. Address the challenges and factors to consider when establishing a smooth and productive IoT ecosystem for educational institutions.

The Role of Network Connectivity Network connectivity is vital in connecting IoT devices in a smart educational environment. It is the communication backbone for exchanging data, sending commands, and enabling monitoring. There are factors to consider when integrating IoT devices into a network (AI and the LinkedIn Community, 2024b; GKM2 Solutions, 2023):

- ***Reliability:*** A stable and dependable network is essential to ensure the uninterrupted functionality of IoT devices.
- ***Bandwidth:*** Having sufficient bandwidth is necessary to handle the data generated by IoT devices and ensure smooth operations.
- ***Low Latency:*** Real-time applications like whiteboards and video conferencing require low latency for seamless user experiences.
- ***Scalability:*** Educational institutions must ensure their networks can expand as more IoT devices are added and data demands increase.

By addressing these aspects of network connectivity, educational institutions can create an environment where IoT devices work seamlessly together.

Managing and Scaling IoT Devices As educational institutions continue to adopt IoT devices, effectively managing and scaling these devices poses a challenge. There are factors to consider (Lanars, 2023; Particle, 2023; Intuz, 2023):

- ***Device Management Platforms:*** It is essential to implement device management platforms that enable monitoring and controlling IoT devices, facilitate firmware updates, and ensure their overall health and security.
- ***Data. Analysis:*** Educators require tools to gather and analyze data from IoT devices, allowing them to gain insights and improve their educational practices.
- ***Interoperability:*** Seamless communication between IoT devices is vital to ensure they can work harmoniously together and provide users with a smooth experience.
- ***Security:*** Safeguarding all IoT devices is crucial to prevent access or potential data breaches.

Ensuring Seamless Integration Integrating IoT devices seamlessly with network infrastructure requires careful planning and coordination. There are aspects to consider (Russel, 2023) (AI and the LinkedIn Community, 2024b):

- ***Compatibility:*** IoT devices must align with the network infrastructure regarding protocols, security standards, and data formats.
- ***Network Management:*** Effective network management includes monitoring bandwidth limitations, identifying security vulnerabilities, and ensuring device health.
- ***Training for Educators:*** Teachers and administrators must receive training to utilize and troubleshoot IoT devices, ensuring a smooth and practical learning experience.
- ***Scalability and Future Proofing:*** The network infrastructure should be designed with scalability in mind, allowing for the addition of devices and technologies in the future.

Integrating IoT devices into network infrastructure requires regular maintenance, updates, and adaptations to meet educational institutions' changing needs.

Collaboration between IT professionals, educators, and administrators is necessary to ensure that technology continues to enhance mart education.

5.7 Future Trends and Innovations

Smart education is constantly changing and driven by technological advancements and innovative approaches. In this section, we will delve into the emerging trends and groundbreaking ideas shaping the future of education, emphasizing the role of network infrastructure.

Emerging Technologies in Smart Education The integration of IoT and network infrastructure in education is the beginning. There are emerging technologies that are set to revolutionize the educational landscape. Here are some of the trends to keep an eye on:

- ***Artificial Intelligence (AI):*** AI will continue to play a vital role in tailoring learning experiences, automating administrative tasks, and enhancing educational content.
- ***Augmented Reality (AR) and Virtual Reality (VR):*** AR and VR will bring about immersive and interactive educational experiences, allowing students to delve into complex subjects and historical events firsthand.
- ***5G Connectivity:*** Implementing 5G networks will provide more reliable internet connections, making real-time communication and high-quality video streaming the standard in education.
- ***Blockchain for Credentials:*** Blockchain technology will enable verification of credentials, ensuring they cannot be tampered with. This will make it easier for students to share their achievements with employers and institutions.

Predictions for the Future Looking ahead, we can anticipate several trends and predictions that will shape the future of smart education:

- ***Personalized Learning:*** AI and big data analytics will be vital in tailoring learning experiences to meet each student's unique needs and preferences. This means adapting content and resources for them.
- ***Global Collaboration:*** The Internet of Things (IoT) and advanced connectivity will foster global collaboration, enabling students worldwide to collaborate on projects and share cross-cultural experiences.
- ***Blending Online and Physical Education:*** The line between physical classroom learning and online education will become increasingly blurred as more educational institutions adopt blended learning models combining both approaches.
- ***Emphasis on Skill Development:*** Education will emphasize skill development and lifelong learning. This shift aims to equip students with the skills to thrive in a changing job market.

- ***Digital Literacy:*** Digital literacy and critical thinking will become core educational competencies. Students will be taught how to navigate the digital landscape effectively and responsibly.

Adapting to Future Challenges While these promising emerging trends offer opportunities, they also pose challenges. Educational institutions will need to address issues in the future, including;

- Ensuring all students have fair access to technology and internet connectivity regardless of background or location.
- Dealing with data privacy and security concerns in an interconnected educational ecosystem.
- Equipping educators with the training to utilize technologies and teaching methods in their classrooms effectively.
- Managing the impact of technology in education, such as energy consumption and electronic waste.

As we embrace the future of smart education, it becomes evident that IoT and network infrastructure will remain components of this transformative journey. The dynamic relationship between technology and education will shape how we learn and influence the skills and knowledge we acquire. Rather than distant possibilities, the emerging trends and innovations we have discussed serve as elements for a more inclusive, personalized, and digitally proficient educational future.

5.8 Challenges and Considerations

Incorporating the Internet of Things (IoT) and network infrastructure into educational environments offers several advantages. Still, it poses various challenges that must be addressed to ensure smart education's successful implementation and sustainability.

- ***Bridging Connectivity Gaps:*** One obstacle in many areas is narrowing the digital divide and ensuring fair access to the internet and technology. Unequal connectivity can result in disparities in accessing resources and opportunities. Educational institutions and policymakers should collaborate to provide connectivity solutions to underserved regions and communities.
- ***Accessibility and Inclusivity:*** While technology has the potential to enhance education, it also presents accessibility challenges for students with disabilities. Educational institutions must ensure that digital resources and IoT devices are designed with accessibility in mind while offering support for students with needs to promote inclusivity in smart education.
- ***Training and Capacity Development:*** Introducing IoT devices and network infrastructure into the educational ecosystem requires a significant shift in teaching methods and administrative practices. Educators and staff require training opportunities and professional development programs to utilize these technolo-

gies effectively. Continuous support and capacity building are crucial for educational institutions to fully leverage smart education's potential.

- ***Data Privacy and Security:*** Safeguarding student data privacy and institutional information security is a vital priority. Data breaches and privacy violations can have severe consequences. Educational institutions must implement security measures, comply with data protection regulations, and regularly audit their systems to protect data.
- ***Integration and Compatibility:*** With the introduction of IoT devices and technologies, ensuring they can seamlessly communicate and work together is crucial. Challenges in interoperability and integration may arise when different devices and platforms are used within an educational setting. Institutions must carefully plan for compatibility and easy integration.
- ***Financial Considerations:*** Establishing and maintaining network infrastructure, such as implementing IoT devices, can be expensive. Educational institutions must allocate resources effectively while considering the sustainability of their smart education initiatives. This includes budgeting for device maintenance, software updates, and infrastructure upgrades.
- ***Digital Literacy and Cybersecurity:*** Both students and educators need to develop digital literacy skills while being aware of cybersecurity practices. Students should be educated about safe online behavior, while educators should understand how to protect digital resources and data from cyber threats.
- ***Adaptation to Change:*** Rapid technological advancements in education require educational institutions to be adaptable and responsive. They must be prepared to embrace technologies and teaching methods while adjusting their strategies based on evolving needs and trends.
- ***Ethical considerations:*** Ethical concerns come into play when technology is used in education, specifically regarding data collection, monitoring students, and the possibility of bias in algorithms. Establishing and adhering to ethical frameworks is vital to ensuring the ethical use of technology.

Successfully addressing these challenges and considerations is vital for implementing smart education initiatives. Educational institutions need to plan, execute, and continuously assess their strategies to navigate the landscape of integrating technology into education. By doing so, they can fully harness the potential of IoT and network infrastructure to deliver inclusive, high-quality education that looks toward the future.

5.9 Conclusion

In summary, combining IoT technology and network infrastructure has created an era called smart education. This innovative approach enhances learning experiences, tailors education to students' needs, enhances accessibility, and optimizes resource allocation. Educational institutions can use IoT devices, data analysis, and network connections to create effective learning environments. However, this evolution in education also poses challenges, such as data privacy concerns, security issues, accessibility barriers, and the need for literacy. Educational institutions must tackle these challenges while embracing emerging trends and innovations to ensure the implementation and sustainability of smart education initiatives. By overcoming these obstacles and fully utilizing technology and network infrastructure, education can adapt to meet the demands of learners in the digital era by promoting inclusivity, creativity, and lifelong learning opportunities. Smart education will continue shaping the landscape by preparing students for success in a rapidly changing world.

References

AI and the LinkedIn Community. (2024a). *How can you ensure data privacy and security when selecting educational technology tools?* LinkedIn. https://www.linkedin.com/advice/0/how-can-you-ensure-data-privacy-security-zerkc

AI and the LinkedIn Community. (2024b). *What do you do if your computer networking system needs to incorporate Internet of Things (IoT) devices?* LinkedIn. https://www.linkedin.com/advice/0/what-do-you-your-computer-networking-system-hnipc

Alexa, J. (2021). *The network infrastructure revolution in education* (Issue March).

Bach, R. (2015). *Benefits of smart education with smart learning in schools*. ChampionTutor. https://www.championtutor.com/blog/benefits-of-smart-education-with-smart-learning-in-schools/

Best Education Sikar. (2024). *5 brilliant benefits of smart education in schools!* Best Education Sikar. https://www.besteducationsikar.com/5-brilliant-benefits-of-smart-education-in-schools/

Buzzapp. (2024). *The challenges of implementing a digital smart classroom solution*. Buzzapp. https://www.linkedin.com/pulse/challenges-implementing-digital-smart-classroom-solution/

Cambridge Spark. (2023). *7 benefits of data analytics in higher education*. Cambridge Spark. https://www.cambridgespark.com/info/7-benefits-of-data-analytics-in-higher-education

Deetya Education. (2023). *Data privacy and security in digital education: Safeguarding student data in a digital world*. Deetya Education. https://deetya.education/2023/09/08/data-privacy-and-security-in-digital-education-safeguarding-student-data-in-a-digital-world/

Demir, K. A. (2021). Smart education framework. *Smart Learning Environments, 8*(29), 1–36. https://doi.org/10.1186/s40561-021-00170-x

Dua, A. (2018). *Smart education is more than just advanced learning methods*. LinkedIn. https://www.linkedin.com/pulse/smart-education-more-than-just-advanced-learning-methods-amit-dua/

GKM2 Solutions. (2023). *9 things to consider when setting up IoT devices on your network*. GKM2 Solutions. https://gkm2.com.au/setting-up-iot-devices-on-your-network/

Intuz. (2023). *IoT device management: Importance, challenges, solutions*. Intuz. https://www.intuz.com/guide-on-iot-device-management

Jiang, Y., Zhang, L., & Ma, Q. (2022). A study on the components of a smart education system. In *7th International Conference on Distance Education and Learning* (pp. 7–10).

Lanars. (2023). *Scaling IoT the right way: Challenges & solutions*. Lanars. https://lanars.com/blog/iot-scalability

Particle. (2023). *IoT scalability: What it means, common challenges, and how to scale effectively?* Particle. https://www.particle.io/iot-guides-and-resources/iot-scalability/

Russel, S. (2023). *IoT integration in network infrastructure*. LinkedIn. https://www.linkedin.com/pulse/iot-integration-network-infrastructure-stanley-russel-ar1wc/

Terzieva, V., Ilchev, S., & Todorova, K. (2022). The role of Internet of Things in smart education. *IFAC PapersOnLine, 55*(11), 108–113. https://doi.org/10.1016/j.ifacol.2022.08.057

UNESCO. (2011). *Classroom revolution through SMART education in the Republic of Korea*.

Chapter 6
Intelligent IoT-Based Tutoring Systems, Including AR, VR

Abstract This chapter delves into how technologies like Intelligent Tutoring Systems (ITS), Augmented Reality (AR), Virtual Reality (VR), and the Internet of Things (IoT) are being integrated into education to improve learning experiences. It discusses the importance of these technologies in creating personalized learning environments, monitoring student engagement, and providing adaptive instruction. The chapter also explores using IoT devices and sensors to track student participation, utilizing learning analytics and the tools needed for AR and VR applications. Furthermore, it covers strategies for implementing IoT, AR, and VR in educational settings, creating content tailored to IoT-based learning, and offering personalized learning opportunities. Case studies showcase the use of ITS and real-world instances of AR and VR in classrooms. The chapter also examines methods for assessing learning outcomes influenced by IoT, AR, and VR in education. It addresses challenges such as technical constraints, privacy issues, and inclusivity concerns in design considerations while discussing future trends in educational technology advancements in AR and VR for improved learning experiences and predictions concerning the future generation of ITS.

Keywords Intelligent Tutoring Systems (ITS) · Augmented Reality (AR) · Virtual Reality (VR) · Internet of Things (IoT) · Personalized learning environments · Learning analytics · Implementation strategies

6.1 The Emergence of Intelligent Tutoring Systems (ITS)

This section will focus on Intelligent Tutoring Systems (ITS), an approach to learning driven by technology.

Introduction to Intelligent Tutoring Systems Intelligent Tutoring Systems (ITS) belong to a category of educational technology that aims to provide adaptable learning experiences for students. These systems are designed to mimic the role of a human tutor by offering guidance and feedback tailored to each learner's needs.

M. Kurni, Srinivasa K. G., *The Internet of Educational Things*,
https://doi.org/10.1007/978-3-031-67387-0_6

Leveraging artificial intelligence (AI) and machine learning, ITS evaluates students' knowledge, skills, and progress to delivering relevant content and activities (Sedlmeier, 2001; Wong, 2024).

While the origins of ITS can be traced back to computer-assisted instruction programs, the current implementations have evolved significantly. Today, ITS can dynamically adapt according to a student's requirements, making them an invaluable tool in modern education.

Benefits of ITS Intelligent Tutoring Systems offer several advantages. They provide personalized instruction that caters to every learner's unique needs and pace. This personalization increases engagement, retention, and improved learning outcomes (Nucleoo, 2023).

Moreover, ITS offers instant feedback that enables students to rectify their mistakes while reinforcing their understanding of the material—an aspect often challenging in traditional classroom settings.

The Convergence of IoT and ITS The combination of IoT technologies and ITS enhances these systems by providing valuable data. IoT devices can gather information about students' interactions with content, their assessment performance, and their emotional state during the learning process. This data is precious for personalizing and adapting ITS. It enables the system to tailor its methods based on real-time information, offering previously unattainable customization (Adel, 2024).

6.2 The Role of Augmented Reality (AR) and Virtual Reality (VR) in ITS

As we explore how technology impacts education, let us focus on the captivating realms of Augmented Reality (AR) and Virtual Reality (VR).

Introduction to AR and VR in Education AR and VR bridge the gap between the digital and physical worlds. AR allows us to overlay digital content in the real world, while VR immerses users in entirely virtual environments. These technologies have found their place in education, offering avenues for engaging learners and providing interactive experiences (Vection Technologies, 2024).

In an educational context, AR and VR empower students to journey to historical sites, dissect organisms within virtual realms, or even venture into distant planets. All without leaving their classrooms. These extraordinary tools possess the potential to revolutionize how students learn and comprehend concepts (Verizon, 2024).

Enhancing ITS with AR and VR Although highly effective, intelligent Tutoring Systems (ITS) lack the interactive elements that can enrich learning experiences. Herein lies a solution. Integrating AR and VR into ITS creates captivating environments where students can apply their knowledge while receiving instant feedback.

By incorporating AR and VR into ITS, educators can provide students with opportunities to practice and reinforce their skills through virtual scenarios. These technologies can also enhance the learning experience, which is particularly important for students (Hamza-lup, 2019; Bezanson et al., 2023).

Research and Current Developments Incorporating augmented reality (AR) and virtual reality (VR) into ITS is an ever-evolving research area. Researchers and educators continuously explore leveraging these technologies to enhance educational outcomes. The possibilities are extensive, whether using VR for training or AR for reenactments.

6.3 Principles of Intelligent Tutoring Systems

Intelligent Tutoring Systems (ITS) are based on principles (as shown in Fig. 6.1) that form the foundation of their design and functionality to provide adaptable learning experiences. These principles involve integrating advanced technologies, cognitive science, and educational theory (Wikipedia, 2024).

- ***Personalization:*** The key principle of ITS revolves around personalization, where instruction is tailored to meet each student's needs, preferences, and learning pace. Utilizing artificial intelligence (AI) and machine learning algorithms, ITS assesses a student's knowledge, skills, and progress to create a customized learning path.
- ***Adaptability:*** One of ITS's strengths is its adaptability. It dynamically adjusts instructional strategies based on real-time feedback and learner interactions. This ensures that the system can respond effectively to changes in a student's understanding or pace of learning, resulting in an optimized learning experience.
- ***Feedback Mechanisms:*** Providing constructive feedback is crucial in ITS. These systems assess students' performance by identifying areas of strength and weakness. This instant feedback helps correct errors and reinforce understanding—a feature that can be challenging to replicate in traditional educational settings.
- ***Domain Expertise:*** Successful ITS are developed with an understanding of the subject matter or domain they address. Whether in math, language arts, or science, the system needs the expertise to guide and support learners.
- ***Interactivity:*** Engaging learners through interactivity is crucial. The system utilizes simulations, virtual scenarios, and hands-on activities to create an immer-

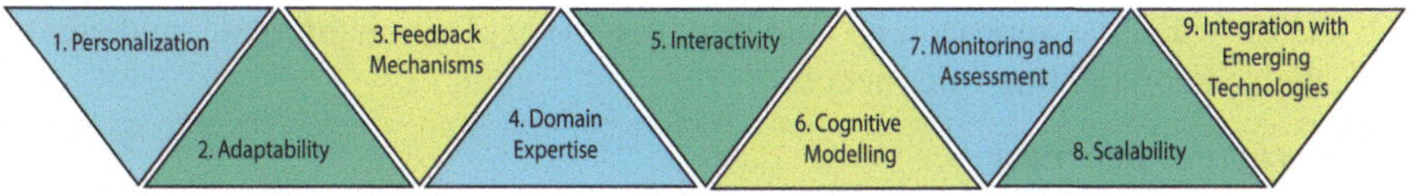

Fig. 6.1 Principles of intelligent tutoring systems

sive learning environment. This not only maintains student interest but also enhances understanding through practical application.
- ***Cognitive Modelling:*** Built on science insights, the system incorporates cognition models to understand better how students learn and remember information. These models help the system adapt instructional methods that align with individual learning styles and cognitive processes.
- ***Monitoring and Assessment:*** Monitoring and assessment are crucial for the ITS system's success. By evaluating student progress, the system can determine the effectiveness of instructional methods and adjust strategies accordingly to ensure ongoing improvement.
- ***Scalability:*** An effective ITS system should accommodate various classroom to remote/online learning environments. This scalability ensures that personalized learning experiences are accessible to various students.
- ***Integration with Emerging Technologies:*** By embracing advancements like IoT (Internet of Things), AR (Augmented Reality), and VR (Virtual Reality), the ITS system stays at the forefront of innovation. Integrating these technologies enriches learning experiences and creates new opportunities for educational engagement.

With a commitment to these principles, Intelligent Tutoring Systems aims to transform education by offering technology-driven learning experiences for students in various disciplines and environments.

6.4 Pedagogical Theories Behind AR and VR Learning

In education, augmented Reality (AR) and Virtual Reality (VR) are driven by pedagogical theories (as shown in Fig. 6.2) that enhance learning experiences. These immersive technologies are beyond tools; they provide platforms for implementing strategies aligned with established educational theories. Here are some essential educational theories behind the integration of AR and VR into learning (Marougkas et al., 2023; Zhao et al., 2020):

- ***Constructivism:***
  - *Principle:* Learning is an active process where individuals construct knowledge based on their experiences and interactions with the environment.
  - *Application in AR and VR:* AR and VR offer hands-on, experiential learning opportunities. Learners can actively engage with content overlayed in the real world (AR) or immerse themselves in virtual environments (VR). This fosters a constructivist approach by enabling them to explore, manipulate, and create their understanding of concepts.
- ***Experiential Learning:***
  - *Principle:* Learning is most effective when it involves experiences followed by reflection on those experiences.

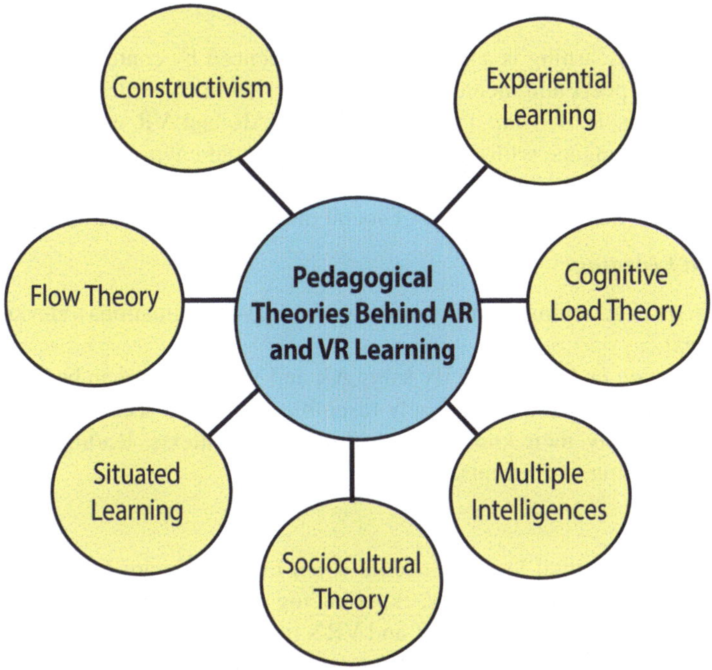

Fig. 6.2 Pedagogical theories behind AR and VR learning

  - *Application in AR and VR:* AR and VR create scenarios that allow learners to experience situations that may be difficult, dangerous, or impractical in the real world. This hands-on experience promotes understanding and skill development through participation.

- ***Cognitive Load Theory:***
  - *Principle:* Effective learning occurs when learners can manage their load appropriately, allowing them to focus on understanding and applying new information.
  - *Application in AR and VR:* These technologies can potentially optimize load by presenting information in engaging and contextually relevant ways. Cognitive resources can be utilized more efficiently by integrating information into the user's AR environment or providing VR experiences.

- ***Multiple Intelligences:***
  - *Principle:* Individuals possess various types of intelligence, and learning experiences must cater to diverse strengths and preferences.
  - *Application in AR and VR:* AR and VR offer various input and interaction modes that accommodate different learning styles and intelligences. These technologies provide stimuli that benefit auditory and kinesthetic learners, among others.

- ***Sociocultural Theory:***
  - *Principle:* Learning is a social activity influenced by context, where interactions with peers and mentors play a critical role in constructing knowledge.
  - *Application in AR and VR:* Collaborative AR and VR experiences enable learners to engage with each other in their virtual environments. This fosters learning, communication, and collaboration. All are aligned with principles that highlight the significance of social interaction in the learning process.
- ***Situated Learning:***
  - *Principle:* Learning is most effective in real-life situations relevant to the context.
  - *Application in AR and VR:* By using AR and VR, learners can be immersed in virtual environments that closely resemble real-world scenarios. This allows them to apply their knowledge within those contexts, leading to a deeper understanding of concepts.
- ***Flow Theory:***
  - *Principle:* Optimal learning occurs when individuals are fully engaged and deeply involved in an activity, experiencing a flow state.
  - *Application in AR and VR:* AR and VR's immersive nature can create a sense of engagement, where learners become entirely absorbed in the learning process. This aligns with the principles of flow theory, which highlight the importance of finding the balance between challenge and skill level to maintain focus and enjoyment.

By incorporating these theories into the design and implementation of AR and VR learning experiences, educators can fully utilize these technologies to create effective learner-centered educational environments.

6.5 System Architecture and Design

The successful integration of IoT in education and Intelligent Tutoring Systems (ITS) heavily depends on a robust system architecture and careful design considerations. In this section, we will explore the components of IoT-based ITS, the considerations for incorporating Augmented Reality (AR) and Virtual Reality (VR) into tutoring systems, and the crucial role of user interface and experience design in ITS.

Key Elements of IoT-based ITS Architecture Here are the key elements typically found in the architecture (Mokmin & Masood, 2017).

- ***IoT Infrastructure:*** IoT-based Intelligent Tutoring Systems are built on a foundation of IoT infrastructure. This includes a network of devices and sensors that gather data on students' interactions with educational content and their learning environment. These devices send the collected data to a central platform, which then processes and analyzes it to provide personalized insights and recommendations for personalized instruction.

- ***Data Processing and Analysis:*** Data processing and analysis play vital roles in IoT-based ITS. Machine learning algorithms and artificial intelligence techniques interpret the data collected from IoT devices. These algorithms can identify patterns in learning behavior, evaluate student performance, and offer adaptive content and interventions in real time.
- ***Personalization Engine:*** The personalization engine is at the core of an IoT-based ITS. This component utilizes data analysis insights to personalize each student's learning experience. It adjusts the content, difficulty level, and pace of instruction according to individual student needs and preferences, resulting in a tailored learning journey.

Design Considerations for Augmented Reality (AR) and Virtual Reality (VR) in Intelligent Tutoring Systems The following considerations are crucial for designing effective AR and VR experiences in tutoring systems (Herbert et al., 2018).

- ***Content Integration:*** The content must be carefully considered when integrating AR and VR into tutoring systems. Designers must ensure that the content aligns with learning objectives, is captivating, and fully utilizes the nature of AR and VR. Whether it involves simulations in AR or virtual science experiments in VR, the content should enhance the learning experience.
- ***Interaction Design:*** Thoughtful interaction design is vital for AR and VR systems. This includes enabling users to navigate and interact seamlessly within the environment. Intuitive, user-friendly interfaces minimize barriers to learning, ensuring that students can focus on content rather than struggle with technology.
- ***Immersion and Engagement:*** AR and VR's true potential lies in their ability to create captivating experiences. Designers should prioritize creating environments and scenarios that capture students' attention and ignite curiosity, keeping them motivated to learn. This includes utilizing realistic visuals, spatial sound, and interactive elements.

Designing User Interfaces and Enhancing User Experience for Intelligent Tutoring Systems Creating user interfaces (UI) and improving user experience (UX) for Intelligent Tutoring Systems (ITS) requires planning to make sure the system is easy to use, inclusive, and beneficial for students (Granić et al., 2000; CAPM, 2024). Let us explore these considerations in detail.

- ***Prioritizing Users:*** Intelligent Tutoring Systems (ITS) must prioritize users by following user-centric design principles. This approach ensures the system is user-friendly, easy to navigate, and aligns with users' preferences and needs. User testing and feedback play a vital role in refining the user interface.
- ***Accessibility and Inclusion:*** Designing for inclusivity is paramount in educational systems. ITS should be designed to cater to a diverse range of learners, including those with disabilities. Factors like screen readers, alternative input methods, and ensuring content accessibility for all students are considered.

- ***Providing Feedback and Monitoring Progress:*** A compelling user experience design in ITS involves providing feedback mechanisms and enabling progress tracking. Learners should receive timely feedback on their performance, allowing them to monitor their progress and make improvements. This feedback loop serves as an essential aspect of motivating and aiding students.

6.6 Technologies Enabling Intelligent Tutoring

To fully unlock the potential of Intelligent Tutoring Systems (ITS), it is essential to comprehend the underlying technologies that support these systems in education. In this section, we will delve into the significance of IoT devices and sensors in education, as well as explore the hardware and software tools used for Augmented Reality (AR) and Virtual Reality (VR), along with how Artificial Intelligence (AI) and Machine Learning are integrated into ITS.

The Role of IoT Devices and Sensors in Education Incorporating IoT devices and sensors into education offers advantages and possibilities for enhancing the learning atmosphere and boosting educational results. Below are some functions that IoT devices and sensors serve in education (Arduino, 2024; Terzieva et al., 2022):

- ***Classroom Monitoring with IoT Sensors:*** IoT sensors play a vital role in gathering data about various aspects of the classroom environment. They can monitor temperature, humidity, lighting conditions, and air quality. This data is crucial for creating a learning environment that fosters focused engagement among students.
- ***Tracking Student Engagement:*** IoT sensors also enable tracking student engagement levels. By monitoring students' use of materials and interactions with IoT-enabled devices, educators can gain valuable insights into which resources are most effective and how actively students are involved in the learning process. This data aids in refining instructional strategies.
- ***Leveraging Adaptive Learning Analytics:*** The wealth of data collected by IoT sensors serves as a treasure trove for learning analytics. These analytics utilize data-driven insights to personalize instruction based on individual student needs. For instance, if Internet of Things (IoT) sensors detect a student struggling with a particular concept, the system can adapt by providing support or offering alternative learning materials.

Augmented Reality (AR)/Virtual Reality (VR) Hardware and Software Tools Augmented Reality (AR) and Virtual Reality (VR) Rely Heavily on Tools, both Hardware and Software, to Enhance Learning Experiences (LinkedIn, 2024). Let us Delve into the Equipment and Programs Typically Utilized in AR and VR Applications

- ***AR Hardware and Software:*** Augmented Reality relies on hardware and software tools such as AR glasses, smartphones, and tablets. Software tools like

ARKit and ARCore are used to develop AR applications. Additionally, educators can create custom AR learning experiences using AR authoring platforms.
- ***VR Hardware and Software:*** Virtual Reality requires hardware and software tools like Oculus Rift, HTC Vive, etc., to provide immersive experiences. Unity3D and Unreal Engine are VR content creation tools that enable the development of VR content. Integrated learning management systems help educators manage and deliver VR experiences effectively.
- ***Content Curation and Integration:*** Curating and integrating content is crucial when incorporating AR and VR in educational settings. Educators should develop content that aligns with learning objectives. Various content integration tools and platforms facilitate the inclusion of AR/VR experiences into the curriculum.

AI and ML in ITS Artificial Intelligence (AI) and Machine Learning (ML) play vital roles in Intelligent Tutoring Systems (ITS). They analyze the data gathered from IoT sensors and user interactions within Augmented Reality (AR) and Virtual Reality (VR) systems. ITS uses AI and ML algorithms to identify student performance patterns and learning behaviors, forming the basis for personalized recommendations (Sapna, 2024; Naveenkumar, 2023).

AI and ML power ITS's adaptive instruction capabilities. These technologies can dynamically assess a student's strengths and weaknesses, adjusting the difficulty level and content of instruction in time. For instance, if a student excels in an area, the system can provide challenging material to keep them engaged while promoting further growth (Naveenkumar, 2023; Sapna, 2024).

Another vital aspect enabled by Natural Language Processing (NLP), a subset of AI, is that ITS can interact with students using natural language. NLP technology allows students to ask questions, receive explanations, and engage in dialogues with the system, creating a learning experience resembling human interaction (Alisher, 2023).

6.7 Implementation Strategies

Successful implementation of the Internet of Things (IoT) in education and Intelligent Tutoring Systems (ITS) requires careful planning and effective strategies. This section will explore strategies for integrating IoT into the curriculum, developing content for IoT-based learning, and providing personalized learning experiences.

Integrating Augmented Reality (AR) and Virtual Reality (VR) into the Curriculum Incorporating Augmented Reality (AR) and Virtual Reality (VR) into the educational program necessitates planning and thoughtful deliberation to guarantee harmony with learning objectives, interdisciplinary cooperation, and inclusivity for all learners (Stemrobo Technologies, 2023; Singh, 2023). Here are a few essential factors to bear in mind.

- ***Alignment with Learning Goals:*** To effectively integrate AR and VR into the curriculum, aligning them with learning goals is essential. Educators should identify how these technologies can enhance understanding of specific topics and skills.
- ***Collaboration Across Subjects:*** Implementing AR and VR often involves collaboration across subjects. Educators from different disciplines can collaborate to create cross-disciplinary experiences that bridge traditional subject boundaries, providing students with a comprehensive perspective on complex issues.
- ***Considerations for Accessibility:*** When incorporating AR and VR into the curriculum, accessibility should be a priority. This includes ensuring all students have access to the technology that suits their abilities or available resources. Educators should also address equity-related concerns.

Developing Content for IoT-Based Learning Creating content for Internet of Things (IoT) learning entails using data-driven methods, interactive tools, and multimedia components to craft impactful learning experiences (Kapoor, 2023; Matellio, 2024). Below is the process of developing content for IoT-based learning;

- ***Data-Driven Content:*** Developing content for IoT-based learning heavily relies on data analysis. Educators and content creators can utilize Internet of Things (IoT) data to identify areas where students may face challenges or excel. This data-driven approach enables the development of tailored material that addresses learning needs.
- ***Interactive Learning Resources:*** IoT-based learning benefits from the inclusion of interactive resources. These resources can be simulations of real-world experiments or interactive applications that engage students in hands-on learning. Creating learning resources requires collaboration between subject matter experts and instructional designers.
- ***Rich Media:*** Incorporating multimedia and rich media elements can enhance content within IoT-based learning experiences. Videos, animations, and other visual elements can make the content more engaging and effective. Designers should ensure that multimedia content aligns with the educational objectives.

Strategies for Personalized Learning Experiences Strategies for personalized learning aim to adjust materials, speed, and assistance to cater to the requirements and interests of every student (Rourke, 2024; School of Scholars, 2023; Alter Learning, 2024). Below are methods for attaining personalized learning experiences:

- ***Adaptive Learning Pathways:*** Personalized learning experiences in Intelligent Tutoring Systems (ITS) are achieved through adaptive learning pathways. These pathways involve adjusting the content and assessments based on student progress and performance. Strategies for creating adaptive pathways include utilizing AI algorithms to identify areas for improvement and providing tailored content.
- ***Continuous Assessment:*** Continuous assessment is vital in effectively personalizing learning. This strategy evaluates student performance and progress, enabling feedback and adaptive adjustments. Continuous evaluation methods can encompass quizzes, assignments, and formative assessments.

- ***Learner Feedback and Reflection:*** Gathering feedback from learners and encouraging self-reflection are elements of personalizing the learning experience. Students need opportunities to share their thoughts on their learning journey and reflect on their progress. This exchange of feedback between educators and instructional technology systems helps determine the effectiveness of personalized strategies.

6.8 Case Studies and Applications

To understand how IoT impacts education and its potential, examining real-life examples and applications in Intelligent Tutoring Systems (ITS) is valuable. In this section, we will explore instances of IoT-based ITS uses of augmented reality (AR) and virtual reality (VR) in classrooms, as well as interdisciplinary applications of intelligent tutoring.

Successful Instances of IoT-Based ITS Intelligent Tutoring Systems (ITS) based on the Internet of Things (IoT) have been effectively utilized in various fields to improve learning outcomes. Below are two examples showcasing instances of implementation.

Case Study: Adaptive Math Tutoring The adaptive Math Tutoring system, which can be employed in a middle school setting, illustrates implementing IoT-based ITS. IoT sensors collect data on students' engagement and progress in the classroom. The ITS system then utilizes this data to tailor math exercises and provide feedback. Consequently, students will demonstrate improvement in their math performance.

Case Study; Language Learning Application A mobile app can use IoT to track user interactions in language learning. The app adjusts lesson difficulty based on progress while incorporating enabled features such as speech recognition to offer pronunciation feedback. Users will benefit from increased motivation and proficiency in acquiring languages.

AR and VR, in Action: Real-life Examples in Classrooms Educators incorporate AR and VR technologies in real-life settings to enrich the learning experience (Proven Reality, 2023; Marr, 2021). Here are two instances where these technologies are making a difference in classrooms.

- ***Virtual Field Trips:*** In a high school geography class, students experience virtual field trips using VR headsets. These trips virtually transport students to locations worldwide, offering an immersive educational experience. This approach can significantly boost student engagement and deepen their understanding of geography.

- ***Medical Training Simulations:*** AR and VR revolutionize medical students' learning of medical procedures. Medical schools can now use VR simulations for training, enabling students to practice and refine their skills in a virtual environment. This technology has contributed to enhanced proficiency among aspiring medical professionals.

Applications of Intelligent Tutoring Across Subjects Intelligent Tutoring Systems (ITS) provide tailored guidance and assistance in various subjects, addressing each individual's learning requirements and preferences. Here are some instances where ITS applications are utilized in various fields (Wang et al., 2023; Alrakhawi et al., 2023).

- ***STEM Education:*** Intelligent Tutoring Systems have been widely implemented in STEM (Science, Technology, Engineering, and Mathematics) education. Students benefit from instruction and targeted practice exercises that help them comprehend STEM concepts. These systems can effectively improve student retention rates and performance within STEM disciplines.
- ***Creativity:*** Intelligent Tutoring Systems will also expand into creative domains. For instance, music education employs an ITS platform that offers music lessons tailored to each student's abilities and preferences. This approach will increase student engagement and enhance musical proficiency.
- ***Language Arts and Literature:*** Intelligent Tutoring Systems can also be used in language arts and literature education. These systems assess students' reading comprehension, writing, and literature analysis abilities. The personalized approach to teaching enhances students' understanding of literature. It helps them improve their writing skills.

6.9 Evaluation and Assessment

Evaluation and assessment processes play a vital role in measuring the influence of innovative technologies like IoT, Intelligent Tutoring Systems (ITS), augmented reality (AR), and virtual reality (VR) applications in education. This section delves into approaches for assessing learning outcomes, evaluating the impact of IoT, AR, and VR in education, and assessing the significance of data analytics and reporting in ITS.

Approaches to Assess Learning Outcomes Evaluating student progress and the effectiveness of teaching methods relies on assessing learning outcomes. Below are three methods used for this purpose (Cornell University, 2024, 24 CE; Bronx Community College, 2018).

- ***Traditional Evaluation:*** Evaluation methods such as quizzes, tests, and assignments remain crucial to gauging learning outcomes. These methods serve as a foundation for measuring knowledge acquisition and skill development.
- ***Formative Evaluation:*** Formative evaluation techniques offer insights into students' progress throughout the learning journey. These assessments can be integrated within ITS IoT systems or AR/VR platforms to provide feedback and tailor instruction accordingly.
- ***Project Evaluation:*** Project-based evaluations encourage students to apply their knowledge and skills to real-world problems. This type of assessment proves invaluable in subjects where practical application is key.

Assessing the Impact of IoT, AR & VR in Education To understand how IoT, AR, and VR influence education, a comprehensive strategy involving assessments, qualitative insights, and comparative research is essential (Fitria, 2023; Sapale & Banerjee, 2023). Let us look into how each of these methods helps us grasp the implications of these technologies.

- ***Quantitative Analysis of Data:*** When evaluating the impact of IoT, AR, and VR on education, it is essential to analyze quantitative data. This involves examining student performance data, measuring engagement metrics, and assessing proficiency gains.
- ***Qualitative Feedback:*** Obtaining feedback can provide insights into the effects of these technologies. Surveys, interviews, and focus groups allow students and educators to share their experiences and perspectives.
- ***Comparative Studies:*** Comparative studies compare the outcomes of students who have experienced IoT, AR, and VR-enabled education with those who have not. This approach helps evaluate the value of these technologies.

Data Analytics and Reporting in Intelligent Tutoring Systems (ITS) In Intelligent Tutoring Systems (ITS), data analytics and reporting are essential for educators to gain insights into student progress, system effectiveness, and instructional enhancements (Educase, n.d.). Let us explore how data analytics and reporting contribute to ITS.

- ***Learning Analytics:*** Learning analytics is a vital aspect of ITS that involves collecting and analyzing student data. This information helps educators understand progress and areas for improvement, enabling personalized instruction.
- ***Performance Metrics:*** Performance metrics in ITS evaluate not only student learning but also the effectiveness of the ITS itself. These metrics may include student engagement levels, completion rates, and proficiency gains.
- ***Reporting and Feedback Loops:*** Reporting mechanisms and feedback loops ensure educators can access real-time data and insights. ITS provides insights into student performance and engagement, allowing for interventions and improvements in instruction.

6.10 Challenges and Considerations

While integrating IoT in education and using Intelligent Tutoring Systems (ITS) show potential, some important challenges and considerations must be considered for successful implementation. This section will explore the hurdles and limitations of ethical privacy concerns and the significance of accessibility and inclusivity in design.

Technical Challenges and Limitations Dealing with obstacles and constraints is crucial for incorporating and running educational technologies like the Internet of Things (IoT) and Intelligent Tutoring Systems (ITS). Below are a few hurdles.

- ***Infrastructure and connectivity:*** One major technical challenge involves ensuring connectivity and robust infrastructure in areas with limited high-speed internet access. Connectivity issues may hinder seamless data transmission, which is essential for devices and ITS platforms.
- ***Compatibility and Interoperability:*** IoT and ITS ecosystems often encompass a range of devices and platforms. Ensuring compatibility and interoperability among these systems can be complex since different technologies and protocols need to work to provide a cohesive learning experience.
- ***Data. Privacy:*** Safeguarding student data is crucially important. Data breaches or privacy violations can have severe consequences. Maintaining data security measures while adhering to regulations continues to be a challenge within the digital education landscape.

Ethical Concerns Regarding Privacy Privacy issues are a priority in educational environments, mainly as technology is widely used to tailor learning experiences. Here are a few important ethical factors to keep in mind.

- ***Data Privacy and Consent:*** Collecting and analyzing student data for personalization purposes or assessments necessitates transparent data privacy policies, such as obtaining informed consent from students, parents, or guardians. Ensuring the legal use of data presents a challenge.
- ***Ethical Considerations for Personalization:*** Using personalization in ITS is crucial. Customized learning experiences should never be exploited commercially or perpetuate biases or discrimination.
- ***Balancing Personalization with Student Agency:*** Finding the balance between learning and student agency is essential. Students should have a voice in their learning experiences and be able to explore pathways to achieve their educational goals.

Designing for Accessibility and Inclusivity Ensuring that educational technology is designed with accessibility and inclusivity is crucial for enabling all students to actively engage and gain from opportunities, regardless of their abilities or backgrounds. Here are a few important principles and factors to keep in mind.

- ***Universal Design:*** When designing technologies such as IoT, AR, VR, and ITS, universal access must be considered. Universal design principles ensure that all students, including those with disabilities, can benefit from these technologies.
- ***Digital Equity:*** Ensuring digital equity means giving all students equal access to technology. Addressing disparities and the lack of access to devices and high-speed internet is necessary to eliminate inequities.
- ***Inclusive Pedagogy:*** Incorporating inclusive pedagogy into educational technology design is crucial. This approach prioritizes accommodating learners' needs by adapting strategies to different learning styles and abilities.

6.11 Future Trends and Directions

The field of education is constantly changing, and technology plays a vital role in shaping its future. In this section, we will explore the trends in technological advancements in augmented reality (AR) and virtual reality (VR) for improved learning experiences and predictions for the next generation of Intelligent Tutoring Systems (ITS).

The Changing Landscape of EdTech and IoT In the changing world of technology (EdTech) and the incorporation of the Internet of Things (IoT), constant advancements influence how education is provided and encountered. Here are a few notable developments in this evolving environment;

- ***Blended Learning:*** The fusion of traditional teaching methods with technology continues to evolve. Blended learning approaches combine face-to-face instruction with digital tools and resources, providing flexibility and personalized learning opportunities.
- ***Mobile Learning:*** Mobile devices have become flexible tools for education. The rise of mobile learning apps and platforms enables students to access educational content and resources whenever and wherever they need them.
- ***IoT-Enabled Classrooms:*** Internet of Things (IoT) integration in education is expected to grow. IoT-enabled classrooms will offer real-time data analysis, personalized learning experiences, and improved interaction among students, teachers, and instructional materials.

Advancements in AR and VR for Enhanced Learning Advancements in augmented reality (AR) and virtual reality (VR) technologies are transforming how we learn, providing engaging and interactive education possibilities. Let us explore some of the developments in AR and VR that are enhancing the learning experience;

- ***Mixed Reality:*** Combining AR and VR into mixed reality (MR) presents exciting possibilities. MR merges the physical and digital worlds with the realm, creating seamless and immersive environments for effective learning.

- ***Haptic Feedback:*** Advances in haptic feedback technology allow students to visualize and hear virtual environments and experience them through touch and physical sensations. This immersive experience enhances comprehension and engagement.
- ***Collaborative VR Learning:*** Collaborative virtual reality (VR) environments encourage student teamwork and social interaction. They can collaborate in virtual spaces, fostering cooperation and problem-solving skills.

Predictions for the Next Generation of Intelligent Tutoring Systems The upcoming wave of Intelligent Tutoring Systems (ITS) is set to transform the field of education with groundbreaking advancements and functionalities. Below are forecasts regarding the trajectory of ITS;

- ***AI-Powered Learning Assistants:*** The upcoming generation of Intelligent Tutoring Systems will introduce AI-powered learning assistants that support and guide students. These assistants will adapt to individual learning styles and preferences.
- ***Enhanced Data Analysis:*** ITS will employ enhanced data analysis techniques, including machine learning, to gain insights into student progress and performance. Predictive analytics will help educators identify students who may be at risk and offer timely interventions.
- ***Personalized Learning Paths:*** The future of ITS lies in personalized learning paths. These systems will use predictive modeling to adjust content and interventions, ensuring each student's educational journey is truly unique.

6.12 Conclusion

In summary, the combination of Intelligent Tutoring Systems (ITS), Augmented Reality (AR), Virtual Reality (VR), and the Internet of Things (IoT) offers possibilities to transform education and improve learning outcomes. Using IoT devices and sensors, teachers can establish personalized learning settings, track student engagement, and deliver tailored instruction based on individual needs. Integrating AR and VR technologies enhances experiences by providing simulations and virtual field trips that promote student involvement and a more profound comprehension of complex ideas. Nevertheless, incorporating these technologies comes with infrastructure limitations, connectivity issues, and ethical concerns related to privacy and inclusivity. Despite these obstacles, progress in technology, AR, VR, and ITS shows potential for the future of education through AI-driven learning aids, advanced data analysis methods, and customized learning pathways that shape an era of educational experiences. By tackling these obstacles head-on and embracing emerging trends, educators can utilize technology to its extent in creating learning environments that empower students for success in the digital era.

References

Adel, A. (2024). The convergence of intelligent tutoring, robotics, and IoT in smart education for the transition from industry 4.0 to 5.0. *Smart Cities, 7*(1), 325–369.

Alisher, P. (2023). *Intelligent tutoring systems: Personalized and adaptive learning with AI and NLP*. Academic Gates. https://www.academicgates.com/blog/intelligent-tutoring-systems-personalized-and-adaptive-learning-with-ai-and-nlp/602

Alrakhawi, H. A., Jamiat, N., & S, S., & Abu-Naser. (2023). Intelligent tutoring systems in education: A systematic review of usage, tools, effects and evaluation. *Journal of Theoretical and Applied Information Technology, 101*(4), 1205–1226.

Alter Learning. (2024). 10 strategies for implementing personalized learning. *LinkedIn.*. https://www.linkedin.com/pulse/10-strategies-implementing-personalized-learning-alterlearning-vhsrf/

Arduino. (2024). *The role of the IoT in education*. 2Arduino. https://www.arduino.cc/education/the-role-of-the-iot-in-education

Bezanson, K., Soberanis, L., Thomas, B., Brooks, R., & Rojas-Muñoz, E. (2023). Towards an intelligent tutoring system for virtual reality learning environments. *IEEE Frontiers in Education Conference (FIE), 2023*, 32–54.

BronxCommunityCollege.(2018).*Assessingstudentlearningoutcomes*.BronxCommunityCollege.. https://www.bcc.cuny.edu/academics/oie/five-step-assessment-process/assessing-student-learning-outcomes/

CAPM, M. G. (2024). *Designing user interfaces and experiences utilizing artificial intelligence (AI) and machine Learning (ML)*. LinkedIn. https://www.linkedin.com/pulse/designing-user-interfaces-experiences-utilizing-ai-machine-gandhi-sllbf/

Cornell University. (2024, 24 CE). *Measuring student learning*. Cornell University. https://teaching.cornell.edu/teaching-resources/assessment-evaluation/measuring-student-learning

Educase. (n.d.). *7 Things you should know about intelligent tutoring systems*. https://library.educause.edu/resources/2013/7/7-things-you-should-know-about-intelligent-tutoring-systems#:~:text=Becausethesesystemsareable,understandthematerialathand

Fitria, T. N. (2023). Augmented Reality (AR) and virtual Reality (VR) technology in education: Media of teaching and learning: A review. *International Journal of Computer and Information System, 4*(1), 14–25. https://doi.org/10.29040/ijcis.v4i1.102

Granić, A., Stankov, S., & Glavinić, V. (2000). User interface aspects of an intelligent tutoring system. In *2000 Proceedings of the 22nd International Conference on Information Technology Interfaces* (pp. 1–8).

Hamza-lup, F. (2019). *Intelligent tutoring systems and augmented Reality*. ELearning Industry. https://elearningindustry.com/role-of-artificial-intelligence-in-elearning-integrating-ai-tech-into-education

Herbert, B., Ens, B., Weerasinghe, A., Billinghurst, M., & Wigley, G. (2018). Design considerations for combining augmented reality with intelligent tutors. *Computers & Graphics, 77*(December), 166–182.

Kapoor, M. (2023). *IoT in education: Fostering personalized and interactive learning experiences*. CognitiveClouds. https://www.cognitiveclouds.com/insights/iot-in-education

LinkedIn. (2024). *What are the key features of AR/VR hardware and software?* LinkedIn. https://www.linkedin.com/advice/0/what-key-features-arvr-hardware-software-skills-virtual-reality-cvqye#:~:text=ARoverlaysdigitalelementson,effectivelyanddeliverengagingexperiences.

Marougkas, A., Troussas, C., Krouska, A., & Sgouropoulou, C. (2023). Virtual reality in education: A review of learning theories, approaches and methodologies for the last decade. *Electronics, 12*(13), 1–21.

Marr, B. (2021). *10 best examples of VR and AR in education*. Forbes. https://www.forbes.com/sites/bernardmarr/2021/07/23/10-best-examples-of-vr-and-ar-in-education/?sh=1f642ab1f482

Matellio. (2024). *A guide to IoT use cases in education: Unlocking the future of Learning*. Matellio. https://www.matellio.com/blog/iot-use-cases-in-education/

Mokmin, N. A. M., & Masood, M. (2017, October). The design and development of an intelligent tutoring system as a part of the architecture of Internet of Things (IoT). In *2017 International Conference on Telecommunications and Communication Engineering* (pp. 92–96). https://doi.org/10.1145/3145777.3145793

Naveenkumar, S. (2023). *Transforming education with machine learning: Personalized learning, intelligent tutoring, and educational games*. LinkedIn. https://www.linkedin.com/pulse/transforming-education-machine-learning-personalized-intelligent-s/

Nucleoo. (2023). *Top 4 benefits and practical examples of Intelligent Tutoring Systems (ITS): An Innovative Approach to optimise learning*. Nucleoo. https://www.nucleoo.com/blog/4-benefits-of-intelligent-tutoring-systems/#:~:text=Immediatefeedbackiskeyto,consolidatetheirunderstandingofconcepts

Proven Reality. (2023). *How are VR and AR used in education: 20 real-life applications*. Proven Reality. https://provenreality.com/education/how-are-vr-and-ar-used-in-education/

Rourke, S. O. (2024). *Top 9 strategies to support personalized learning*. RingCentral. https://www.ringcentral.com/us/en/blog/top-9-strategies-to-support-personalized-learning/

Sapale, S., & Banerjee, S. (2023). Empowering education: Exploring the impact of IoT in smart learning environments. *International Journal for Multidisciplinary Research, 5*. https://doi.org/10.36948/ijfmr.2023.v05i05.7474

Sapna, S. B. (2024). *Artificial intelligence and Intelligent Tutoring Systems (ITS)*. LinkedIn. https://www.linkedin.com/pulse/artificial-intelligence-intelligent-tutoring-systems-its-bhandari-byvpc/

School of Scholars. (2023). *6 personalized learning strategies for students with customized learning environments & resources*. School of Scholars. https://schoolofscholars.edu.in/blog/personalized-learning-strategies/

Sedlmeier, P. (2001). Intelligent tutoring systems. *International Encyclopedia of the Social & Behavioral Sciences*. https://doi.org/10.1016/B0-08-043076-7/01618-1

Singh, P. (2023). *Virtual Reality (VR) and Augmented Reality (AR) revolutionize education*. LinkedIn. https://www.linkedin.com/pulse/virtual-reality-vr-augmented-ar-revolutionize-education-singh/

Stemrobo Technologies. (2023). *AR VR curriculum for schools*. Stemrobo Technologies. https://www.stemrobo.com/ar-vr-curriculum-for-schools/

Terzieva, V., Ilchev, S., & Todorova, K. (2022). The role of Internet of Things in smart education. *IFAC PapersOnLine, 55*(11), 108–113. https://doi.org/10.1016/j.ifacol.2022.08.057

Vection Technologies. (2024). *Virtual reality, augmented reality, and 3D technologies in the education industry: How are learning processes revolutionizing?* Vection Technologies. https://vection-technologies.com/solutions/industries/education/#

Verizon. (2024). *How will AR and VR in classrooms affect the future of education?* Verizon. https://www.verizon.com/about/blog/vr-in-education

Wang, H., Tlili, A., Huang, R., & Cai, Z. (2023). Examining the applications of intelligent tutoring systems in real educational contexts: A systematic literature review from the social experiment perspective. *Education and Information Technologies, 28*(7), 9113–9148). Springer US. https://doi.org/10.1007/s10639-022-11555-x

Wikipedia. (2024). *Intelligent tutoring system* (pp. 1–23). https://en.wikipedia.org/wiki/Intelligent_tutoring_system

Wong, C. (2024). *What is an AI intelligent tutoring system and why you should use it*. Noodle Factory. https://articles.noodlefactory.ai/what-is-an-ai-intelligent-tutoring-system-and-why-you-should-use-it

Zhao, X., Li, X., Wang, J., & Shi, C. (2020). Augmented Reality (AR) learning application based on the perspective of situational learning: High efficiency study of combination of virtual and real. *Psychology, 11*, 1340–1348. https://doi.org/10.4236/psych.2020.119086

Chapter 7
Online Laboratories Using IoT

Abstract This chapter explores online laboratories' development, benefits, obstacles, use, and incorporation with Internet of Things (IoT) technology in educational environments. It explores the shift from traditional lab experiences to remote online setups, emphasizing accessibility, affordability, safety measures, and adaptability. Integrating IoT with online labs improves real-time data gathering, remote accessibility, interaction, and cooperation to enhance learning. The chapter showcases the diverse applications of online labs by presenting examples across contexts, from K12 schools to professional training. It also examines how IoT enhances traditional labs and hands-on learning experiences by highlighting the distinctions between virtual and remote labs while emphasizing collaboration and inclusivity. Additionally, it offers insights into designing IoT-driven online labs by focusing on defining goals, selecting appropriate IoT devices, establishing infrastructure requirements, ensuring user-friendly interfaces and experiences addressing security and privacy concerns, and adhering to regulations. Practical implementation strategies and case studies illustrate the real-world use of IoT in physics, chemistry, and engineering labs by emphasizing accessibility, safety measures, enriched comprehension, cost efficiency, skill development, and interdisciplinary learning prospects. In managing and upkeeping IoT devices, various factors include monitoring their performance and addressing issues, ensuring they can scale up as needed, managing and analyzing data effectively, complying with regulations, maintaining security measures, and ensuring quality standards. Additionally, discussions on future trends and hurdles like emerging technologies concerns regarding security and privacy, broadening access to resources, and integrating curriculum are held to shed light on enhancing the educational experiences offered through IoT-powered online labs.

Keywords Online laboratories · Internet of things (IoT) technology · Remote accessibility · Hands-on learning experiences · Implementation strategies · Security and privacy concerns · Interdisciplinary learning

M. Kurni, Srinivasa K. G., *The Internet of Educational Things*,
https://doi.org/10.1007/978-3-031-67387-0_7

7.1 Introduction

Virtual or remote online labs play a vital role in education, offering students valuable opportunities to conduct experiments and gain practical knowledge across different subjects. This chapter delves into online laboratories' evolution, advantages, and challenges and highlights their applications. Additionally, we examine the incorporation of Internet of Things (IoT) technology to enhance the learning experience by facilitating real-time data collection, remote access, interactive collaboration, and safety measures.

Overview of Online Laboratories Virtual or remote online labs have become a part of today's education. These digital spaces enable students to conduct experiments, explore concepts, and gain experience across various subjects without needing physical equipment or being in a traditional lab. They bridge the gap between theory and application, making education more accessible and engaging (May et al., 2023).

Online labs can take various forms, including simulations, virtual experiments, and remote access to physical equipment. Integrating Internet of Things (IoT) technology into these virtual learning environments has expanded their capabilities and effectiveness. IoT-enabled online labs can provide real-time data collection, analysis, and interaction, making them an invaluable asset in today's modern education (Labster, 2023).

The Evolution of Online Laboratories Online labs have become a game changer in today's education, ultimately transforming how students interact with technical subjects. The idea of online labs has evolved to meet the evolving needs of both educators and learners.

In the past, lab work was limited to physical labs where students carried out experiments and hands-on activities. While these experiences were invaluable, they often posed challenges such as limited access, scheduling constraints, and the need for costly equipment and resources.

The emergence of online labs aimed to tackle these issues by providing a digital alternative. Early versions of online labs primarily comprised simulations and virtual experiments, allowing students to explore and practice concepts in a cost-effective environment; as time passed, the integration of technologies, like the Internet of Things (IoT), has propelled online labs to new heights (Raman et al., 2022; Fajriah et al., 2023).

Benefits and Challenges of Online Laboratories

Advantages of Online Labs in Education Online laboratories offer the following advantages in the field of education (Kumar, 2024; Science Interactive, 2023):

- ***Accessibility:*** They overcome barriers, allowing students worldwide to access high-quality laboratory experiences. This is especially beneficial for distance learning programs.
- ***Cost-effectiveness:*** Online laboratories eliminate the need for physical equipment, maintenance, and setup costs, providing institutions with a budget-friendly alternative.
- ***Safety:*** In disciplines involving hazardous materials or processes, online laboratories create a safe environment where students can experiment without physical risks.
- ***Flexibility in learning:*** Online laboratories enable students to conduct experiments at their own pace, promoting personalized learning and catering to different learning styles.
- ***Real-time feedback:*** The Internet of Things (IoT) enabled online laboratories to offer immediate data and feedback to assist students in grasping concepts and troubleshooting problems in time.

Challenges of Online Laboratories Even though online laboratories have benefits, they also come with their share of challenges (Science Interactive, 2023) (Assem, 2023):

- ***Technical Requirements:*** To make the most of online laboratories, students and educators must have access to reliable internet connections and appropriate devices.
- ***Lack of Physical Interaction:*** While online laboratories provide simulations and remote access to equipment, they cannot fully replicate the hands-on experience of working with physical apparatus.
- ***Privacy:*** Ensuring the security and privacy of online laboratory users is a paramount concern that should not be taken lightly.
- ***Quality:*** Developing top-notch online laboratories that cater to the requirements of different courses and subjects can be pretty demanding.

Use Cases in Various Educational Settings Online labs play a role in educational settings, from K12 schools to higher education and vocational training. Let us explore instances where online labs are making a difference;

- ***K12 Education:*** Online labs have become a part of school curriculums, enhancing science and technology education. Students can now engage in experiments and delve into scientific concepts virtually, even from the comfort of their homes.
- ***Higher Education:*** Colleges and universities have seamlessly integrated online labs into physics, chemistry, engineering, and biology courses. Students can supplement their in-person learning with access to virtual or remote labs.
- ***Distance Learning:*** For distance education programs, online labs serve as a lifeline by providing students with practical experiences of their geographical location.
- ***Professional Training:*** Industries like healthcare and engineering greatly benefit from online labs, which offer professionals a practical platform for training and enable them to enhance their skills and knowledge.

The evolution of online labs in education has been remarkable. They constantly enrich the learning experience. With IoT technology integration, these virtual laboratories open avenues for hands-on learning and foster innovation.

Role of IoT in Advancing Online Laboratories The Internet of Things (IoT) refers to a network of interconnected devices and sensors that gather and exchange information via the Internet. This technology has brought about changes in various industries, including education. In the realm of online labs, IoT plays a vital role in enriching the learning experience in several ways (Perkel, 2017; Stemrobo Technologies, 2023):

- ***Real-Time Data Collection:*** Through IoT sensors and devices, students can analyze experimental data as it happens, providing immediate feedback. This fosters a more profound comprehension of concepts and can encourage participation.
- ***Remote Accessibility:*** Online laboratories powered by IoT enable students to access lab equipment and conduct experiments from anywhere, overcoming geographical limitations. This accessibility is particularly valuable for remote or distance learning initiatives.
- ***Interactivity:*** With IoT, students can interact with experiments and devices, control variables and parameters, and make real-time adjustments. Such interactivity simulates a hands-on experience essential for understanding scientific and technical concepts.
- ***Collaboration:*** IoT-equipped online laboratories facilitate collaboration among students and educators across locations. They can collaborate on experiments, share data, and collectively solve problems—an approach that promotes community building and shared learning.
- ***Safety and Cost Efficiency:*** By utilizing IoT-based online laboratories, risks associated with physical experiments are minimized—especially in fields involving hazardous materials or processes—ensuring safety for all involved while reducing costs. Furthermore, they remove the necessity for physical apparatus, thereby enhancing the cost efficiency of education.

7.2 How IoT Technology Enhances Traditional Laboratories and Hands-On Learning Experiences?

This section will explore how IoT technology enhances traditional laboratories and hands-on learning experiences. We will also discuss the differences between remote labs and virtual labs and highlight the collaborative and inclusive aspects of IoT-powered education. This valuable information sheds light on how IoT is revolutionizing educational environments.

Enhancing Traditional Laboratories with IoT Traditional labs have always played a crucial role in science and engineering education, providing students with hands-on experience using physical equipment and conducting experiments.

However, integrating Internet of Things (IoT) technology has revolutionized these setups. Here is how IoT is transforming traditional labs (Prakash et al., 2021; Newton, 2021):

- ***Real-Time Data Gathering and Analysis:*** IoT sensors embedded in lab equipment continuously collect data, offering students instant information about their ongoing experiments. This immediate feedback allows for real-time adjustments and a deeper understanding of the scientific principles explored.
- ***Remote Monitoring and Control:*** Thanks to IoT, students can now remotely access lab equipment. Whether on campus or studying from a distance, they can control experiments and observe results from their devices. This flexibility promotes inclusivity. It makes education more accessible.
- ***Collaborative Learning:*** IoT-powered labs foster student collaboration even when physically apart. Students can collectively interact with experiments, share data, and troubleshoot together. This collaborative approach enhances the learning experience and prepares students for teamwork in professional environments.
- ***Customization and Adaptability:*** Labs equipped with IoT technology enable instructors to customize experiments and data collection methods according to specific learning goals. This adaptability ensures that lab experiences align with the course curriculum and the student's skill level.

Hands-On Learning with IoT Devices The Internet of Things (IoT) revolutionizes traditional laboratory settings and opens educational opportunities through hands-on learning with IoT devices. Students now have the chance to explore a range of applications in this evolving field, gaining a multidisciplinary perspective. Here are some exciting ways students can dive into IoT (Thought-Process, 2023).

- ***Discovering IoT Kits:*** Students can unleash their creativity using IoT development kits, including sensors, microcontrollers, and communication modules, and design their IoT devices. This hands-on approach fosters problem-solving skills and deepens their understanding of the core principles behind IoT.
- ***Exploring Home Automation Projects:*** The concept of smart homes is closely intertwined with IoT technology. Students can embark on projects where they design and build smart home systems, gaining valuable experience in developing real-life IoT applications.
- ***Engaging in Environmental Monitoring:*** IoT devices, from air quality to wildlife tracking, are vital in environmental monitoring projects. Students can get involved by creating and deploying their IoT sensors to gather real-world data and conduct analysis.
- ***Delving into Industrial IoT (IIoT):*** For engineering and computer science students, delving into Industrial IoT (IIoT) projects is incredibly valuable. They can work with IoT devices in manufacturing, logistics, and industrial settings to witness firsthand how this technology transforms industries.

By embracing these hands-on learning opportunities with IoT devices, students gain experience while broadening their horizons in this dynamic field.

Virtual Labs vs. Remote Labs In the realm of IoT and education, it is crucial to differentiate virtual labs from remote labs (Alhalabi et al., 1998; Poo et al., 2023):

- ***Virtual Labs:*** Virtual labs are software-based simulations of experiments and lab environments. They do not require physical equipment or sensors and provide a digital replica of laboratory scenarios. While they are cost-effective and easily accessible, they may lack the realism and hands-on experience of experiments.
- ***Remote Labs:*** Conversely, remote labs grant students access to physical equipment and IoT devices. Students can control sensors and devices, gather data, and interact with physical apparatus from a distance. This approach bridges the gap between traditional labs and virtual simulations by offering a compromise combining both approaches' advantages.

Integrating the Internet of Things (IoT) into virtual and remote laboratories allows educators to select the method that aligns with their educational goals while improving the learning experience.

Collaborative and Accessible Learning One benefit of incorporating IoT into education is its ability to foster collaboration and promote learning. Students from different backgrounds and locations can collaborate on projects, exchanging knowledge, ideas, and experiences. This collaborative approach mirrors real-life scenarios where IoT technology is commonly utilized (Arduino, 2024).

Moreover, IoT-based education promotes inclusivity by catering to students with disabilities or specific needs. Students can actively participate in laboratory work irrespective of physical limitations through access to laboratories and adaptable interfaces, helping to democratize education (Gerlée, 2023).

Furthermore, the influence of IoT in education extends beyond subjects. It encompasses emerging fields such as data science, cybersecurity, and artificial intelligence. Thus, IoT becomes a part of education and equips learners for future workforce requirements (Kapoor, 2023).

7.3 Designing IoT-Powered Online Laboratories

Creating online laboratories that utilize IoT technology is vital for providing a smooth and enriching learning journey. Whether you are an educator or involved in curriculum development, grasping design principles is crucial for creating impactful online laboratory environments (Poongothai & Arumugam, 2018; Nelke et al., 2023). This section will delve into the elements (see Fig. 7.1) of crafting IoT-powered online laboratories.

Identifying Educational Objectives Before you start the design process, it is crucial to understand your goals. What do you want your students to learn or achieve through the online lab experience? These objectives will guide the process from selecting IoT devices to experiments and activities. Here are some essential factors to consider.

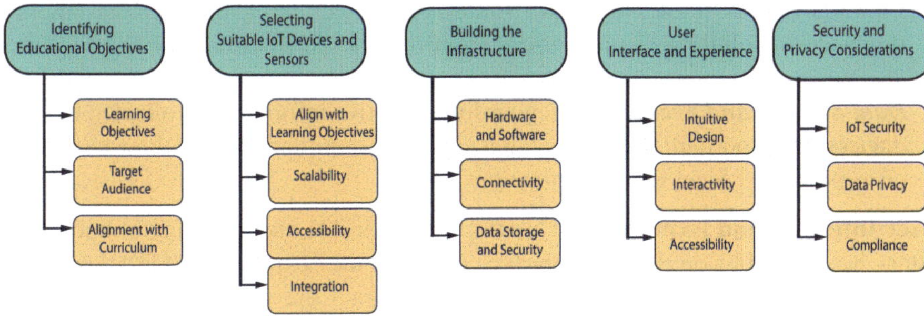

Fig. 7.1 Steps in designing IoT-powered online laboratories

- ***Learning Objectives:*** Define outcomes you want your students to achieve, such as grasping concepts, mastering lab techniques, or applying IoT technology to solve real-world problems.
- ***Target Audience:*** Consider your student's level of knowledge, prior experience, and preferred learning methods. Design the lab to meet their needs.
- ***Alignment with Curriculum:*** Ensure the lab activities align with educational standards and curriculum requirements.

Selecting Suitable IoT Devices and Sensors Selecting the IoT devices and sensors is crucial when designing an online laboratory experience. These components play a vital role in shaping the extent and quality of the online laboratory learning experience. Here are some factors to consider while choosing IoT devices:

- ***Align with Learning Objectives:*** Ensure the IoT devices and sensors you choose directly align with your goals. They should support the concepts and skills you intend to teach.
- ***Scalability:*** Consider scalability, especially if you anticipate several students. Opt for devices easily deployed for both small- and large-scale usage.
- ***Accessibility:*** It is important to ensure students can access the IoT devices in a physical laboratory or remotely. Assess their user friendliness and availability to ensure inclusivity among all students.
- ***Integration:*** Verify that the selected IoT devices and sensors can seamlessly integrate into your chosen laboratory platform. Compatibility with your software and hardware infrastructure is vital.

Considering these factors, you can decide which IoT devices best suit your laboratory requirements.

Building the Infrastructure The success of your IoT-powered online laboratory relies heavily on its infrastructure. This encompasses both the physical and digital components required for operation. Here are some important factors to consider.

- ***Hardware and Software:*** Invest in hardware and software infrastructure to handle real-time device data. A user-friendly, robust laboratory platform is crucial.

- ***Connectivity:*** A stable, high-speed internet connection ensures remote laboratory access. Solutions to minimize disruptions caused by connectivity issues are also wise.
- ***Data Storage and Security:*** Safeguarding sensitive information collected by IoT devices is important. Implement data storage solutions that follow best data encryption and access control practices.

User Interface and Experience Creating an accessible and engaging online laboratory heavily relies on the user interface (UI) and user experience (UX) design. A well-designed UI/UX ensures students can navigate the platform smoothly and focus on their learning goals. Here are some important factors to consider.

- ***Intuitive Design:*** Developing an intuitive and user-friendly interface that guides students effortlessly through laboratory activities is crucial. By minimizing complexity, we can reduce the learning curve and prevent frustration.
- ***Interactivity:*** To enhance engagement and facilitate learning, students must have tools to control IoT devices, adjust parameters, and observe real-time data. Maximizing interactivity is key.
- ***Accessibility:*** Ensuring all students can access the UI/UX is vital, including those with needs or disabilities. This involves offering alternate content formats and supporting assistive technologies.

Security and Privacy Considerations Security and privacy are important for IoT devices and student data. Addressing these concerns during the design phase is crucial to safeguarding your laboratory and students. Here are some key factors to keep in mind.

- ***IoT Security:*** Implement IoT device security practices to prevent unauthorized access or potential data breaches. Regularly updating firmware and software is essential to address potential vulnerabilities.
- ***Data Privacy:*** You must communicate your data usage and privacy policies with your students. Whenever necessary, obtain their consent. For added protection, anonymize or pseudonymize their data.
- ***Compliance:*** Ensure your online laboratory follows all regulations, including data protection laws and industry-specific standards.

By considering these considerations when designing IoT-powered online laboratories, you can create a compelling, engaging, and secure learning environment for all your students.

7.4 Implementation and Case Studies

The effective adoption of online laboratories powered by the Internet of Things requires planning, resource allocation, and strategic decision-making. This section will investigate the considerations in implementing these laboratories and analyze real-life examples demonstrating their practical applications.

Case Study 1: IoT in Physics Labs In Case Study 1, we delve into incorporating technology within physics laboratories. This case study sheds light on how this integration facilitates student access, broadens the availability of distance learning opportunities, improves understanding of concepts through real-time data collection, and brings about substantial cost savings by reducing the need for physical lab space and equipment upkeep in a prominent university environment.

- ***Implementation Details***: IoT sensors and devices can be integrated into a university's physics lab to enhance traditional experiments. This integration allows students to remotely access top-notch physics equipment and conduct experiments with an internet connection. With real-time sensor data, they could analyze data as if they were physically present in the lab.
- ***Results - Increased Accessibility:*** Thanks to IoT technology, students from different locations can gain access to the physics lab, enabling them to engage in remote and distance learning.
- ***Enhanced Understanding:*** The ability to collect and analyze real-time data will help students grasp principles more deeply, resulting in greater engagement and improved learning outcomes.
- ***Cost Savings:*** The university can save by reducing the need for physical lab space and equipment maintenance.

Case Study 2: IoT in Chemistry Labs Case Study 2 demonstrates how IoT technology can be utilized in a chemistry lab class to improve safety by monitoring chemical reactions. It also broadens students' ability to conduct experiments and offers a real-world experience that prepares them for careers in chemistry and related fields.

- ***Implementation Details:*** In a chemistry lab course, we can use sensors and devices to monitor chemical reactions and handle materials. This allows students to manipulate variables remotely and observe reactions through video feeds. We can have safety protocols to ensure everyone's well-being during the experiments.
- ***Results—Improved Safety Measures:*** IoT technology will significantly reduce the risks of handling chemicals, ensuring that students and instructors are safe.
- ***Expanded Experimental Opportunities:*** With the help of IoT, students may have the chance to conduct various experiments exploring chemical reactions that were previously limited due to safety concerns.
- ***Real-Life Application:*** The IoT devices will mirror real-world practices for chemical monitoring, providing an experience for students pursuing careers in chemistry or related fields.

Case Study 3: IoT in Engineering Labs In Case Study 3 of an engineering program, students can have the opportunity to incorporate IoT devices and sensors into their hands-on projects. They could use development kits to create smart systems and devices that will help them develop technical skills and foster creativity, problem-solving abilities, and interdisciplinary learning experiences.

- ***Implementation Details:*** An engineering program can integrate IoT devices and sensors into projects. To gain hands-on experience, students can use development kits to create smart systems and devices while learning to design and implement IoT solutions.
- ***Results—Skills Development:*** This approach will equip students for careers in the IoT industry by enabling them to acquire skills in programming IoT devices, integrating sensors, and analyzing data.
- ***Creativity and Problem Solving:*** The hands-on projects allow students to think critically and unleash their potential. By utilizing the power of IoT technology, they can tackle real-world challenges.
- ***Interdisciplinary Learning:*** The engineering labs' IoT projects often foster collaboration and encourage students to collaborate across fields and apply their knowledge innovatively.

Lessons Learned and Best Practices The integration of online laboratories powered by IoT has resulted in important lessons and recommended approaches:

- ***Training:*** It is crucial to train students and instructors on IoT devices and the laboratory platform to ensure smooth operation.
- ***Support and Technical Assistance:*** Support and assistance during laboratory sessions are essential for students with technical difficulties.
- ***Privacy:*** Robust security measures should be implemented to safeguard data and devices while complying with privacy regulations.
- ***Regular Maintenance:*** Maintenance and updates for IoT devices and the laboratory platform are necessary to maintain a well-functioning system.
- ***Feedback and Improvement:*** Continuously gather feedback from students and instructors to enhance the laboratory experience.
- ***Scalability:*** Design the laboratory to accommodate increasing users as demand grows.

The case studies and recommended approaches demonstrate how IoT enhances learning across fields of study. These experiences highlight IoT's potential to revolutionize education while providing insights for those considering implementing similar systems.

7.5 Managing and Maintaining Online Laboratories

Once online laboratories powered by the Internet of Things (IoT) are put into operation, ensuring their management and maintenance to sustain their success becomes crucial. This section will delve into overseeing and preserving these cutting-edge educational environments.

Monitoring and Troubleshooting IoT Devices Ensuring smooth online laboratory operations requires monitoring of IoT devices. Here are some important factors to consider when managing and troubleshooting these IoT devices (JRPanel, 2021; Intuz, 2023; Shiksha Online, 2023):

- ***Remote Monitoring:*** It is crucial to establish a system that allows us to monitor IoT devices, enabling us to monitor their status, connectivity, and functionality.
- ***Alert Systems:*** Implementing alert systems and notifications will help identify device malfunctions or abnormal data readings. This proactive approach ensures the detection and resolution of issues.
- ***Regular Diagnostics:*** Conducting routine diagnostics and testing is essential for potentially preventing problems. We should replace faulty sensors or devices as necessary.
- ***Technical Support:*** It is vital to offer channels for students and instructors to seek support when faced with IoT device-related issues.

Scalability and Upgrades As the demand for online laboratories grows, designing a system that can handle increased usage is essential. Here are some considerations for managing scalability and upgrades (Kewaunee, 2023):

- ***Infrastructure Scalability:*** Ensure the hardware and software infrastructure accommodates more users and allows growth.
- ***Updates:*** Stay updated with the latest IoT technology and software updates. Upgrade the system regularly to take advantage of new features, security patches, and improvements.
- ***User Feedback:*** Consider user feedback on performance and usability. Use this information to decide on upgrades and enhancements.

Implementing these strategies ensures your online laboratory system remains scalable while meeting users' evolving needs.

Data Management and Analysis To ensure valuable insights are derived and enhance the laboratory experience, managing and analyzing the data generated by IoT devices is crucial. Here are some key considerations (Trusted Twin, 2024; Gerber & Kansal, 2020):

- ***Data Storage:*** Establish a data storage system with backups to safeguard experimental data.
- ***Data Analysis Tools:*** Use data analysis tools that empower students to comprehend and interpret the information collected during laboratory activities.
- ***Data Sharing:*** Foster an environment by enabling students and instructors to share their findings, facilitating analysis and productive discussions.
- ***Data Privacy:*** We will prioritize student data security and privacy and ensure compliance with relevant regulations.

Compliance and Regulation Running an online laboratory involves adhering to data protection rules. Here are some important things to consider (Microlit, 2023).

- ***Safeguarding Data:*** Following data protection regulations is essential to protect students' information and privacy.

- ***Accessibility Matters:*** It is crucial to ensure that the online laboratory platform is accessible for students with disabilities. This means following accessibility standards and guidelines.
- ***Curriculum Alignment:*** To meet educational requirements, laboratory activities must be reviewed and aligned with curriculum standards.
- ***Security Protocols:*** Continuously assessing and updating security protocols helps safeguard against cyber threats and data breaches.
- ***Ensuring Quality:*** Establishing quality assurance processes ensures that the laboratory consistently meets objectives and performance standards.

By addressing these aspects of managing and maintaining online laboratories, educators and administrators can create an effective learning environment for students.

7.6 Future Trends and Challenges

With the progress of technology and the changing landscape of education, online laboratories powered by IoT are encountering promising possibilities and enduring obstacles. This section delves into the future trends and challenges associated with IoT-based online laboratories.

Emerging Technologies in IoT and Education The fusion of emerging technologies is shaping the future of learning in the Internet of Things (IoT) and education.

- ***Integration of AI and Machine Learning***: By incorporating intelligence (AI) and machine learning into IoT devices, we can achieve smarter data analysis, personalized learning experiences, and predictive analytics. Students will receive personalized recommendations and insights based on their performance and interactions with IoT-powered laboratories.
- ***Integration of Virtual Reality (VR) and Augmented Reality (AR):*** Combining IoT with VR and AR technologies opens up possibilities for immersive laboratory experiences. Students can engage with virtual experiments in 3D, making science and engineering concepts more tangible and captivating.
- ***Embracing Edge Computing:*** Using a centralized cloud, edge computing processes data locally on IoT devices. This approach reduces latency and provides real-time feedback, which is precious in online laboratory settings where low latency is crucial.

Integrating these emerging technologies holds promise for revolutionizing how we learn in the IoT era.

Addressing Security and Privacy Concerns IoT devices in educational settings are targets for cyberattacks. As the use of online labs increases, it is crucial to prioritize addressing security and privacy concerns. Here are some key measures to consider.

- ***Data Encryption:*** Employ robust encryption protocols to safeguard data transmission between IoT devices and the lab platform.
- ***Access Control:*** Implement access controls to ensure authorized individuals can interact with IoT devices and access student data.
- ***Regular Security Audits:*** Conduct periodic security audits and vulnerability assessments to identify and mitigate potential threats.
- ***Promoting cybersecurity awareness:*** Educate instructors about cybersecurity practices and the importance of safeguarding data in online labs.

Expanding Access to Online Laboratories Online labs can potentially make hands-on learning more accessible, thus democratizing education. To ensure increased access, educational institutions can consider implementing the following strategies.

- ***Mobile-Friendly Platforms:*** Ensure that online labs are compatible with smartphones and tablets for easy accessibility.
- ***Global Partnerships:*** Foster global partnerships with institutions and organizations worldwide to share resources and provide lab access to a broader audience.
- ***Internet Connectivity Initiatives:*** Advocate for improved internet connectivity in underserved areas, ensuring all students can access online labs.
- ***Cloud-Based Solutions:*** Explore cloud-based solutions as they can help reduce hardware requirements and increase accessibility for institutions with constrained resources.

Integrating IoT into the Curriculum Educational institutions must prioritize integrating IoT-powered online laboratories into the curriculum to ensure they remain practical and relevant. Here are some key strategies.

- ***Collaboration with Industry:*** Work closely with industry partners to align laboratory activities with real-world technology applications. This collaboration will ensure that students gain the skills and knowledge for careers in the IoT field.
- ***Curriculum Updates:*** Laboratory exercises and materials must be updated to keep pace with the ever-evolving IoT technology and trends. This will ensure that students receive up-to-date education that prepares them for challenges.
- ***Interdisciplinary Approach:*** Encourage the integration of IoT into a wide range of disciplines, such as engineering, computer science, biology, and environmental studies. By incorporating concepts across subjects, students can better understand their applications.
- ***Assessment and Continuous Improvement:*** Implement assessment methods to evaluate how well online laboratories meet learning objectives. Collect feedback from students and instructors to identify areas for improvement and make adjustments.

Addressing these trends and challenges in the landscape of IoT-powered online laboratories is crucial for providing high-quality educational experiences that prepare students for the future.

7.7 Conclusion

Integration of online labs with the Internet of Things (IoT) in education has transformed learning, providing students with hands-on learning experiences regardless of location or available resources. This chapter delved into the development, benefits, obstacles, uses, future directions of online labs, and how IoT improves traditional lab setups. Online labs have become invaluable educational tools connecting conceptual knowledge with practical applications in a cost-effective, secure, and adaptable educational environment. Technology integration has enhanced these digital learning spaces to facilitate real-time data gathering, remote access capabilities, interaction opportunities, collaborative work environments, and individualized feedback mechanisms. The versatility and effectiveness of online lab applications have been showcased across levels—from K12 institutions to universities and professional training programs. Whether in physics, chemistry, engineering, or other subjects, incorporating IoT has resulted in accessibility to resources, enhanced safety measures, improved comprehension levels, and interdisciplinary learning prospects. Successful deployment, administration, supervision, and upkeep of IoT-driven online laboratories are crucial for ensuring their efficacy and functionality. Teachers and school leaders must focus on defining goals, choosing appropriate IoT devices, establishing robust infrastructure, and creating easy-to-use interfaces addressing security and privacy issues following regulations and incorporating feedback to enhance learning continuously. New technologies like AI virtual reality (VR) and augmented reality (AR) are set to improve online labs by offering personalized learning opportunities. However, challenges such as ensuring security and privacy, increasing group access, and integrating IoT into the curriculum remain areas that require careful consideration. In summary, online labs powered by IoT are changing education by giving students hands-on skills, promoting teamwork and creativity, and preparing them for success in the digital era. By embracing these technologies and following best practices, educational institutions can deliver top-quality inclusive education that prepares students for the future.

References

Alhalabi, B., Hamza, M. K., Hsu, S., & Romance, N. (1998). Virtual labs VS remote labs: Between myth & reality. In *Florida Higher Education Consortium Statewide Conference* (pp. 1–5).

Arduino. (2024). *The role of the IoT in education*. Arduino. https://www.arduino.cc/education/the-role-of-the-iot-in-education

Assem, S. (2023). *The most important advantages and disadvantages of virtual*. PraxiLabs. https://praxilabs.com/en/blog/2018/03/01/important-advantages-impediments-use-virtual-lab/

Fajriah, N., Maulida, P., Agung, T., Marida, C., & Prasetya, A. (2023). A decade evolution of virtual and remote laboratories. *Bulletin of Social Informatics Theory and Application, 7*(1), 63–73.

Gerber, A., & Kansal, S. (2020). *Making sense of IoT data storing*. IBM. https://developer.ibm.com/tutorials/iot-lp301-iot-manage-data/

Gerlée, K. (2023). *IoT in education: Transforming learning environments*. Freeeway. https://freeeway.com/iot-in-education-transforming-learning-environments/
Intuz. (2023). *IoT device management: Importance, challenges, solutions what is IoT device management?* Intuz. https://www.intuz.com/guide-on-iot-device-management
JRPanel. (2021). *6 important factors for managing IoT devices*. JRPanel. https://www.jrpanel.com/engineerhome/keyword/JRPanel__Important_Factors_for_Managing_IoT_Devices.html
Kapoor, M. (2023). *IoT in education: Fostering personalized and interactive learning experiences*. CognitiveClouds.. https://www.cognitiveclouds.com/insights/iot-in-education
Kewaunee. (2023). *Infrastructure considerations for modern labs*. Kewaunee International Group. https://www.kewaunee.in/blog/infrastructure-considerations-for-modern-labs/
Kumar, S. (2024). *Benefits and need of virtual laboratories in the education system*. Linkedin. https://www.linkedin.com/pulse/benefits-need-virtual-laboratories-education-system-santosh-kumar-w0a0c/?trk=article-ssr-frontend-pulse_more-articles_related-content-card
Labster. (2023). *The complete guide to virtual labs what are virtual labs?* Labster. https://www.labster.com/how-it-works#:~:text=in modern pedagogy.-,What Are Virtual Labs%3F,tosolverealworldproblems
May, D., Jahnke, I., & Moore, S. (2023). Online laboratories and virtual experimentation in higher education from a sociotechnical-pedagogical design perspective. *Journal of Computing in Higher Education, 35*, 203–222.
Microlit. (2023). *Why data security is vital for laboratories?* Microlit. https://www.microlit.com/why-data-security-is-vital-for-laboratories/
Nelke, S. A., Khomyakov, M., Mhmad, S., Winokur, M., & Benis, A. (2023). Designing and developing a remote IoT lab for enhanced lab classes pedagogical study. In *2023 Pre-ICIS SIGDSA Symposium, February 2024*.
Newton, E. (2021). *How is the IoT improving laboratori and research?* IoT Times. https://iot.eetimes.com/how-is-the-iot-improving-laboratories-research/
Perkel, J. M. (2017). The Internet of Things toolbox. *Nature, 542*, 125–126. https://doi.org/10.1038/542125a
Poo, M. C.-P., Lau, Y., & Chen, Q. (2023). Are virtual laboratories and remote laboratories enhancing the quality of sustainability education? *Education Sciences, 13*(11), 1–13.
Poongothai, M., & Arumugam, R. A. (2018). Design and implementation of IoT based smart laboratory. In *2018 5th International Conference on Industrial Engineering and Applications Design, April 2018* (pp. 10–15). https://doi.org/10.1109/IEA.2018.8387090
Prakash, K. R., Santhosh, M. S., Purushothama, G. K., & Ramya, M. V. (2021). An approach to convert conventional laboratories into IoT-enabled laboratories. *International Journal of Web-Based Learning and Teaching Technologies, 16*(5), 108–120. https://doi.org/10.4018/IJWLTT.20210901.oa6
Raman, R., Achuthan, K., & Kumar, V. (2022). Virtual laboratories – A historical review and bibliometric analysis of the past three decades. In *Education and information technologies*. Springer US. https://doi.org/10.1007/s10639-022-11058-9
Science Interactive. (2023). *The pros & cons of virtual labs based on 1,614 instructors & students the drawbacks of virtual science labs*. Science Interactive. https://www.scienceinteractive.com/the-pros-cons-of-virtual-labs-based-on-1614-instructors-students/
Shiksha Online. (2023). *IoT device management fundamentals*. Shiksha Online. https://www.shiksha.com/online-courses/articles/iot-device-management/
StemroboTechnologies.(2023).*AIandIoTlabs:Transformingschoolsintoinnovationhubs*.Stemrobo Technologies.. https://www.stemrobo.com/ai-and-iot-labs-in-schools-ai-and-iot-in-education/
Thought-Process. (2023). *IoT connectivity corporate training for employees*. Thought-Process. https://thought-process.in/iot-connectivity-corporate-training-for-employees/
Trusted Twin. (2024). *How to manage large data sets from IoT devices*. Trusted Twin.. https://trustedtwin.com/data-sharing/iot-data/

Chapter 8
Technology-Based Learning Experiences with IoT in Education

Abstract This chapter explores how IoT technology is being incorporated into the education sector, examining its impacts on remote learning, data analysis, upcoming trends, obstacles, and recommended approaches for implementation. Students can use virtual remote experiments and IoT-enabled distance learning to engage in practical activities, flexible assessments, and real-time discussions to create inclusive and globally connected learning environments. Data analysis with IoT supports predictive analytics, personalized learning experiences, and data-informed decision-making. Future trends hint at adaptive learning methods, augmented reality applications, and blockchain credentials within educational settings. Nonetheless, challenges such as data security concerns, integration complexities, and accessibility issues need to be managed alongside considerations of collaboration efforts and adherence to regulations. Effective strategies involve setting goals, investing in infrastructure upgrades, emphasizing data protection measures, and providing training for staff members. By addressing these hurdles, educational institutions can leverage the power of IoT to improve the quality and availability of education for students worldwide.

Keywords IoT technology · Distance learning · Data analysis · Adaptive learning methods · Data security concerns · Infrastructure upgrades · Data protection measures

8.1 Introduction

Technology has become a part of our lives in education. One noteworthy advancement is the Internet of Things (IoT), which has brought about environmental changes and opportunities. The IoT refers to a network of objects or "things" that gather and share data, revolutionizing how we approach teaching and learning.

Importance of IoT in Education Integrating IoT into education is more than a passing trend; it has become necessary due to the growing demand for personalized,

M. Kurni, Srinivasa K. G., *The Internet of Educational Things*,
https://doi.org/10.1007/978-3-031-67387-0_8

efficient, and technology-driven learning experiences. IoT allows educational institutions to leverage data, connectivity, and automation to serve their students and faculty better. It can revolutionize traditional educational models by making them more adaptable, responsive, and effective. The integration of IoT in education offers various benefits, which are listed below (Intuz, 2023).

- ***Improved Learning Experiences:*** Connecting students with various digital resources and IoT tools empowers educators to create more engaging and interactive learning environments. It enables real-time feedback, customized content delivery, and personalized learning paths tailored to each student's needs and progress.
- ***Efficient Campus Management:*** IoT simplifies administrative tasks beyond the classroom by optimizing facility management. It can help optimize energy consumption, enhance campus security measures, and improve resource allocation while reducing costs and environmental impact.
- ***Informed Decision-Making through Data Analysis:*** The wealth of data generated by IoT can be harnessed to enhance the experience. Through data analytics, educators can gain insights into student performance, evaluate the effectiveness of teaching methods, and make informed decisions to improve learning outcomes.
- ***Enhanced Student Engagement:*** IoT devices and applications can make learning more interactive and enjoyable. Educators can leverage gamification elements, real-world applications, and collaborative tools to increase student engagement and motivation.
- ***Support for Remote Learning:*** IoT is important in today's online education era. It enables virtual labs, remote proctoring, and seamless content delivery to learners worldwide.

IoT is not another tool but a transformative force that has the potential to shape the future of education by making it more inclusive, adaptable, and effective.

IoT Applications in Education The Internet of Things (IoT) in education is vast and diverse, offering possibilities to transform how we teach and learn. This section will explore some of the innovative IoT applications in educational environments. These applications exemplify how IoT technology can create efficient and compelling learning experiences for students and educators (Kumar, 2023; Wattley, 2023).

- ***Smart Classrooms:*** One remarkable application of IoT in education is "smart classrooms." These advanced learning spaces have various devices and sensors that enhance teaching and learning. Here are some key features found in smart classrooms.
  - *Interactive Whiteboards:* With interactive whiteboards enabled, teachers can deliver engaging lessons, annotate content, and share digital resources with students. Additionally, these devices can gather data on student interactions for real-time feedback and assessment.

  - *Smart Projectors:* Smart projectors incorporate sensors that detect gestures and objects. This enables an interactive and dynamic teaching style where teachers can directly interact with content displayed on the screen.
  - *IoT Connected Devices:* In smart classrooms, devices such as tablets, laptops, and smartphones can also be connected to the Internet. This connectivity enables learning and the sharing of resources.
  - *Environmental Control Sensors:* IoT sensors can monitor and regulate the classroom environment, adjusting lighting, temperature, and air quality to create a more comfortable and conducive learning atmosphere.

- ***Smart Campus:*** Beyond classrooms, IoT technology extends its advantages to the campus, resulting in what is commonly known as a "smart campus." A smart campus utilizes IoT technology to streamline operations, enhance security measures, and create a more efficient and sustainable environment. Here are some key applications within a campus.

  - *Energy Management:* IoT sensors can control energy usage across all campus buildings. They automatically adjust lighting, heating, and cooling systems based on occupancy levels, optimizing energy efficiency while reducing costs.
  - *Security and Access Control:* Security systems enabled by IoT provide advanced access control capabilities alongside surveillance. They can detect access attempts in time and promptly notify security personnel to ensure the safety of students and staff.
  - *Resource Optimization:* Smart campuses use IoT technology to manage resources more effectively. This includes optimizing the utilization of classrooms, laboratories, and library spaces. Sensors provide real-time information on occupancy levels and usage patterns, enabling resource allocation.
  - *Navigation and wayfinding:* Internet of Things (IoT) applications in navigation can make it easier for students and visitors to navigate around the campus. Interactive maps and mobile apps provide guidance, streamlining campus navigation.

- ***IoT in library and resource management:*** Libraries are vital for the learning experience, and IoT technology can improve their functionality in many ways.

  - *Smart bookshelves:* Libraries equipped with IoT technology can have intelligent bookshelves that keep track of which books are on the shelves and which are checked out. This information is invaluable for managing inventory and planning resources.
  - *Enabled study spaces:* Libraries can offer IoT-enabled study spaces with capabilities that monitor occupancy levels, adjusting lighting and temperature conditions for user comfort while saving energy.
  - *Resource discovery:* IoT can assist in resource discovery, helping users find relevant books, articles, and digital materials within the library's collection through smart searching and personalized recommendations.

- ***Laboratory and equipment management:*** In institutions, laboratories play a vital role in STEM education (science, technology, engineering, and mathematics). IoT can enhance laboratory management through the following methods.
  - *Equipment tracking:* Sensors can effectively track laboratory equipment usage and condition. This helps prevent loss or theft, ensure proper maintenance, and facilitate the scheduling of student experiments.
  - *Safety Monitoring:* IoT technology enables laboratory conditions to be monitored to ensure safety, such as temperature control, gas leak detection, and proper storage of chemicals. Real-time alerts can be sent to prevent accidents.
  - *Remote Access to Lab Resources:* With IoT, students and educators can access laboratory resources remotely, conduct experiments, and gather data. This is particularly beneficial for distance learning and online education.
- ***IoT in School Transportation:*** Educational institutions that provide transportation services can enhance safety, efficiency, and communication through IoT. Some applications include:
  - *GPS Tracking:* School buses equipped with devices can be tracked in time to ensure the safety and security of students during their journeys.
  - *Route Optimization:* Bus routes can be optimized using IoT technology based on traffic conditions and weather forecasts, reducing travel time and fuel consumption.
  - *Parent School Communication:* IoT enables real-time information sharing between parents and schools regarding bus schedules, such as student pick-up and drop-off times.
- ***IoT for Student Well-being:*** Educational institutions prioritize the well-being of their students. IoT can enhance students' mental well-being.
  - *Wearable Devices:* Students can wear IoT-enabled devices that track their activity, sleep patterns, and stress levels. Schools can utilize this data to establish wellness programs and provide support accordingly.
  - *Mental Health Support:* IoT applications can offer students access to resources for managing stress, anxiety, and other mental health issues. Chatbots and apps can guide students and connect them with counselors whenever needed.
  - *Safety Alerts:* In emergencies, IoT technology can send safety alerts to students, ensuring their well-being on and off campus.

These are a few examples of how IoT can be applied in education. This technology's adaptability and scalability enable institutions to customize solutions that cater to their needs and goals.

8.2 Enhancing Classroom Learning

The traditional classroom, characterized by rows of desks and chalkboards, is transforming due to the integration of the Internet of Things (IoT). This section will explore how IoT enhances classroom learning by creating engaging educational environments. These innovative technologies, such as smart boards and connected devices, reshape how students and teachers interact with educational content (NVIT, 2023; Intuz, 2023).

- ***Smart Boards and Interactive Displays:***
  - *Interactive Whiteboards:* Commonly known as smart boards, they have become a part of modern classrooms. These large touchscreen displays are equipped with IoT technology, enabling educators to create captivating and interactive lessons. Students can directly engage with the content displayed on the board, whether it is a math problem, a map, or a science experiment. The features of annotations, multimedia integration, and real-time collaboration foster a dynamic learning experience.
  - *Collaborative Learning:* Smart boards promote learning where students can collaborate on projects, presentations, and problem-solving activities. The ability to instantly share and showcase their work enhances teamwork skills and critical thinking.
  - *Digital Content Delivery:* IoT-enabled smart boards offer effortless access to a range of digital content that can be readily displayed in classrooms. Teachers can seamlessly switch between teaching materials, including videos and online resources, to keep their students engaged and provide diverse learning experiences.
- ***Connected Devices in the Classroom:***
  - *Student Devices:* Many students bring their IoT-enabled devices, such as tablets and laptops, to school. These devices can connect to the classroom network, allowing students to participate in activities, actively submit assignments electronically, and access textbooks and educational apps.
  - *Real-Time Assessment:* Teachers can leverage IoT technology to assess student understanding in real time. Students can provide immediate feedback by conducting quizzes and polls on their devices. This allows teachers to adapt their instruction based on students' responses, leading to enhanced learning outcomes.
  - *Remote Learning:* In situations where physical attendance is impossible, IoT technology enables students to connect remotely. Virtual classrooms and video conferencing tools enable them to join lectures and participate in discussions with an internet connection.

- ***Personalized Learning Experiences:***
  - *Adaptive Learning Platforms:* IoT-powered adaptive learning systems can tailor educational content based on student progress. These platforms analyze data from students' interactions with materials like quizzes and exercises. As students interact with the material, the system adjusts itself to offer supportive content, tailoring it to their needs and learning pace.
  - *Intelligent Tutoring Systems:* Intelligent tutoring systems driven by IoT provide personalized guidance and assistance. These systems analyze data from sources like students' completion of homework, quiz scores, and participation in classroom activities. Based on this data, students receive recommendations, additional resources, or targeted exercises to address their learning difficulties.
- ***Gamification and Interactive Learning:***
  - *Gamification:* IoT has paved the way for learning experiences that incorporate gamification elements. Rewards, badges, and leaderboards make learning captivating and enjoyable. Students are motivated to complete tasks, achieve goals, and compete with their peers while mastering content.
  - *Real-World Applications:* IoT-enabled devices can bridge the gap between classroom education and real-world applications. For example, students can use IoT sensors to gather data or embark on their Internet of Things projects in science and engineering classes. This hands-on approach makes learning more relevant and memorable.

IoT transforms classrooms by making education interactive, engaging, and adaptable to each student's requirements.

8.3 Personalized Learning with IoT

Personalized learning is an approach that customizes content and methods to cater to individual students' needs, preferences, and progress. The Internet of Things (IoT) plays a vital role in bringing learning into reality within educational environments (Kumar, 2015; Ollivachreis, 2024). In this section, we will delve into how IoT enables the delivery of learning experiences, adaptive content, and tailored support for students, ultimately leading to improved outcomes. Figure 8.1 shows how personalized learning is implemented using IoT technologies, which successfully customize educational experiences to meet each student's unique needs.

- ***Adaptive Learning Systems:***
  - *Continuous Assessment:* An essential aspect of learning with IoT is the ability to assess student performance continuously. IoT devices and systems gather data on how students interact with materials through digital textbooks, learning management systems, or interactive software. This data encompasses time

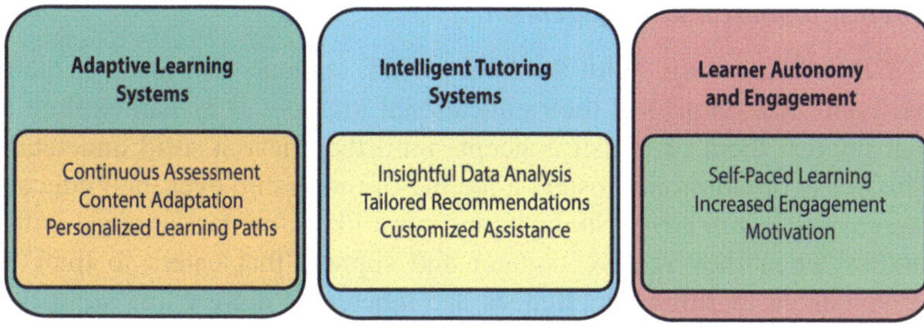

Fig. 8.1 Personalized learning with IoT

spent on specific topics, quiz scores, response times, and even biometric data like heart rate variability (HRV) for monitoring engagement and stress levels.
- *Content Adaptation:* By leveraging this data, adaptive learning platforms adjust the content provided to each student in real time. For instance, if students excel in a subject area, the system can automatically advance them to advanced materials or offer additional challenges. On the other hand, if a student has difficulty understanding a concept, the system can offer explanations, examples, or practice exercises until the student demonstrates mastery.
- *Personalized Learning Paths:* The adaptive learning system designs learning paths for each student. These paths may include resources like text, videos, interactive simulations, and customized assignments that cater to the student's strengths and weaknesses. As a result, students can learn at their own pace and develop a comprehension of the subject matter.

• ***Intelligent Tutoring Systems:***

  - *Insightful Data Analysis:* Intelligent tutoring systems powered by IoT gather data from completed homework, quiz scores, classroom engagement levels, and self-assessment tools. They use this data to gain insights into each student's learning process and identify areas where additional support might be necessary.
  - *Tailored Recommendations:* The intelligent tutoring system can provide students with recommendations based on these insights. These recommendations may include materials, remedial exercises, or challenging tasks. For instance, if a student consistently struggles with math problem-solving skills, the system may suggest practice problems or recommend videos.
  - *Customized Assistance:* Besides content suggestions, intelligent tutoring systems can offer specific support tailored to individual students' needs. This support can be virtual office hours with teachers, online tutoring from peers, or access to specific resources. The main objective is to ensure that students receive the assistance they need to succeed regardless of their level of proficiency in a particular subject.

- ***Learner Autonomy and Engagement:***
  - *Self-Paced Learning:* With the help of IoT, students can learn at their own pace and take control of their educational journey. They can explore topics that interest them or revisit concepts until they have a solid understanding. This sense of autonomy fosters a feeling of ownership over their education.
  - *Increased Engagement:* Students are more likely to stay engaged with their studies when they receive content and support that caters to their needs. Personalized learning experiences are inherently more captivating because they directly relate to the student's level of comprehension, giving them a sense of achievement as they progress.
  - Motivation: Personalized learning through IoT can incorporate gamification elements to motivate students further. Students are encouraged to participate in their journey by earning badges, competing with peers, and tracking their progress.

Personalized learning through IoT empowers students by enabling them to take charge of their education and customize their learning experiences according to their needs and preferences. IoT-driven systems offer personalized support and adaptable content to enhance engagement, motivation, and academic achievements.

8.4 IoT for Campus Management

Integrating IoT (Internet of Things) in education goes beyond the classroom setting and extends to the efficient management of educational institutions. Utilizing IoT technology can bring advantages to campus management, covering various administrative and operational aspects (Wipro, 2024; Joshi, 2021). This section will explore how IoT enhances campus security, optimizes energy management, and improves institutional resource allocation. Figure 8.2 shows how IoT is changing campus life by improving security, managing energy efficiently, and better allocating resources.

- ***Campus Security:*** The safety and security of students, staff, and the entire campus are essential to institutions. Security systems offer tools that effectively monitor, safeguard, and respond to security incidents.
  - *Surveillance Cameras:* Strategically positioned across the campus, connected surveillance cameras provide real-time video feeds for monitoring entrances, exits, hallways, parking lots, and other areas. These cameras have features such as license plate recognition and motion detection to enhance security further.
  - *Access Control Systems:* Access control systems help ensure secure and convenient access to campus facilities. Smart cards or biometric identifiers, like fingerprints or facial recognition, are used to grant access. This technology

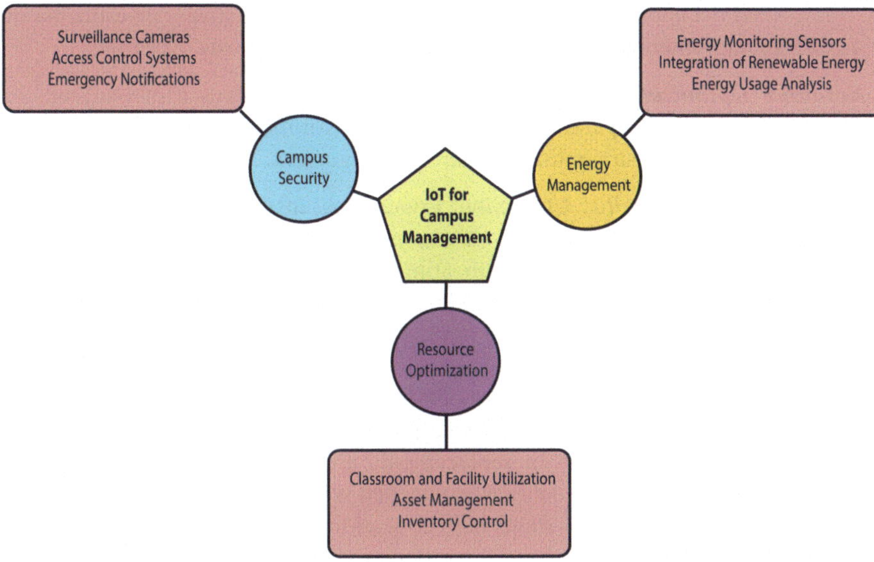

Fig. 8.2 Unlocking campus potential: IoT's triple impact on security, energy, and resources

accurately tracks individuals entering or leaving buildings on campus while enhancing security measures.

- *Emergency Notifications:* Internet of Things (IoT) technology enables the dissemination of emergency notifications. During security threats or natural disasters, automated alerts can be sent to students and staff using text messages, emails, and public address systems. This ensures that people on campus receive crucial information promptly.

- ***Energy Management:*** Effectively managing energy consumption is environmentally responsible and cost-effective for institutions. IoT technology allows for the efficient use of energy on campus.
  - *Energy Monitoring Sensors:* IoT sensors monitor energy usage in buildings across the campus. These sensors collect lighting, heating, cooling, and electrical systems data. The gathered data is then analyzed to identify areas where energy savings can be achieved. For instance, lights can automatically turn off in rooms, and temperature control can be adjusted based on occupancy levels and outdoor conditions.
  - *Integration of Renewable Energy:* IoT facilitates the integration of energy sources like panels and wind turbines into the campus's energy grid. Institutions can optimize energy use by monitoring real-time energy production and consumption while reducing reliance on renewable sources.
  - *Energy Usage Analysis:* IoT technology provides insights into energy consumption patterns. Educational institutions can utilize this data to make

informed decisions regarding energy conservation initiatives, investments in energy equipment, and strategies for reducing energy costs over time.

- ***Resource Optimization:*** Efficient resource allocation plays a pivotal role in ensuring the smooth operation of educational institutions. IoT facilitates data-driven decisions and streamlines resource management.
  - *Classroom and Facility Utilization:* Educational institutions can employ sensors to track the utilization of classrooms, laboratories, libraries, and other facilities. This data assists in allocating resources effectively by optimizing class schedules and events to maximize room usage. It also aids in making decisions about space expansion or renovation.
  - *Asset Management:* IoT technology proves valuable in managing and maintaining assets like computers, projectors, and laboratory equipment. Sensors can monitor asset condition and location, track maintenance schedules, and issue alerts when repairs or replacements are necessary. This ensures that resources are readily available when needed while being well maintained.
  - *Inventory Control:* IoT systems help educational institutions efficiently manage inventory levels. Whether it is textbooks, lab supplies, or office equipment, IoT sensors automatically monitor inventory levels and provide restocking alerts when necessary to prevent resource shortages or thefts.

IoT technology integration presents advantages for campus management within educational institutions. Improved security protocols, energy preservation, and efficient resource management contribute to friendly and economically viable operations.

8.5 IoT and Student Engagement

Student involvement plays a vital role in facilitating learning. When students are engaged, they tend to be more motivated and attentive and achieve outcomes. In specific educational settings, the Internet of Things (IoT) technology is increasingly utilized to enhance student engagement (MKAI International Ltd., 2024; Williamson, 2023). This section will explore strategies and technologies that leverage IoT to encourage student participation and motivation.

- ***Real-time Feedback and Interaction:***
  - *Interactive Learning Tools:* By incorporating IoT-powered learning tools like response systems and smart devices, classrooms can facilitate real-time feedback and interaction. Students can actively engage in discussions, quizzes, and polls by responding through their devices. Educators can promptly assess student comprehension levels and adapt their teaching strategies accordingly based on the feedback received.

  - *In-class Response Systems:* Response systems allow students to answer questions or participate in discussions using their smartphones or dedicated clickers. This technology enables teachers to create quizzes, polls, and surveys. The immediate feedback loop promotes student engagement while providing instructors insights into student understanding.

- ***Gamification***
  - *Gamified Learning Platforms:* Introducing gamification into non-game contexts has proven to be an effective way of increasing student engagement. Learning platforms incorporating gamification elements such as badges, leaderboards, and rewards have proven effective in motivating students. Through task completion, goal achievement, and healthy competition with peers, students are encouraged to participate and make progress in their journey.
  - *Scenario-based Learning:* One valuable aspect of scenario-based learning is that IoT technology creates real-life situations for students to solve. For instance, business course participants could utilize data from a company to make informed decisions, while science class students can engage in virtual experiments leveraging IoT sensor data. These practical scenarios enhance interactivity and relevance in the learning process.

- ***Collaborative Tools:***
  - *Virtual collaboration:* With the help of IoT, students can collaborate regardless of their physical location. Video conferencing, real-time communication tools, collaborative document editing, group work on projects, assignment discussions, and idea sharing enable students to work collaboratively.
  - *Integrating IoT into group projects:* Students are challenged to tackle real-world problems by incorporating technology into group assignments. For example, they might engage in a project focused on environmental sensors to collect and analyze data. This fosters teamwork skills, problem-solving abilities, and critical thinking.

- ***Real World Applications:***
  - *IoT in the Real World:* Examples of IoT technology demonstrate its real-world practicality in the classroom. For example, students can use sensors to gather data, analyze it, and draw conclusions. In a biology class, they can monitor wildlife behavior through IoT sensors. In an engineering class, they can program IoT devices for applications. These hands-on experiences bridge the gap between theory and practice, making learning more engaging and applicable.
  - *Career Relevance:* Technology's relevance extends beyond the classroom walls, as many industries and careers heavily rely on it. By exposing students to applications during their education, they acquire skills and insights directly transferable to future job opportunities. This enhances their motivation to learn and equips them with practical knowledge that aligns with real-world demands.

Incorporating technology into education offers avenues to enhance student engagement. Real-time feedback mechanisms, gamification elements, collaborative tools, and real-world applications create a motivating learning environment.

8.6 Remote Learning and IoT

The education field has changed with the rise of remote and online learning. IoT (Internet of Things) technology plays a vital role in facilitating remote learning experiences (p3aservices, 2024; Kumar, 2023). This section will explore how IoT enhances education delivery to students learning remotely, bridging gaps and creating opportunities for an inclusive educational experience.

- ***Virtual Labs and Remote Experiments:***
  - *Enhanced Virtual Labs with IoT:* Virtual labs use IoT technology to allow students to conduct experiments and engage in hands-on activities from their homes. These labs replicate laboratory setups, allowing students to interact with real-world phenomena online. IoT sensors collect data and provide feedback, significantly improving the learning experience.
  - *Accessibility:* Virtual labs make education more accessible for learners who may not have access to physical laboratories. They ensure that students can actively participate in learning activities without constraints.
  - *Ensuring Safety:* Virtual chemistry and biology labs enhance safety by eliminating potential risks of handling hazardous materials or conducting experiments requiring specialized equipment. Students can explore concepts without being exposed to any dangers.
- ***Remote Proctoring and Assessments:***
  - *Proctoring Solutions Based on IoT:* Remote proctoring ensures the integrity of online exams by monitoring students through cameras and microphones enabled. Advanced algorithms detect suspicious behavior, creating an environment for students to take their exams from wherever they are.
  - *Flexible Assessment:* One advantage of proctoring is its flexibility in assessment scheduling. Students can choose the time they take exams based on their learning preferences, while educators can offer a variety of assessment types, including traditional tests, essays, and oral examinations.
  - *Eliminating Geographical Barriers:* Another benefit is that IoT-enabled proctoring eliminates the need for students to travel to test centers. This is particularly advantageous for international students who may face difficulty reaching a testing location.
- ***IoT-enabled Distance Education:***
  - *Virtual Classrooms:* IoT technology supports virtual classrooms where students and instructors can participate in real-time discussions, presentations,

and collaborative activities. Features like video conferencing, screen sharing, and interactive whiteboards help create an online learning environment.
- *IoT-equipped Learning Management Systems (LMS):* LMS equipped with IoT capabilities provide a comprehensive distance education platform. Educators can efficiently manage course materials, track student progress, and deliver content using these systems. Data analytics can provide insights into student engagement and academic performance.
- *Interactive Learning:* IoT technology enables students to actively participate in learning by engaging in virtual science experiments, exploring museums, or immersing themselves in field-specific simulations.

• ***Inclusive Education:***

  - *Meeting Diverse Learner Needs:* Remote learning with IoT caters to individuals with unique requirements, such as those who must balance work or family commitments, face physical limitations, or seek specialized courses unavailable locally.
  - *Creating a Global Learning Community:* IoT-powered distance education fosters a global learning community where students from various countries and cultures can interact, collaborate, and learn from each other, enhancing the overall educational experience.

IoT technology enables remote learning. It provides students with practical experiences through virtual labs, ensures the integrity of assessments through remote proctoring, and promotes an inclusive and globally connected learning environment. IoT will remain instrumental in offering students engaging learning opportunities as the educational landscape evolves.

8.7 Data Analytics and IoT in Education

Data analytics is an education tool that empowers institutions to gain insights into student performance, teaching effectiveness, and the overall educational experience. The Internet of Things (IoT) technology gathers, processes, and analyzes data within educational settings (SAS Institute Inc., 2023). This section will explore how IoT contributes to educational data analytics and its transformative impact on decision-making and educational enhancement.

• ***Collecting Data with IoT:***

  - *Comprehensive Data Streams:* IoT devices have sensors and connectivity features that generate a data flow. Within an educational context, this data can encompass a wide range of information, such as student interactions with digital learning materials, classroom attendance records, environmental conditions, and campus resource utilization.

  - *Real-time Data:* IoT provides real-time information that is vital for making decisions. Educators and administrators can access up-to-date details about student progress, facility usage, or resource availability, enabling them to act promptly and responsively.
  - *Diverse Data Sources:* IoT technology collects data from sources, allowing for a holistic view of educational activities. Whether it involves tracking student behavior patterns, monitoring energy consumption levels, or assessing resource utilization efficiency, IoT systems provide an ecosystem of data.

- ***Data Analysis and Insights:***

  - *Predictive Analytics:* The data collected from IoT can be used to predict student needs and performance trends. By analyzing patterns of student engagement and assessment results, educators can anticipate which students may need support to avoid falling.
  - *Personalized Insights:* IoT enables the creation of personalized insights for students. Analyzing their learning behaviors and interactions with content institutions can provide tailored recommendations and interventions to help students succeed.
  - *Evaluating Teaching Methods:* IoT data provides insights into the effectiveness of teaching methods. Through student performance and engagement data analysis, educators can refine their teaching strategies to determine what works best for groups of students.

- ***Data-Driven Decision Making:***

  - *Resource Allocation:* Utilizing IoT data allows educational institutions to make informed decisions about resource allocation. By analyzing the utilization of classrooms, library resources, and laboratory equipment, institutions can optimize resource distribution, resulting in cost savings while delivering services.
  - *Curriculum Enhancement:* Data analytics using IoT can inform curriculum enhancements. By examining student performance data, institutions can adjust course content, teaching methods, and assessments to meet students' needs better and improve learning outcomes.
  - *Institutional Enhancement:* IoT data allows educational institutions to evaluate their performance. By monitoring student achievements and faculty effectiveness, campus management institutions can identify areas for improvement and make changes to enhance the quality of education.

- ***Ethical Considerations:***

  - *Data Privacy:* Institutions must strictly adhere to privacy regulations when collecting data, including students' information. Consent should be obtained before collecting and analyzing any data.
  - *Transparency:* Maintaining transparency with students, faculty, and staff regarding data collection and utilization is essential. Clear communication about the purpose of data collection and how it will be used is vital.

  - *Data Security:* Strong security measures must be in place to safeguard the collected data. This includes encryption, access controls, and security protocols that protect information.

Leveraging data analytics through IoT technology in education has valuable effects. It provides insights for educators, administrators, and policymakers alike. It aids decision-making processes, supports learning experiences, and enables institutions to improve their practices continuously. As IoT technology advances alongside data analytics capabilities, it holds the potential to shape a future of education that's more adaptable, driven by data insights, and ultimately more effective.

8.8 Future Trends and Possibilities of IoT in Education

As technology advances and educational approaches change the role of IoT (Internet of Things), education is poised to expand and diversify. In this section, we will explore trends and possibilities of IoT in education, providing insights into advancements and innovations that may reshape the educational landscape.

- ***Personalized Learning Pathways:***
  - *Advanced Adaptive Learning:* Integrating IoT technology will contribute to developing more sophisticated adaptive learning systems. These systems will adapt content and assess students' emotional states, levels of engagement, and learning preferences. This comprehensive personalization ensures that students receive tailored content and support to meet their emotional needs.
  - *AI-driven Tutoring:* Intelligent tutoring systems powered by IoT will be enhanced with advanced AI algorithms. These systems will engage in natural language interactions with students while providing personalized guidance. Students may have access to AI tutors who offer round-the-clock support, adjusting their approach based on each student's learning journey.
- ***Augmented and Virtual Reality:***
  - *Immersive Learning Experiences:* The convergence of IoT with augmented reality (AR) and virtual reality (VR) technologies will enable the creation of immersive learning experiences. Students can engage with 3D models, delve into historical sites through virtual reality, and conduct science experiments in a virtual environment. These innovative technologies will make the learning experience more captivating and memorable.
  - *Real-time Collaboration:* Real-time collaboration is another perk of using augmented reality (AR) and virtual reality (VR) alongside Internet of Things (IoT) integration. Students can now collaborate on projects, examine specimens, or explore data sets together in shared AR/VR environments regardless of their physical locations.

- ***IoT in Assessment and Accreditation:***
  - *Blockchain Credentials:* IoT data is crucial in assessment and accreditation. Combining IoT with blockchain technology can make academic credentials more secure and easily verifiable. Students will have access to tamper-proof certificates, transcripts, and badges that can be effortlessly shared with employers and educational institutions.
  - *Competency-based Assessment:* IoT technology also enables competency-based assessment, in which students are evaluated based on their mastery of skills and knowledge. This approach promotes personalized pathways toward acquiring credentials and degrees.
- ***Enhanced Campus and Resource Management:***
  - *Smart Campuses:* Implementing IoT technology will also improve campus management. Smart campuses with sensors will monitor foot traffic efficiently while effectively managing energy consumption. Furthermore, enhanced environmental security measures will be implemented. For instance, classrooms and study areas can automatically adjust their lighting and temperature based on the number of people present.
  - *Resource-sharing Networks:* One exciting aspect of IoT in education is the potential for resource-sharing networks. Educational institutions like schools and universities can collaborate with neighboring institutions to share resources such as laboratories, equipment, or specialized faculty expertise. This collaboration will make education more cost-effective and efficient in terms of resources.
- ***Inclusivity and Accessibility:***
  - *Accessible Learning Environments:* Technologies in the education sector will significantly enhance inclusivity and accessibility. Smart assistive devices and platforms driven by IoT will provide support and accommodations for students with disabilities, creating inclusive learning environments.
  - *Remote Learning Evolution:* Furthermore, remote learning experiences will evolve significantly with the help of IoT. Improved virtual classrooms, remote laboratory experiences, and increased opportunities for collaboration will make remote learning more effective and engaging.

The future of IoT in education is filled with immense possibilities. As technology continues to advance, educational institutions have the opportunity to create personalized, engaging, and inclusive learning environments. By staying updated on these emerging trends and possibilities, educators, administrators, and policymakers can harness the power of IoT to enhance the quality of education for learners worldwide.

8.9 Challenges and Considerations in Implementing IoT in Education

Implementing IoT (Internet of Things) technology in education offers several benefits but brings its fair share of challenges. Educational institutions need to consider factors to ensure the integration of IoT to enhance learning experiences. This section will explore some obstacles and considerations when implementing IoT in education.

- ***Data Privacy and Security:***
  - *Concerns about Privacy:* One primary concern with IoT devices is collecting student data, which can raise privacy concerns. Institutions must establish policies and procedures to protect information and ensure responsible data usage.
  - *Risks to Security:* IoT devices not correctly configured and secured can be vulnerable to security breaches. Robust cybersecurity measures are essential for networks and student information to prevent device access.
- ***Costs Associated with Implementation***
  - *Infrastructure Expenses:* Setting up the IoT infrastructure entails costs for sensors, devices, and network infrastructure. Educational institutions must allocate budgets for equipment procurement, software acquisition, and ongoing maintenance.
  - *Training and Skill Development:* Staff members may require training to manage and use IoT technology. This additional training can be costly and require time and resource allocation.
- ***Integration with Existing Systems:***
  - *Compatibility:* It is important to ensure that IoT systems seamlessly integrate with learning management systems (LMS) and educational technology platforms. This integration process can be quite intricate and requires careful consideration.
  - *Legacy Systems:* Many educational institutions still rely on legacy systems. Incorporating IoT technology into these existing systems may demand effort and investment.
- ***Accessibility and Inclusivity:***
  - *Digital Divide:* While IoT technology assumes that all students have access to devices and a reliable internet connection, this is not the reality for everyone. Ensuring inclusivity and accessibility for all students, regardless of their resources or circumstances, is essential.
  - *Assistive Technologies:* Educational institutions must also address how IoT systems can be accessible to students with disabilities. Providing assistive technologies and accommodations becomes crucial in this regard.

- ***Ethical Use of Data:***
  - *Data Ethics:* The ethical use of data generated by IoT devices is a growing concern. Institutions must guarantee that the collected data is used solely for educational purposes without leading to consequences or biases.
  - *Transparency:* Open communication regarding data collection, analysis, and utilization becomes vital. Students, faculty members, and staff should be appropriately informed about data collection objectives and potential impacts.
- ***Scalability and Maintenance:***
  - *Scalability:* As educational institutions expand, it is vital to have an IoT infrastructure to accommodate the growing number of students, devices, and data. Planning for scalability right from the start is crucial.
  - *Maintenance and Upkeep:* Ongoing maintenance is required to ensure that the IoT system's sensors and devices remain in working condition. Educational institutions must allocate resources and staff members to maintain the ecosystem properly.
- ***Integration with Teaching Practices:***
  - *Alignment with Learning Objectives:* Ensuring IoT technology aligns with educational goals and desired learning outcomes is essential. Technology should enhance teaching practices rather than replace them.
  - *Training for Educators:* Faculty members should receive training on incorporating IoT technology into their teaching methods. It is crucial to support educators in using IoT for pedagogical purposes.
- ***Compliance with Legal and Regulatory Requirements:***
  - *Data Regulations:* Educational institutions must adhere to data protection regulations and privacy laws. Failure to comply with these laws can lead to legal consequences.
  - *Accessibility Laws:* Compliance with accessibility laws, such as the Americans with Disabilities Act (ADA), is necessary to ensure equal access to educational resources for all students.

While implementing IoT in education holds potential, it also comes with challenges and considerations. Educational institutions must address factors to utilize IoT in education and effectively enhance the learning experience. These include data privacy, security, cost management, compatibility with existing systems, inclusivity for all students, ethical considerations, scalability of solutions, integration into teaching methods, and compliance with requirements. By navigating these challenges with a strategic approach, institutions can fully leverage the transformative potential of IoT in education.

8.10 Best Practices and Implementation

Planning and following best practices are crucial to incorporating IoT (Internet of Things) technology into education. This section will outline recommendations and best practices for institutions implementing IoT in their learning environments.

- ***Define Objectives:*** Establishing clear objectives before implementing IoT in education is important. Identify the goals you aim to achieve through the utilization of IoT technology. Whether enhancing student engagement, improving campus management, or advancing data analytics, having defined objectives will guide the implementation process.
- ***Invest in Infrastructure:*** Ensuring the required infrastructure is available to support IoT implementation is essential. This encompasses network connectivity, sensors, and IoT devices. Investing in quality and scalable infrastructure will enable accommodating future growth.
- ***Prioritize Data Privacy and Security:*** Establishing data privacy and security protocols is paramount when dealing with IoT devices that collect sensitive information. Implement encryption and access controls and conduct security audits to safeguard data from unauthorized access.
- ***Consider Accessibility and Inclusivity:*** When implementing IoT solutions, consider accessibility and inclusivity factors. Providing assistive technologies and accommodations when necessary ensures that all students benefit from this technology regardless of disabilities or diverse technology access.
- ***Training for Staff:*** Provide training and professional development opportunities for educators and staff members to ensure they are proficient in utilizing IoT technology in teaching and administrative tasks. This training includes device usage, data analysis, and problem-solving skills.
- ***Integration into Teaching Methodology:*** Incorporate IoT technology into the pedagogical approach to ensure alignment with educational objectives and enhance the teaching and learning experience. Encourage faculty members to develop lesson plans that leverage IoT for engaging activities.
- ***Start Small and Expand Gradually: Begin with pilot projects or limited-scale implementations to test the effectiveness of the IoT technology. Once thriving, use cases can be*** identified, and the implementation can be expanded across the institution if any issues have been addressed. This approach allows for learning from experiences and improving before full-scale deployment.
- ***Ethical Use of Data:*** Promote ethical data collection, analysis, and utilization practices. Ensure that data is used solely for purposes without consequences or biases.
- ***Collaboration with Stakeholders:*** Engage all stakeholders, including students, faculty members, administrators, and IT staff in the implementation process. Foster collaboration between these groups to gather input, address concerns effectively, and ensure that IoT technology meets the needs of everyone involved.

- ***Ongoing Evaluation and Adaptation:*** Regularly assess the effectiveness of IoT implementations to gauge their impact on education. Based on evaluation results, adjustments or adaptations can be made.
- ***Budgeting and Sustainability:*** Plan for the long-term sustainability of initiatives by allocating resources for maintenance, upgrades, and staff training. Ensure that IoT technology remains viable and up to date.
- ***Compliance and Regulations:*** Adhere to data privacy regulations, accessibility laws, and other legal requirements. Stay updated on any changes to ensure that your IoT implementations remain compliant.

By following these recommended practices and guidelines, educational institutions can successfully incorporate IoT into their learning environments, unlocking this technology's potential. Through careful planning and considering these factors, IoT can enhance the experience for students and educators while meeting the evolving needs of modern education.

8.11 Conclusion

The potential of incorporating IoT technology in education is a significant offering to revolutionize the learning process and enhance results. Schools can overcome distance limitations through IoT-based solutions, improve access, and create inclusive learning environments. Real-time data analysis provides insights into student progress, teaching effectiveness, and resource allocation, enabling institutions to make data-driven decisions and continually enhance their remote-learning methods. Despite obstacles such as concerns over data privacy and integration challenges, following best practices and fostering collaboration among stakeholders can help address these issues. Future trends like customized learning paths, augmented reality experiences, and blockchain-based credentials suggest a future where education is more adaptable, engaging, and accessible to all. By seizing these opportunities and tackling challenges proactively, educational institutions can leverage the potential of IoT to shape the future of learners worldwide.

References

Intuz. (2023). *IoT in the education industry: Embracing the new way of learning*. LinkedIn. https://www.linkedin.com/pulse/iot-education-industry-embracing-new-way-learning-intuz-1f/

Joshi, N. (2021). *Building smart university campuses with IoT technology*. LinkedIn. https://www.linkedin.com/pulse/building-smart-university-campuses-iot-technology-naveen-joshi/

Kumar, S. (2015). *Technology and education – Enabling personalized learning using IoT*. LinkedIn. https://www.linkedin.com/pulse/technology-education-enabling-personalized-learning-sawan-kumar/

Kumar, A. (2023). *IoT in education: A future of smart and sustainable learning*. LinkedIn. https://www.linkedin.com/pulse/iot-education-future-smart-sustainable-learning-ankit-kumar/

MKAI International Ltd. (2024). *How IoT can help increase student interest and engagement*. MKAI InternationalLtd.https://mkai.org/how-iot-can-help-increase-student-interest-and-engagement/

NVIT. (2023). *Transforming education: The internet of things in the classroom*. LinkedIn. https://www.linkedin.com/pulse/transforming-education-internet-things-classroom-nvitech/

Ollivachreis. (2024). *IoT revolutionizing education from smart classrooms to personalized learning*. Medium. https://medium.com/@oliviachris5567/iot-revolutionizing-education-from-smart-classrooms-to-personalized-learning-522ad42f1be0

p3aservices. (2024). *Can the Internet of Things (IoT) enhance classroom learning experiences?* P3aservices. https://p3aservices.com/can-the-internet-of-things-iot-enhance-classroom-learning-experiences.php

SAS Institute Inc. (2023). *IoT analytics for education*. SAS Institute. https://www.sas.com/en_in/industry/education/technology/iot.html

Wattley, E. B. (2023). *Unlocking the future technology, teaching: Embracing the transformative power of IoT in K–12 education*. LinkedIn2. https://www.linkedin.com/pulse/unlocking-future-technology-transportation-teaching-b-dr-erica-b%2D%2Duftjc/

Williamson, R. (2023). *IoT in education — Smart ways to improve engagement and efficiency*. Medium. https://ryanwilliamsonc.medium.com/iot-in-education-smart-ways-to-improve-engagement-and-efficiency-54dcfcfa18c8

Wipro. (2024). *Smart i – Campus*. Wipro. https://www.wipro.com/infrastructure/smart-i-campus/

Chapter 9
Remote Experiments and Assessments Using IoT

Abstract The chapter explores how education is changing due to remote learning driven by technology and the impact of COVID-19. It discusses the pros and cons of remote learning in practical fields like STEM. To tackle these issues, the chapter introduces IoT-enabled experiments that use IoT technology to offer hands-on learning experiences integrated with remote learning platforms. IoT-enabled experiments involve interconnected sensors, devices, and tools across subjects, giving students access, control, visualization, collaboration, and feedback. The chapter looks into both commercial and DIY platforms that educators can use to conduct remote experiments and enhance learning. It also delves into IoT-based assessment methods that transform evaluation in education by providing types of assessments, such as formative and summative assessments, through projects and evaluation tools. Real-world examples demonstrate how IoT technology is successfully incorporated IoT technology into remote experiments and assessments, demonstrating its uses and effectiveness. Despite technical issues and varying access levels, future directions for IoT-based remote experiments include incorporating AR/VR technology, adaptive learning techniques, standardized approaches, advanced analytics methods, and ongoing research to encourage innovation in remote education.

Keywords Technology-driven learning · COVID-19 impact · IoT technology · Hands-on learning experiences · Assessment methods · AR/VR technology · Adaptive learning techniques

9.1 Introduction

The field of education has changed in recent years due to advancements in technology and evolving learning environments. One significant transformation is adopting remote learning, enabling students to access educational resources and engage in learning activities anytime, anywhere. The COVID-19 pandemic further expedited this shift, compelling educational institutions to adapt quickly to new instruction and assessment methods.

M. Kurni, Srinivasa K. G., *The Internet of Educational Things*,
https://doi.org/10.1007/978-3-031-67387-0_9

Remote learning offers advantages such as flexibility, accessibility, and the ability to reach a wider audience. However, it also presents its challenges. The absence of physical presence in a classroom can be problematic for STEM (Science, Technology, Engineering, and Mathematics) education and other practical disciplines that require hands-on experiments and assessments. This is where the Internet of Things (IoT) comes into play.

The Shift to Remote Learning The traditional model of education, which involved traditional classrooms and face-to-face interactions, has changed in recent times. This transformation was triggered by digital technological progress and global events like the COVID-19 pandemic, which have accelerated the adoption of remote learning.

Remote learning or e-learning refers to delivering educational content and instruction to students not physically present in a traditional classroom. It encompasses online courses, virtual classrooms, video lectures, and self-paced learning (Talespin Team, 2023). There are drivers behind this shift.

- ***Technological advancements:*** The widespread availability of high-speed internet, mobile devices, and digital platforms has made remote learning more accessible and efficient.
- ***Flexibility:*** Remote learning allows students to learn at their own pace from anywhere, catering to the needs and schedules of learners.
- ***Accessibility:*** It provides opportunities to individuals facing geographical or physical limitations that hinder their access to traditional education.
- ***Cost efficiency:*** Remote learning can be cost-effective for students and institutions by reducing transportation, accommodation, and physical infrastructure expenses.

Advantages and Disadvantages

Advantages of Remote Learning The advantages of remote learning are as follows (Telespin Team, 2023; Splashtop Team, 2023):

- ***Flexibility:*** Remote learning allows students to learn at their own pace, making it convenient for those juggling work, family, or other commitments.
- ***Accessibility:*** Remote learning makes education accessible to a broader audience, eliminating geographical barriers and allowing individuals from different locations to access quality education.
- ***Diverse Resources:*** Remote learning provides multimedia resources that enrich the learning experience and foster greater student engagement.
- ***Personalization:*** Adaptive learning technologies in education can personalize content according to student needs, ensuring a tailored approach to learning.
- ***Safety:*** During COVID-19, remote learning ensures students' and educators' safety and well-being.

Disadvantages of Remote Learning The disadvantages of remote learning are as follows (Telespin Team, 2023; Splashtop Team, 2023):

- ***Lack of Physical Interaction:*** One downside is the absence of face-to-face interactions, which may reduce engagement levels and lead to students' feelings of isolation.
- ***Technical Challenges:*** Internet connectivity issues, device compatibility problems, and limited digital literacy can hinder the learning experience.
- ***Limited Hands-On Experiences:*** Some subjects, such as science and engineering, heavily rely on hands-on experiences that are difficult to replicate in a remote setting.
- ***Assessment Difficulties:*** Evaluating students' understanding and skills can become more complex when physical proctoring or experiments are impossible.

The Need for Remote Assessments The rise of remote learning highlighted the importance of remote assessments. Traditional assessment approaches like in-person exams, lab experiments, and practical demonstrations posed difficulties in the learning context. Educators and institutions had to adjust to ensure reliable and secure assessments. Here are the main reasons for the necessity of remote assessments (McCarthy, 2011; Senel & Senel, 2021).

- ***Ensuring fairness:*** Remote assessments should provide students with an equitable experience regardless of location, resource access, or personal circumstances.
- ***Continuity of learning:*** Assessments play a vital role in the learning process, and disruptions in assessment methods can impact educational quality.
- ***Security and integrity:*** Maintaining assessment security and integrity is essential to prevent cheating and ensure fair evaluation of students.
- ***Improvement:*** Assessments offer valuable feedback to students and educators, guiding enhancements and tracking student progress.

Various innovative assessment methods and technology integration have emerged in response to these needs. These advancements facilitate the evaluation of students' knowledge and skills in remote learning environments.

9.2 IoT-Enabled Remote Experiments

To address the difficulties posed by remote learning, IoT-powered experiments leverage the Internet of Things technology to transform education. They offer practical learning opportunities in STEM fields seamlessly integrated with remote learning platforms, enhancing students' accessibility, collaboration, and assessment.

What Are IoT-Enabled Experiments? In traditional educational settings, experiments have always been crucial for students to apply what they learn in theory and develop practical skills. These hands-on experiences offer an understanding of scientific principles, engineering concepts, and other subjects. However, the shift towards remote learning has posed a challenge in providing these important learning opportunities. This is where IoT-enabled experiments come into play (Geilings, 2023).

IoT-enabled experiments are conducted by integrating Internet of Things (IoT) technology. These experiments use interconnected sensors, devices, and data collection tools to facilitate hands-on learning experiences when students are not physically present. With IoT technology, data from experiments can be transmitted, allowing students to observe, analyze, and draw conclusions from wherever they are located.

Real-World Applications IoT has revolutionized experiments across disciplines, especially in science, technology, engineering, and mathematics (STEM) (Kumar et al., 2019). Here are some notable examples;

- ***Physics Experiments:*** In physics, IoT technology allows students to conduct experiments related to motion, electricity, magnetism, and more. For instance, they can remotely control IoT-enabled devices to simulate motion or free fall experiments. Real-time data from these experiments can be analyzed for insights.
- ***Chemistry Experiments***: Chemistry experiments enable IoT-enabled sensors to monitor real-time chemical reactions, temperature changes, and gas releases. This provides students with data that helps them analyze and understand physical and chemical properties.
- ***Biology and Environmental Science Experiments:*** IoT technology facilitates data collection in biology and environmental science. For example, ecosystem sensors can monitor temperature, humidity, pollution, and other environmental parameters. Students can access this data remotely to analyze the impact of environmental changes on ecosystems.
- ***Engineering Projects:*** IoT-enabled projects offer engineering students opportunities to build and test circuits and mechanical systems with automation capabilities. Sensors and actuators in the Internet of Things (IoT) realm can assist in gathering real-time data, managing controls, and monitoring a range of engineering prototypes.

Integration with Remote Learning Platforms IoT-enabled experiments become more effective when seamlessly integrated into online learning platforms. These platforms are the backbone for students to access experiment data, control experiment parameters, and collaborate with peers and educators (Mershad et al., 2020). The integration of IoT-enabled experiments with learning platforms includes several essential elements:

- ***Experiment Accessibility and Control:*** Students should be able to access IoT experiments conveniently through a user-friendly interface. They should also be able to control experiment parameters, start data collection, and make real-time adjustments whenever necessary.

- ***Data Visualization and Analysis:*** Experiment data should be presented comprehensibly. IoT-enabled platforms often provide tools for visualizing and analyzing the data, allowing students to interpret the results effectively.
- ***Collaboration and Feedback:*** Remote learning platforms should facilitate collaboration among students, enabling them to work on experiments and share their findings. Educators can provide real-time feedback and guidance during this process.
- ***Integration with Assessments:*** The data collected from IoT-enabled experiments can be utilized for assessments. Educators can design quizzes, assignments, and projects that evaluate students' understanding and analysis of experiment results.

By incorporating IoT technology into remote learning, these experiments address the challenges associated with distance education and enhance the overall learning experience. They provide students with hands-on opportunities previously limited to physical classrooms or laboratories.

9.3 Components of IoT-Enabled Experiments

The various elements of IoT-driven experiments include sensors that gather environmental data, tools for processing and analyzing data, mechanisms for real-time control, and connectivity solutions like internet connectivity, wireless communication, and cloud storage. These components (as shown in Fig. 9.1) create the basis for engaging and successful remote learning experiences (Azad, 2020).

Sensors and Data Acquisition In enabled experiments, sensors and data acquisition devices play a vital role in gathering information from the physical world. These sensors can measure parameters depending on the nature of the experiment. Here are some types of sensors:

- **Temperature Sensors:** These sensors detect temperature changes, which is significant for experiments involving chemical reactions, material science, and environmental monitoring.

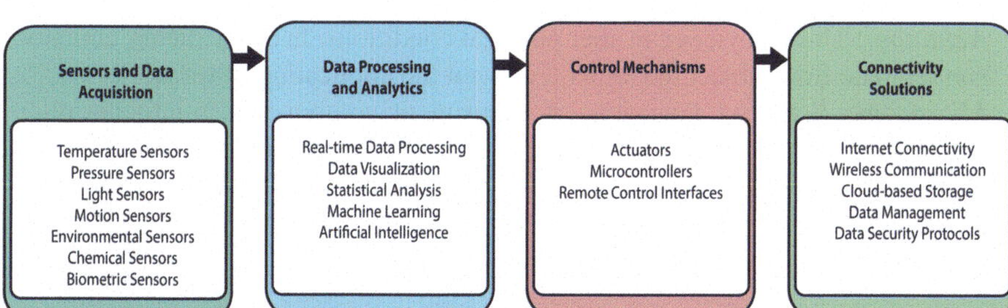

Fig. 9.1 Components of IoT-enabled experiments

- **Pressure Sensors:** Designed to monitor changes in pressure, these sensors are well-suited for experiments that involve gases, liquids, and fluid dynamics.
- **Light Sensors:** Light sensors measure illumination levels and have applications in optics, photography, and electronics experiments.
- ***Motion Sensors:*** Motion sensors can detect position, acceleration, or velocity alterations. They prove invaluable for physics experiments that require motion analysis.
- ***Environmental Sensors:*** Environmental sensors can track humidity, air quality, and pollution levels, which are helpful in biology research, environmental science, and sustainability studies.
- ***Chemical Sensors:*** Employed to monitor changes in chemical properties during chemistry experiments and research activities.
- ***Biometric Sensors:*** Biometric sensors encompass a range of devices, such as heart rate monitors or electroencephalography (EEG) sensors. They can be utilized in experiments involving physiological data.

Data Processing and Analytics Once the sensor data has been gathered, it must undergo processing and analysis. Data processing units and software transform data into meaningful information in IoT-enabled experiments. Data analytics tools offer benefits such as:

- ***Real-time Data Processing:*** Real-time data processing enables students to observe immediate experiment results, particularly valuable in interactive and dynamic scenarios.
- ***Data Visualization:*** Visualization tools understandably present data, often utilizing graphs, charts, and tables. This facilitates students' comprehension of patterns and trends within the data.
- ***Statistical Analysis:*** Data analytics software can perform analysis to extract insights and draw conclusions from the collected information, thereby enhancing the value of experiments.
- ***Machine Learning & Artificial Intelligence:*** Machine learning and AI can automate data analysis and generate predictive models in advanced applications.

Control Mechanisms Control mechanisms play a vital role in IoT-enabled experiments, allowing students to manipulate variables and conditions actively in real time. These mechanisms encompass:

- ***Actuators:*** These devices can alter physical conditions. In experiments, actuators can regulate flow, object movement, or even the application of force.
- ***Microcontrollers:*** As managers of experiment components, microcontrollers can be programmed to respond to various conditions and inputs.
- ***Remote Control Interfaces:*** Students need to be able to adjust experiment parameters remotely through a user interface. This may involve modifying temperature, pressure, or other variables.

Connectivity Solutions In experiments facilitated by the Internet of Things (IoT), the ability to establish connections and transfer data is essential. Important connectivity solutions include:

- ***Internet Connectivity:*** IoT devices typically connect to the Internet for remote access and data transmission. Reliable internet access is crucial.
- ***Wireless Communication:*** Sensors and actuators can communicate wirelessly, allowing for flexible experiment setups and reducing the need for physical wiring.
- ***Cloud-based Storage and Data Management:*** Storing data in the cloud ensures accessibility and security. Experiment data can be accessed by students and educators from any location.
- ***Data Security Protocols:*** Implementing security measures like encryption and authentication is vital to protect experiment data from access or tampering.

Understanding these IoT-enabled experiment components forms the foundation for compelling remote learning experiences. When properly designed and integrated with remote learning platforms, these components enable students to perform experiments, gather data, and draw conclusions—all from the convenience of their remote locations. The successful incorporation of IoT technology in education relies on planning, considering these components, adhering to best practices, and respecting data privacy regulations.

9.4 Design and Implementation

Careful planning is required when designing and conducting IoT-enabled experiments for remote learning environments. This includes setting educational objectives addressing safety and ethical considerations and choosing sensors and equipment that prioritize accuracy, connectivity, and affordability. Additionally, it is important to consider the hardware, software, and safety measures to create an accessible educational experience (Hamieh & Mershad, 2019).

Planning and Designing IoT-Based Experiments To achieve educational goals, various factors must be considered when planning and implementing IoT-enabled experiments in remote learning environments. Here are some important points to consider during the planning and design process.

- ***Educational Objectives:*** Clearly define the learning goals and outcomes you intend to accomplish through the IoT-enabled experiment. What do you want students to learn or demonstrate from this experiment?
- ***Experiment Scope:*** Determine the extent of the experiment. Which variables will be manipulated? What kind of data will be collected? It is important to assess the complexity level and suitability for remote learning.
- ***Safety and Ethical Considerations:*** Ensure safety considerations when designing the experiment, primarily if students conduct it at home. Additionally, address any concerns related to handling living organisms.

- ***Accessibility:*** Ensure all students can access and participate in the experiment, considering their needs and potential disabilities. This includes ensuring that the IoT experiment interface is user-friendly.
- ***Equipment:*** Compile a list of materials and equipment required for experimenting. Ensure these resources are readily available or can be provided to students beforehand.
- ***Experiment Procedures:*** Create detailed protocols that guide students through each process step, from setup to data collection and analysis.

Considering these aspects when planning and designing IoT-enabled experiments in remote learning environments, you can optimize educational outcomes while maintaining safety, accessibility, and ethical standards.

Choosing Suitable Sensors and Equipment When conducting IoT-enabled experiments, selecting the appropriate sensors and equipment is crucial. Consider the following factors when making your choices.

- ***Experiment Requirements:*** Ensure your chosen sensors and equipment align with your experiment's needs. For instance, if you are monitoring temperature, opt for temperature sensors.
- ***Accuracy and Precision:*** Ensure that the selected sensors offer accuracy and precision to gather data.
- ***Connectivity Options:*** Evaluate the connectivity options available with the sensors, such as Wi-Fi, Bluetooth, or other wireless protocols. This will ensure easy integration into your ecosystem.
- ***Data Format:*** Verify that the sensors provide data in a format that can be efficiently processed and analyzed within your chosen platform.
- ***Budget***: Consider your experiment constraints while selecting sensors and equipment.

Hardware and Software Requirements To conduct IoT-based experiments, you will require both hardware and software elements.

- ***Hardware Specifications:*** The sensors, actuators, microcontrollers, and any physical devices utilized in the experiment must be functional and well-maintained.
- ***Software Specifications:*** The software should encompass the control interface, data acquisition, analysis, and visualization tools. Cloud-based solutions are often favored to facilitate students' access.
- ***User-Friendly Interface:*** The interface should be intuitive and easy for students to navigate while interacting with the experiment.
- ***Compatibility Considerations:*** It is important to verify that the hardware and software components are compatible with each other and the chosen remote learning platform.

Safety Considerations Safety is essential when conducting IoT-enabled experiments, mainly when students perform experiments remotely. To achieve this, the following safety measures should be implemented.

- Conduct an assessment of risks to identify and address any hazards. This is particularly crucial for experiments involving chemicals, electricity, or equipment that may pose dangers.
- Provide students with safety guidelines, including how to use protective equipment, handle hazardous materials, and respond to emergencies.
- Establish protocols for emergencies such as fires, spills, or accidents. Students need to be aware of how to respond when an emergency occurs.
- Consider any ethical considerations regarding living organisms or sensitive data related to the experiment.

Adopting a comprehensive approach encompassing educational objectives, safety measures, equipment requirements, and user-friendly interfaces is important when designing and implementing IoT-enabled experiments for remote learning purposes. By planning and executing these experiments, educators and institutions can offer students hands-on experiences that enrich their learning outcomes and equip them with practical skills applicable to real-world situations.

9.5 Remote Experiment Platforms

Educators and institutions can use various platforms to enhance the learning experience in IoT-enabled remote experiments. These platforms include Labster's Virtual Labs, RealLab for controlling equipment, LabArchives for digital documentation, LabXchange for open educational resources, and DIY solutions like Raspberry Pi and Arduino. Commercial solutions from PASCO Scientific, Vernier, National Instruments, and Quanser also cater to science, technology, and engineering fields. These solutions provide the infrastructure for creating, managing, and conducting remote experiments (Viswanadh et al., 2024).

Overview of Existing Platforms Several platforms and solutions aim to streamline the process and enhance the learning experience when implementing IoT-enabled remote experiments. These platforms offer the infrastructure and tools for students and educators to conduct experiments and assessments remotely. Let us take a look at some of the existing platforms.

- ***Labster:*** Labster provides various virtual labs covering various scientific disciplines. It allows students to experiment and explore concepts in a virtual environment. The labs offered by Labster are designed with specific learning objectives in mind. They can be easily integrated into different learning management systems (LMS).
- ***Labster's RealLab:*** Building upon their virtual labs, RealLab from Labster offers a platform enabling students to control laboratory equipment available in partner institutions remotely. This provides a hands-on experience when students are physically far away from the actual lab.

- ***Labster's Lab Manager:*** Labster's Lab Manager platform empowers educators to create and customize virtual labs according to their curriculum goals, ensuring that experiments align perfectly with educational objectives.
- ***LabArchives:*** LabArchives is a digital lab notebook platform designed to document and manage experiments, observations, and research findings for students and researchers. It facilitates collaboration among peers while maintaining data security within the digital environment.
- ***Labsters LabXchange:*** LabXchange is a platform for open educational resources that provides interactive learning opportunities. It offers virtual labs, simulations, and educational materials that educators and institutions contribute worldwide.

DIY Solutions If educators and institutions want to develop remote experiment platforms with Internet of Things (IoT) capabilities, do-it-yourself (DIY) solutions and open-source tools are available (Editorial Staff, 2024). These options offer flexibility and customization to cater to specific educational needs.

- ***Raspberry Pi and Arduino:*** Raspberry Pi and Arduino are well-known single-board computers and microcontrollers that can be utilized to create IoT experiments. Educators and students can construct their experiments and interfaces, taking advantage of the wide support provided by these platforms and online communities.
- ***Open-source IoT Platforms:*** Open-source platforms like Node-RED, ThingsBoard, and OpenHAB enable the creation and management of IoT experiments. These platforms offer the flexibility to design experiments according to specific requirements.
- ***GitHub and Collaborative Tools:*** Collaborative platforms like GitHub facilitate the sharing, collaboration, and documentation of IoT experiments. This approach allows educators and students to create and modify experiments in alignment with their educational objectives.

Commercial Solutions In addition to do-it-yourself solutions, there are options for educators and institutions seeking to incorporate IoT-enabled remote experiments and assessments.

- ***PASCO Scientific:*** PASCO Scientific offers various physics, chemistry, biology, engineering experiment kits, sensors, and software. Their SparkVue software allows for data collection and analysis, making it suitable for remote and in-person experiments.
- ***Vernier Technology:*** Vernier provides sensors and data collection tools for science and engineering experiments. Their Logger Pro software enables students to collect and analyze data remotely.
- ***National Instruments (NI):*** NI's LabVIEW software and hardware solutions facilitate the development of customized experiments across various fields. The LabVIEW platform can be adapted for remote experimentation.

- ***Quanser:*** Quanser specializes in engineering and control systems experiments. Their platform enables students to remotely control real-world experiments related to robotics, mechatronics, and control systems.

Whether available commercially or open-source, these platforms enable remote experiments and assessments through IoT technology. They provide the infrastructure, tools, and resources to create, manage, and execute experiments effectively while enhancing the remote learning experience for students and educators.

9.6 IoT-Based Assessment Methods

The use of IoT technology changes the way assessments are conducted in remote learning. It allows for formative feedback during the learning process and thorough summative evaluations. This promotes authentic assessments through projects like engineering tasks and environmental monitoring. It also highlights the significance of rubrics and evaluation criteria. Platforms such as Learning Management Systems, customized assessment tools, data analytics software, and remote monitoring facilitate these assessment processes, ensure efficiency, and provide streamlined insights.

Formative and Summative Assessments IoT technology presents innovative ways to conduct formative and summative assessments in remote learning environments. These assessments serve the following purposes.

- ***Formative Assessments:*** These assessments are carried out during learning to provide feedback and guide instruction. IoT can enable real-time feedback by using data collected during experiments. For instance, in a chemistry experiment, students can receive immediate feedback on the progress of a reaction, which helps them adjust their approach.
- ***Summative Assessments:*** These assessments are conducted at the end of a learning period to evaluate students' overall learning outcomes. IoT technology can analyze experiment data to accurately evaluate students' understanding and skills.

Authentic Assessments IoT-enabled experiments provide an opportunity to conduct authentic assessments that simulate real-world situations and difficulties. These assessments aim to assess students' understanding and capacity to apply that knowledge in practical contexts. For instance:

- ***Engineering Projects:*** Students may be tasked with designing and constructing an IoT-based system to address a real-world problem. The assessment evaluates their ability to conceptualize, implement, and troubleshoot such a system.
- ***Environmental Monitoring:*** Students can employ IoT sensors to monitor environmental conditions, collect data, and propose solutions for mitigating environmental issues. The assessment measures their ability to apply scientific principles to real-world challenges.

- ***Data Analysis:*** IoT-generated assessments can require students to analyze and interpret data sets. This approach tests their critical thinking skills.

Rubrics and Evaluation Criteria Rubrics and evaluation criteria must be in place to ensure a fair and consistent evaluation process. These tools provide guidelines for grading. Enable educators to measure how well students are meeting specific learning objectives. When conducting assessments using IoT technology, it becomes more important to establish well-defined rubrics and criteria tailored to the experiment's unique nature. Some examples of these may include:

- ***Interpretation of Data:*** Criteria that assess how effectively students interpret and draw conclusions from the data generated by IoT sensors.
- ***Experimental Procedures:*** Rubrics designed to evaluate students' understanding of procedures, including setup, data collection, and safety precautions.
- ***Problem Solving Skills:*** Criteria used to measure students' problem-solving ability, mainly when unexpected challenges arise during experiments.
- ***Communication Skills:*** Assessment methods that gauge students' proficiency in communicating their findings through written reports or oral presentations.
- ***Critical Thinking Abilities:*** Evaluation criteria assessed students' critical thinking skills and ability to analyze experiment results.

Evaluation Platforms and Tools Incorporating IoT technology often involves using built-in assessment platforms or integrating learning management systems (LMS) to make the evaluation process more efficient. These platforms assist in collecting, analyzing, and providing feedback on assessment data. Here are some examples of commonly used tools.

- ***Learning Management Systems (LMS):*** Platforms like Moodle, Blackboard, and Canvas can seamlessly integrate with IoT-enabled experiments to manage assessment tasks, gather data, and offer student feedback.
- ***Custom Assessment Tools:*** IoT platforms provide customized assessment tools for specific experiments. These tools collect data, generate reports, and support the assessment process.
- ***Data Analytics Software:*** Data analytics tools can process and analyze the data gathered during experiments. They provide insights for assessments.
- ***Remote Monitoring and Control:*** Some IoT platforms enable educators to monitor students' progress remotely during experiments, allowing them to offer real-time support and guidance.

Using IoT-based assessment methods offers an authentic approach based on data analysis to evaluate student learning in remote education settings. These methods provide educators with insights into student performance and engage students in practical experiences that deepen their understanding of the subject matter.

9.7 Case Studies and Examples

Looking at real-life examples demonstrates how IoT technology has revolutionized remote learning. For instance, Labster has introduced labs and instant assessments, while LabXchange offers an open educational resource. Verniers Logger Pro software also seamlessly integrates IoT features into traditional lab experiments. These platforms showcase the applications and effectiveness of IoT for various purposes in various settings.

Case Study 1: Labster's Virtual Labs Labster is a platform offering various virtual labs for various scientific fields. These labs allow students to conduct experiments in a simulated environment. Schools and universities worldwide have embraced Labsters Labs as an example of how IoT technology can revolutionize remote experimentation and evaluation.

- ***Implementation:*** Labster's virtual labs encompass subjects like biology, chemistry, physics, and engineering. Students can access these labs online and interact with a virtual laboratory setup. These labs replicate real-life experiments by utilizing IoT sensors and data collection mechanisms, enabling students to engage in hands-on activities from afar.
- ***Assessment:*** Labster's virtual labs incorporate built-in assessments that offer students feedback on their experiment performance. This real-time evaluation assists educators in gauging student progress and identifying areas where improvement is needed.
- ***Benefits:*** The Labsters platform has empowered students to participate in hands-on experiences that overcome remote learning challenges. Additionally, it equips educators with data-driven insights into student performance, fostering instruction and assessment.

Case Study 2: LabXchange by Labster LabXchange is an open educational resource platform developed by Labster that provides various interactive learning opportunities, including virtual labs and simulations.

- ***Implementation:*** LabXchange offers interactive experiments and simulations utilizing Internet of Things (IoT) technology. These experiences cover various subjects, allowing students to explore concepts and principles from afar. Educators can customize and integrate these experiences into their curriculum.
- ***Assessment:*** LabXchange includes assessments designed to evaluate students' comprehension of the material presented in labs and simulations. These assessments are aligned with learning objectives, providing educators with data for performance evaluation.
- ***Benefits:*** LabXchange provides educators with an open, accessible platform for accessing top-notch experiments and assessments enabled by IoT. Its open educational resource model encourages collaboration among institutions while promoting accessibility for all.

Case Study 3: Vernier Software & Technology Vernier Software & Technology specializes in creating sensors and tools for collecting data in science and engineering experiments. One of their examples is the Logger Pro software, which demonstrates how IoT technology can be incorporated into laboratory experiments for remote learning.

- ***Implementation:*** Vernier's sensors and data collection tools are utilized in physical experiments. These sensors allow students to gather data while conducting experiments connected to the Logger Pro software, which empowers students to visualize and analyze the collected data on their computers.
- ***Assessment:*** The Logger Pro software offers tools that enable students to analyze and interpret the data they collect during experiments. Educators can assess students' understanding and skills based on their data analysis as their conclusions.
- ***Benefits:*** Vernier technology brings IoT capabilities to traditional laboratory experiments. Students gain experience collecting and analyzing data, while educators have a tool for evaluating student performance in remote or in-person learning environments.

These examples demonstrate how IoT technology has been successfully integrated into remote experiments and assessments showcasing its applications. They highlight platforms and solutions that provide students with engaging, hands-on learning experiences while offering educators assessment tools. Implementing such solutions requires planning, customization, and alignment with educational goals and objectives.

9.8 Challenges and Future Directions

Although there are advantages, it is crucial to utilize IoT technology for remote experiments and assessments to address specific challenges, such as technical problems, security risks, and disparities in accessibility. Integrating IoT with AR/VR, adaptive learning methods, standardized approaches, advanced analytics, gamification techniques, and ongoing research will undoubtedly contribute to the improvement and accessibility of this technology. As a result, remote education will continue to evolve and foster innovation in remote education.

Challenges in IoT-Based Remote Experiments and Assessments While there are benefits to using IoT-based remote experiments and assessments, several challenges need to be addressed.

- ***Technical Challenges:*** One obstacle is dealing with issues like internet connectivity, hardware compatibility, and software reliability. These factors can potentially hinder the success of remote experiments and assessments.
- ***Privacy:*** Ensuring the security and privacy of student data in remote assessments is of utmost importance. Robust measures must be in place to protect against data breaches and unauthorized access.

- ***Equity:*** Ensuring all students have equal access to technology and remote experiments is crucial. Addressing disparities in device access, internet connectivity, and technology skills is essential in promoting fairness.
- ***Teacher Training:*** Educators require training and professional development opportunities to effectively design, implement, and assess IoT-based experiments in remote learning environments.
- ***Cost Considerations:*** Implementing IoT technology and developing or acquiring suitable platforms can be expensive. Institutions must allocate resources to support these initiatives effectively.

Future Directions IoT-based remote experiments and assessments are expected to grow and innovate. There are directions for the ongoing development of this educational technology.

- Combining IoT technology with augmented reality (AR) and virtual reality (VR) can create immersive and interactive learning experiences, making it easier for students to engage with and understand.
- Adaptive Learning Systems integrating IoT can customize content and assessments according to each student's needs, providing a more personalized learning experience.
- Standardizing IoT protocols and ensuring interoperability among devices and platforms will simplify implementing and integrating IoT technology in education.
- Leveraging advanced data analytics and machine learning techniques can offer deeper insights into student performance and automate the assessment process.
- Developing educational games and simulations using IoT technology can enhance learning by making learning more enjoyable and interactive.
- Continued research and development in IoT technology and the creation more affordable hardware and software solutions will drive innovation in remote experiments and assessments.

Integrating IoT technology into remote experiments and assessments is an ever-evolving field with exciting opportunities for educators, students, and institutions. By tackling the obstacles and exploring these paths, we can guarantee that remote education continues to be efficient, captivating, and available to students all over the globe.

9.9 Conclusion

Incorporating Internet of Things (IoT) technology into remote learning settings has emerged as a game-changing approach to tackling education methods' limitations in hands-on subjects like STEM. This chapter has highlighted the significance of IoT-enabled remote experiments in delivering practical learning experiences seamlessly integrated with remote learning platforms. Educators can use IoT technology to overcome physical distance barriers and empower students to engage in, control, and collaborate on experiments from anywhere. The conversation has stressed the

ranging applications of IoT-enhanced experiments across diverse fields such as physics, chemistry, engineering, and environmental science. Furthermore, IoT-driven assessment techniques have transformed the evaluation process in remote learning by providing instant feedback, authentic assessments through projects, and robust evaluation tools. Real-world examples have showcased implementations that illustrate how IoT technology enhances the journey. Although challenges like technical glitches and accessibility gaps remain prevalent, prospects for IoT-based experiments and assessments show great potential. The integration of augmented reality (AR) and virtual reality (VR) adaptive learning systems, standardized protocols, advanced analytics, and continuous research are set to foster innovation in remote education. Incorporating IoT technology into remote learning represents a change towards enhanced, customized, and easily accessible educational interactions. By embracing these innovations and tackling obstacles, teachers can guarantee that remote learning progresses, equipping students with the abilities and information for thriving in the digital era.

References

Azad, A. K. M. (2020). Use of Internet of Things for remote laboratory settings. In *2020 ASEE Virtual Annual Conference Content Access* (pp. 1–19).

Editorial Staff. (2024). *Top IoT platforms to empower your projects for smarter solutions*. Geekflare. https://geekflare.com/best-iot-platforms/

Geilings, A. (2023). *The smart laboratory: How IoT is redening lab sterilization*. Tuttnauer USA. https://tuttnauer.com/blog/smart-laboratory-how-iot-redefining-lab-sterilization#:~:text =SmartlaboratoriesuseIoT-enabled,ratherthanondatacollection

Hamieh, A., & Mershad, K. (2019). Using Internet of Things to enhance remote experiments in learning management systems. In *IEEE International Smart Cities Conference* (pp. 1–4).

Kumar, S., Tiwari, P., & Zymbler, M. (2019). Internet of Things is a revolutionary approach for future technology enhancement: A review. *Journal of Big Data, 6*(111), 1–21. https://doi.org/10.1186/s40537-019-0268-2

McCarthy, A. (2011). *Assessment in a remote learning environment: What have we learned?* NACE. https://www.nace.co.uk/blogpost/1761881/367399/Assessment-in-a-remote-learning-environment-what-have-we-learned

Mershad, K., Damaj, A., Wakim, P., & Hamieh, A. (2020). LearnSmart: A framework for integrating internet of things functionalities in learning management systems. *Education and Information Technologies, 25*, 2699–2732. https://doi.org/10.1007/s10639-019-10090-6

Senel, S., & Senel, H. C. (2021). Remote assessment in higher education during COVID-19 pandemic. *International Journal of Assessment Tools in Education, 8*(2), 181–199.

Splashtop Team. (2023). *Pros and cons of remote learning*. Splashtop. https://www.splashtop.com/blog/pros-cons-remote-learning

Talespin Team. (2023). *The full rundown on what remote learning means*. Talespin Reality Labs, Inc. https://www.talespin.com/reading/the-full-rundown-on-what-remote-learning-means

Telespin Team. (2023). *Exploring the pros and cons of remote learning*. Talespin Reality Labs, Inc. https://www.talespin.com/reading/exploring-the-pros-and-cons-of-remote-learning

Viswanadh, K., Gureja, A., Walchatwar, N., Agrawal, R., Sinha, S., Chaudhari, S., Vaidhyanathan, K., Choppella, V., Bhimalapuram, P., Kandath, H., & Hussain, A. (2024). Engineering end-to-end remote labs using IoT-based retrofitting. *ArXiv:2402.05466*, 1–30.

Chapter 10
IoT-Enabled Gamification for Education

Abstract This chapter provides a practical exploration of the blend of Internet of Things (IoT) technology and gamification in educational settings, underlining its ability to reshape learning experiences. It begins by discussing the practical role of assessment and feedback in IoT-driven gamification, focusing on immediate insights, personalized learning paths, and ongoing student progress tracking. With features like real-time data analysis, progress dashboards, and adaptive learning journeys, teachers can easily customize their teaching methods to engage students and support academic development. Real-world examples demonstrate the practicality of IoT-powered gamification in transforming classrooms into vibrant learning spaces. From classroom solutions to apps enhanced with IoT features and interactive study environments, these instances showcase how IoT technology seamlessly complements teaching practices to boost engagement levels, academic achievements, and student enthusiasm. Despite its benefits, integrating IoT-enabled gamification poses practical challenges related to technology complexities, privacy, and ethical considerations in game design. The chapter addresses these issues while exploring practical future trends, such as incorporating AI and machine learning technologies offering augmented reality (AR) and virtual reality (VR) experiences and utilizing learning analytics. Moreover, it provides practical suggestions and top strategies encouraging teachers and creators to integrate gamification into curriculum objectives, with goals focused on enhancing user experience, ensuring data protection, promoting diversity, and consistently assessing impact. By adopting these practical ideals, individuals can confidently leverage the possibilities of IoT-driven gamification to transform education, establish engaging learning atmospheres, and encourage lifelong learning.

Keywords Internet of Things (IoT) technology · Gamification · Assessment and feedback · Personalized learning paths · Real-time data analysis · Augmented reality (AR) and virtual reality (VR) experiences · Learning analytics

M. Kurni, Srinivasa K. G., *The Internet of Educational Things*,
https://doi.org/10.1007/978-3-031-67387-0_10

10.1 Introduction

The field of education is constantly adapting to meet student's needs in the digital age. One exciting development in recent years has been integrating technology into classrooms. This integration has the potential to transform how we teach and learn entirely. Specifically, combining Internet of Things (IoT) technology with gamification has emerged as a powerful approach to enhancing learning experiences.

Gamification, which involves incorporating game design elements into non-game settings, has gained popularity in education due to its ability to engage and motivate learners. IoT, conversely, refers to a network of interconnected devices and sensors that collect, transmit, and analyze data. Combined, these two concepts create a synergy that can revolutionize education.

This chapter introduces the innovative field of IoT-enabled gamification in education. We will explore the potential of this combination's practical applications and its benefits to educators, students, and the entire education system.

Definition of Gamification A gamification approach integrates game design and mechanics into non-game settings like education. Its primary educational objective is to enhance learning by making it more captivating, motivating, and interactive. It incorporates game elements such as points, badges, leaderboards, challenges, and rewards to encourage participation and boost student motivation (Inspiroz, 2022; Jonathan., 2022). Essential aspects of gamification in education include (Ramesh & Sadashiv, 2019):

- ***Points and Rewards:*** Students earn points or rewards when they complete tasks or achieve learning goals. These rewards can be virtual (like badges or in-game currency) or tangible (certificates or prizes).
- ***Objectives:*** Gamified learning often involves challenges, quests, or objectives students must accomplish. These challenges mimic the structure of games and provide a sense of progression.
- ***Competition and Collaboration:*** Leaderboards and competitive elements can promote healthy competition among students, while collaborative tasks foster teamwork and cooperation.
- ***Feedback and Progress Tracking:*** Gamification systems offer immediate feedback to students so that they can monitor their progress and understand their performance. This real-time feedback serves as a vital motivator.
- ***Narrative and Storytelling:*** Many gamified educational experiences incorporate storytelling elements to create an engaging narrative that immerses students in learning.

Benefits of Gamification in Education Gamification has become an attractive approach in classrooms due to its numerous benefits (Inspiroz, 2022; Smithsonian Science Education Center, 2023; Savonin, 2022).

- ***Increased Engagement:*** One key advantage of gamification is its ability to engage students actively. By incorporating game mechanics and rewards, learning becomes more enjoyable, encouraging students to participate and invest in their education as if it were a game.

- ***Improved Motivation:*** Gamification taps into both intrinsic and extrinsic motivation. Students are motivated to earn points, achieve badges, and climb leaderboards. This motivation translates into increased effort and commitment towards their studies.
- ***Enhanced Learning Retention:*** Game-based learning experiences often result in information retention. When students are actively involved and invested in the learning process, they are likelier to remember and apply what they have learned.
- ***Immediate Feedback:*** Gamification provides immediate feedback, allowing students to assess their performance in time. This feedback loop helps them understand their strengths and weaknesses, enabling them to adjust their learning strategies.
- ***Personalized Learning Paths:*** Gamified systems can be tailored to meet each student's needs and progress. This personalization accommodates learning styles and progress, ensuring a customized approach for every learner.
- ***Encourages Critical Thinking and Problem-Solving:*** Students often encounter challenges that require critical thinking skills. They solve puzzles and problems that foster the development of these abilities.

By incorporating gamification into education, classrooms can benefit from increased student engagement, motivation, improved retention rates, immediate feedback mechanisms, personalized learning paths, and the promotion of critical thinking and problem-solving abilities. This fosters the development of these skills, which are crucial for lifelong learning.

Challenges and Criticisms While there are advantages to implementing gamification in education, it is important to acknowledge the challenges and criticisms associated with it (Huseman, 2023; Savonin, 2022):

- ***Overemphasis on Rewards:*** Relying heavily on rewards and external motivators can result in a surface-level understanding of the subject matter. Some students may prioritize earning points over truly delving into the material.
- ***Sustaining Motivation:*** Maintaining student engagement and motivation over time can be difficult. Gamified systems need to introduce challenges and incentives to sustain interest.
- ***Catering to Individual Differences:*** Gamification might not align with students' preferences or learning styles. Some learners may not find gamified experiences captivating, and a one-size-fits-all approach may not suit everyone.
- ***Assessments and Grading:*** Determining how to assess and grade gamified activities can be complex. Educators must strike a balance between fostering motivation and ensuring evaluation methods.
- ***Ethical Considerations:*** Poor implementation of gamification can raise ethical concerns, such as data privacy, competitiveness, and the potential exclusion of certain student groups.

Understanding these gamification aspects is crucial when exploring its integration with IoT technology in education.

10.2 Integration of IoT and Gamification

In the changing world of education, two factors come together: Internet of Things (IoT) technology and gamification—which hold great promise in transforming how we educate and acquire knowledge (Pappas et al., 2022). This section dives into the fusion of IoT and gamification in education, delving into the possibilities that arise when interactive games meet the interconnectedness provided by IoT devices. As we embark on this exploration, we reveal a world of potential for creating learning experiences that are personalized and filled with data going beyond the traditional confines of education.

The Synergy Between IoT and Gamification Integrating the Internet of Things (IoT) and gamification in education can potentially create immersive learning experiences. By combining these two concepts, educators can tap into the best of both worlds, providing students with captivating journeys enriched with real-world data.

Advantages of Synergy (as shown in Fig. 10.1) (ANTT Robotics Ltd, 2024; Xiao et al., 2022):

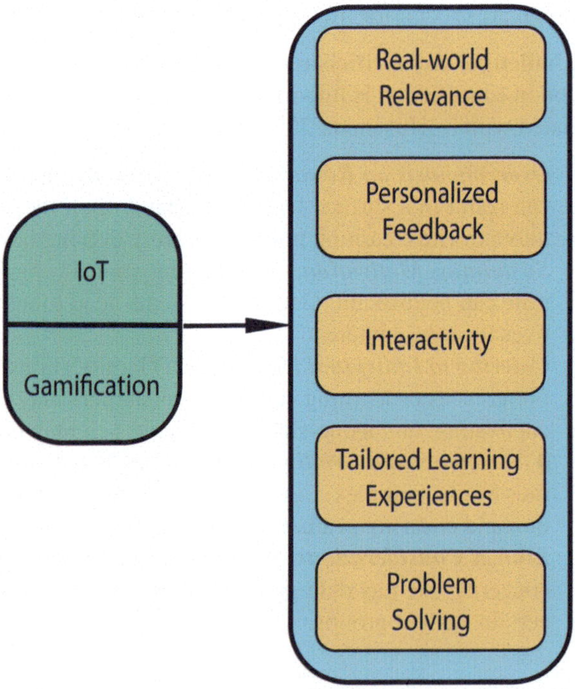

Fig. 10.1 The advantages of synergy between IoT and Gamification

- ***Real-world Relevance:*** By incorporating IoT devices and sensors, students can experience relevant scenarios in their educational environment and gain valuable hands-on experience.
- ***Personalized Feedback:*** Leveraging the data collected by IoT technology allows for immediate and personalized feedback, enhancing the engaging nature of gamified learning.
- ***Interactivity:*** Gamification elements, like challenges and rewards, motivate and captivate students. Using IoT devices that respond to student actions creates an interactive and responsive learning atmosphere.
- ***Tailored Learning Experiences:*** Combining IoT data and gamification enables customized learning journeys. Students can progress at their own pace while receiving content that caters to their needs.
- ***Problem Solving:*** Gamification often involves problem-solving tasks. The support of IoT technology presenting real-world problems and challenges encourages critical thinking skills and innovation.

Examples of IoT-Enhanced Gamification in Education To demonstrate the potential of combining IoT and gamification in education, let us explore a few examples (Wang & Nunes, 2020):

- ***Adventure in Environmental Science:*** In an environmental science course, students receive IoT-enabled devices that measure air quality, temperature, and humidity. They then embark on a journey to tackle challenges like pollution and climate change by gathering data from their IoT devices. Points are awarded for data collection and innovative problem-solving. Students can track their progress on leaderboards and earn badges for completing missions.
- ***A Smart Tour of History Museums:*** During a history class, students visit museums equipped with IoT beacons near exhibits. As they approach each exhibit, their smartphones or tablets receive information about the artifacts. They answer quiz questions related to the exhibits and can collect artifacts along the way. These virtual artifacts unlock mysteries and allow students to delve into deeper narratives. Students can compete for scores and collaborate in solving historical puzzles.
- ***Language Learning in a Connected World:*** Language learning becomes an experience by integrating IoT and gamification techniques. Students are provided with IoT devices that enable them to interact with speakers worldwide. These devices facilitate conversations by translating languages and offering language challenges. Points are earned for communication and achieving language milestones. Leaderboards showcase the language learners, fostering healthy competition and collaboration.
- ***Physics Lab of the Future:*** We can see how IoT sensors are cleverly placed on equipment in a physics lab. As students conduct their experiments, these smart IoT devices collect real-time data on velocity, acceleration, and temperature variables. This data is then used to participate in a game's physics challenges! Students who make predictions and execute their experiments well receive

rewards. Can even see their scores displayed on a leaderboard. It is about promoting competition while creating an engaging and immersive learning experience.

These examples beautifully showcase how IoT-enabled gamification can revolutionize education. By integrating technology with gamification mechanics, educators can create thrilling learning experiences that encouraging active participation, critical thinking, and learning driven by fundamental data.

10.3 Designing IoT-Enabled Gamified Learning Experiences

Creating educational experiences that engage and motivate requires a combination of pedagogical objectives, technological progress, and motivational techniques. This section will explore the intricacies of crafting learning journeys by integrating IoT and gamification. From defining learning goals to selecting gamification elements incorporating technologies and ensuring a smooth user experience—each step is like adding brushstrokes to the canvas of educational innovation.

Identifying Learning Objectives Establishing learning goals is essential before designing IoT-enabled gamified learning experiences. These goals should align with your objectives and the desired outcomes you hope to achieve. Start by considering the knowledge or skills you want students to acquire or enhance through the experience. These objectives will be a foundation for selecting devices, game mechanics, and assessment strategies. Here are some examples of learning objectives.

- Enhancing student's comprehension of factors and their impact on health.
- Developing problem-solving abilities through physics experiments.
- Promoting cultural communication and language proficiency.
- Expanding historical knowledge and fostering critical thinking skills.

Selecting Appropriate Gamification Mechanics When designing your educational content, it is important to select gamification mechanics that align with your learning objectives and the context of the material. The chosen mechanics should effectively engage students while reinforcing the desired learning outcomes. Some common gamification mechanics include:

- ***Points and Rewards:*** Students can earn points, badges, and game currency as they achieve milestones or complete tasks.
- ***Challenges and Objectives:*** Assigning missions or challenges that guide students through their learning journey.
- ***Competition and Collaboration:*** Encouraging competition through leaderboards or fostering collaboration on group projects.
- ***Narrative and Storytelling:*** Creating a narrative that provides context and immerses students in the learning experience.
- ***Feedback and Progress Tracking:*** Providing immediate feedback to help students monitor their performance and adjust their learning strategies.

- ***Achievement Unlocks:*** Unlocking new content, challenges, or rewards for students as they progress in their learning.

Incorporating these gamification mechanics into your educational content can create an environment that enhances student motivation and engagement.

Choosing IoT Technologies and Sensors Selecting IoT technologies and sensors to enhance the learning experience and align it with your learning objectives is essential. These choices should enable data collection and interaction with the physical environment. Consider factors like accessibility, affordability, and ease of use. Here are some examples of IoT technologies you could consider.

- Environmental sensors that measure air quality, temperature, and humidity.
- Bluetooth beacons that facilitate location-based interactions at museums or historical sites.
- Language translation devices that aid in cultural communication.
- Lab equipment sensors are designed to conduct physics experiments.

User Experience Design Creating an IoT-enabled gamified learning experience relies heavily on effective user experience design. The design should prioritize engaging users, ensuring ease of use, and seamlessly integrating IoT technology and gamification mechanics. Here are some important factors to consider in the design process.

- ***Usability:*** It is essential to ensure that IoT devices and gamified elements are user-friendly and accessible to all students.
- ***Immersion:*** Blending real-world data from IoT devices with the game narrative can create a sense of immersion.
- ***Feedback:*** Providing constructive feedback that guides students towards their learning objectives is crucial.
- ***Progression:*** Designing a clear progression path helps keep students motivated and allows them to track their progress effectively.
- ***Adaptability:*** The learning experience should cater to students' needs and pace.

By considering these aspects during the design phase, educators can create captivating IoT-enabled gamified learning experiences that drive student educational outcomes.

10.4 Data Collection and Analysis

In the evolving world of gamified learning experiences enabled by the Internet of Things (IoT), the combination of real-world connectivity and interactive gameplay creates a wealth of valuable information. This section delves into how data is collected from IoT devices, highlighting the different types of information gathered and emphasizing their crucial role in enriching the learning process. Whether it is data that paints a picture of our surroundings or user interactions that shape personalized experiences, the range and impact of this data are immense.

Data Capture from IoT Devices Integrating Internet of Things (IoT) devices and gamification into education produces a plethora of data that can be utilized to enhance the learning experience. These IoT devices, equipped with sensors, gather data about the physical environment and user interactions. This data serves as the basis for an adaptable educational journey. The types of collected data (IFACET, 2023) are as follows.

- ***Environmental Data:*** IoT sensors can measure parameters such as temperature, humidity, air quality, or movement within the learning environment. For example, environmental data can assist students in comprehending how temperature impacts chemical reactions during a science experiment.
- ***User Interactions:*** IoT devices can log student actions and interactions with the physical world. For example, they could track students' movements in a history museum or manipulate equipment during a physics lab.
- ***Progress and Achievements:*** Gamification elements often generate data on student progress, including earned points, collected badges, and completed challenges.
- ***Response Times:*** IoT devices can record students' task completion times, offering insights into their efficiency and level of engagement.

Data Storage and Processing Information gathered from Internet of Things (IoT) devices is typically stored in databases or cloud servers. Establishing mechanisms for processing and storing this data is crucial to making the most of it. Cloud-based solutions are commonly utilized, providing scalability and accessibility for educators and students. The data processing steps (IFACET, 2023) are as follows.

- ***Data Aggregation:*** The data collected from multiple devices and sensors is organized and prepared for analysis.
- ***Data Analysis:*** The collected data is examined to extract meaningful insights. This analysis may involve statistical techniques, machine learning algorithms, and data visualization methods.
- ***Identifying Patterns:*** Data analysis can detect patterns in student behavior, engagement levels, and learning outcomes. This information can be used to customize each learner's experience.
- ***Predictive Analytics:*** Data analysis enables predictive capabilities such as forecasting student performance or suggesting personalized learning paths.

Data Security and Privacy Concerns Educators and institutions must consider privacy and security when collecting and storing data from IoT devices. The confidentiality and security of student data should be a priority. Here are some important things to consider (Babalola, 2021).

- ***Data Privacy:***
  - Ensure you follow data privacy regulations, such as the Family Educational Rights and Privacy Act (FERPA) in the United States.
  - Get permission from students and their guardians before collecting and using their data.

- ***Data Security:***
  - Put security measures in place to protect the data from unauthorized access or breaches.
  - Keep IoT devices updated with the latest patches to address any vulnerabilities.
  - Use encryption when transmitting or storing data to keep it safe from interception.
- ***Data Ownership:***
  - Clearly define who owns the data, especially when using third-party IoT devices or platforms.
  - Educate students about their rights regarding their data and how it will be used.
- ***Data Retention:***
  - Establish policies on how long student data will be stored and when it will be deleted.

Addressing these privacy and security concerns can ensure that IoT-enabled gamification in education is trustworthy, ethical, and compliant with regulations.

10.5 Assessment and Feedback Mechanisms

We focus on assessment and feedback (as shown in Fig. 10.2) as we explore the intersection of IoT technology and gamification. In this section, we delve into how real-time insights and adaptive pathways empower educators and foster engagement among learners. We examine how continuous monitoring of student progress, prompt feedback, and dynamic adaptive learning create a fulfilling educational journey.

Monitoring Student Progress Tracking student progress is a component of learning experiences enhanced by Internet of Things (IoT) technology. Educators can customize their instruction by monitoring how students engage with the content and making progress. Provide timely feedback. The following are important aspects of monitoring progress (Abiodun et al., 2023).

- ***Real-time Data:*** IoT devices offer up-to-the-minute information on students' interactions, accomplishments, and performance. Both educators and students have access to this data for analysis.
- ***Progress Dashboards:*** Gamification platforms often incorporate progress dashboards that showcase students' points, badges, and completed challenges. These visual displays represent achievement.
- ***Leaderboards:*** Leaderboards display how students rank compared to their peers, fostering competition and motivating learners to excel.

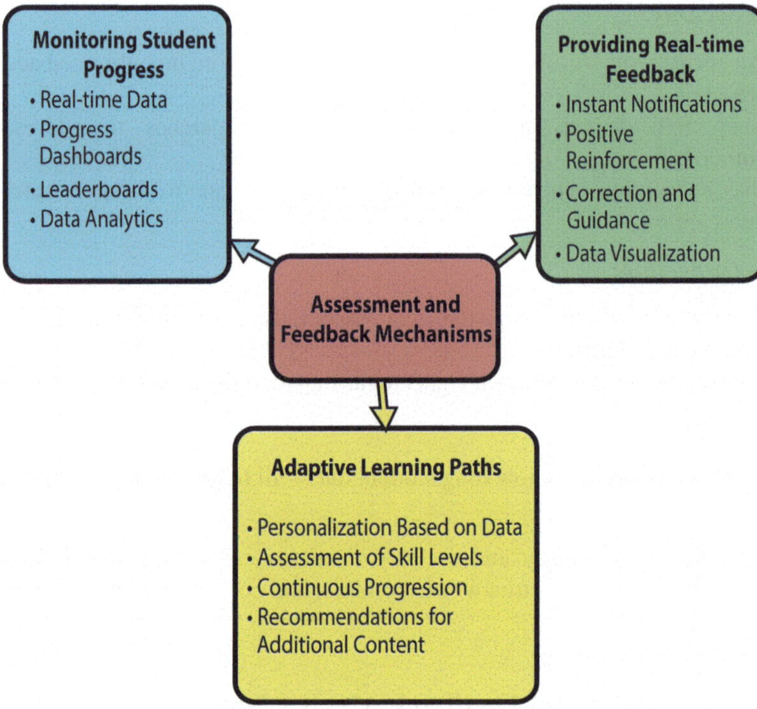

Fig. 10.2 Assessment and feedback mechanisms

- ***Data Analytics:*** Leveraging data analysis tools enables educators to identify student behavior and performance patterns, empowering them to make data-based decisions.

Providing Real-Time Feedback Real-time feedback plays a vital role in making IoT-enabled gamification effective in education. It provides students with insights into their performance areas for improvement and ways to advance in their learning journey (Kumar, 2023; Haleem et al., 2022). The different forms of real-time feedback include:

- ***Instant Notifications:*** Students receive notifications or alerts when they reach a milestone, earn a badge, or complete a challenge. These notifications can be delivered through mobile apps, web platforms, or physical IoT devices.
- ***Positive Reinforcement:*** Encouraging messages, virtual rewards, and praises serve as feedback to reinforce desired behaviors and accomplishments.
- ***Correction and Guidance:*** Constructive feedback helps students identify areas for improvement. It can be given when they make mistakes or when guidance is needed.
- ***Data Visualization:*** Visual representations, like charts and graphs, depict students' progress and enable them to spot patterns and trends.

Adaptive Learning Paths One of the advantages of incorporating IoT-enabled gamification is its ability to provide adaptive learning paths. These paths dynamically adjust the content and challenges according to each student's progress, ensuring learners remain engaged and appropriately challenged. The key elements of adaptive learning paths include (Smart Sparrow, 2023):

- ***Personalization Based on Data:*** By leveraging data collected from IoT devices, educators can tailor the learning experience to meet the needs of every student. For example, if a student excels, the system can present advanced challenges in a subject area.
- ***Assessment of Skill Levels:*** Gamification platforms can evaluate students' proficiency levels and identify knowledge gaps, ensuring they are exposed to content that aligns with their abilities.
- ***Continuous Progression:*** Students can move through the content at their own pace. The system adapts accordingly and introduces new challenges as students achieve specific milestones.
- ***Recommendations for Additional Content:*** IoT data can suggest learning resources like readings, videos, or interactive exercises to enhance the gamified experience.

The combination of real-time feedback and adaptive learning cultivates an environment where students are actively involved and consistently pushed beyond their comfort zones. As students progress, the data from IoT devices contributes to an educational journey enriched with valuable insights.

10.6 Case Studies and Examples

This section will explore case studies and instances of gamified learning experiences utilizing Internet of Things (IoT) technology. These examples demonstrate how the integration of IoT and gamification has been utilized in educational settings to amplify engagement, improve learning outcomes, and ignite student motivation.

Case Study 1: Smart Classroom Solutions

Overview Smart classrooms use IoT technology to create interactive and dynamic learning environments. These classrooms incorporate IoT sensor devices and gamification elements to engage students innovatively.

Example For instance, consider a university that adopts IoT sensors in its classrooms. These sensors keep track of student attendance, participation levels, and environmental conditions. Students are provided with smart devices that connect to the classroom system. To make things more exciting, gamification elements are introduced whereby students earn points for participating and contributing to a comfortable learning environment. Leaderboards showcase the students who positively enhance the classroom experience. This approach motivates students to attend classes regularly, actively participate in discussions, and maintain a conducive environment for learning. Educators can utilize the data collected from sensors and gamification platforms to assess student engagement levels and reward them accordingly.

Case Study 2: IoT-Enhanced Educational Apps

Overview Educational applications enhanced by Internet of Things (IoT) technology provide students with an interactive learning experience. These apps connect objects or environments and virtual content, creating captivating interactions.

Example For example, imagine an educational app specifically designed for elementary science education. This app utilizes technology to connect with microscopes and telescopes. The embedded IoT sensors capture data as students explore the world using these tools and transmit it to the app. The app incorporates gamification elements, transforming the learning experience into an adventure. Students earn points and badges by observing objects, identifying wildlife, or conducting experiments. The app offers feedback based on their observations and challenges them to complete. Additionally, students can share their accomplishments with peers and teachers, fostering a competitive learning environment.

Case Study 3: Interactive Learning Environments

Overview Interactive learning environments like science labs or historical sites leverage IoT technology to enhance the educational experience. Students can explore, learn, and engage by connecting physical spaces to content and incorporating gamification elements.

Example For instance, IoT beacons are utilized in museums or heritage centers to offer interactive tours. Visitors can access content through IoT-enabled devices or their smartphones. The tour incorporates gamification features like quizzes, challenges, and virtual artifact collection. As visitors navigate the site-specific exhibits, related content is triggered via beacons. Points are awarded for answers to questions, and virtual artifacts can be collected along the way. A leaderboard showcases the scoring visitors to foster competition. This interactive learning experience imparts knowledge and immerses visitors in the site's historical significance and cultural aspects.

These real-life scenarios and examples demonstrate the applications of IoT-enabled gamification technology in education. They demonstrate how technology integration, gamification elements, and real-world experiences converge to create captivating learning journeys enriched with data.

10.7 Challenges and Ethical Considerations

Bringing together IoT technology and gamification in education opens up possibilities for innovation. However, it also comes with challenges and ethical considerations that educators, institutions, and developers need to consider and address.

Technical Challenges and Limitations In this section, we delve into the complexities that educators and developers encounter when dealing with challenges such as compatibility issues with IoT devices, connectivity problems, ensuring data accuracy, and considering the financial aspects of scalability.

- ***Compatibility of IoT Devices:*** Ensuring that IoT devices from manufacturers are compatible with the same platforms can be challenging, making standardization and integration challenging.
- ***Connectivity Challenges:*** The reliability of internet connectivity and the smooth functioning of IoT devices may be disrupted in educational environments, impacting the overall gamification experience.
- ***Accuracy and Precision of Data:*** Data collected from IoT devices must be accurate and precise. Inaccurate data can lead to misleading insights and hinder the effectiveness of gamified experiences.
- ***Cost and Scalability:*** Procuring and maintaining IoT devices can be costly, and scaling up to accommodate students or classrooms may pose financial difficulties.

Privacy and Data Security In this section, we will explore the aspects of using IoT-enabled gamification. We will discuss the challenges of balancing data privacy and security risks and the importance of informed consent and transparency in protecting student information.

- ***Concerns about Data Privacy:*** There are valid privacy concerns when collecting data from student IoT devices. Both students and their guardians may be worried about how personal information is collected, stored, and utilized.
- ***Risks to Data Security:*** IoT devices can be susceptible to security breaches, which could lead to access to sensitive data. It is crucial to prioritize safeguarding data against breaches.
- ***Importance of Consent and Transparency:*** Educational institutions must obtain consent from students and their guardians regarding the collection and usage of IoT data. Being transparent about how this data is used is crucial in establishing trust.

Ethical Concerns in Gamification We must shift our focus from relying on rewards to creating gamified experiences and designing game mechanics free from bias.

- ***Balanced Approach:*** Balancing rewards and intrinsic motivation in gamification is crucial. Relying heavily on rewards can result in a shallow understanding of the subject matter and diminish students' internal motivation for learning.
- ***Inclusivity and Competition:*** While gamification can introduce competition, it is vital to ensure that it does not discourage students. To create inclusive experiences, we should consider diverse learning preferences and abilities.
- ***Ethical Game Design:*** When implementing game mechanics like points and leaderboards, it is essential to prioritize ethical considerations. This will help us avoid harmful competition, exclusion, or adding stress on students.
- ***Fairness without bias:*** Grading mechanisms within gamified experiences must be fair for all students and free from bias or favoritism.

Implementing IoT-enabled gamification in education requires addressing these challenges while upholding privacy, security, inclusivity, and ethical standards. Educators and institutions should carefully plan, design, and implement experiences that consider these factors.

10.8 Future Directions and Emerging Trends

The realm of gamifying education through the Internet of Things (IoT) is continually evolving, presenting possibilities and emerging trends on the horizon. Educators, institutions, and developers can anticipate advancements in this approach.

- ***Integration of AI and Machine Learning***: By incorporating artificial intelligence (AI) and machine learning (ML), IoT-based gamification will significantly benefit. AI can analyze the data devices generate, enabling more sophisticated and personalized gamified experiences. ML algorithms can adapt content, challenges, and rewards based on students' learning preferences, enhancing engagement and improving learning outcomes.
- ***Integration of Augmented Reality (AR) and Virtual Reality (VR):*** By combining AR/VR with IoT and gamification, we can create immersive educational experiences. IoT devices can interact with AR/VR environments to provide interactive content. For instance, students may utilize IoT-enabled devices to explore historical sites or conduct virtual science experiments.
- ***Leveraging Learning Analytics for Predictive Insights:*** Educators can gain insights into student performance through IoT-powered learning analytics. These insights help identify at-risk students by allowing for interventions and personalized learning paths. Educators can make data-driven decisions to enhance student outcomes.

- ***Assessments and Certification, in a Gamified Format:*** How we assess and grade students will likely change. Students can earn certifications and badges by completing engaging learning modules, allowing them to showcase their skills and knowledge interactively and tangibly.
- ***Gamification Extending Beyond Formal Education:*** Gamification empowered by IoT technology will extend its reach beyond formal education settings. It will find applications in development, corporate training, and lifelong learning. By incorporating gamified experiences, individuals can acquire new skills to adapt to evolving work environments and maintain competitiveness in the job market.
- ***Social Learning through Gamification:*** IoT-enabled gamification will foster student social learning and collaboration. Students will engage in challenges within gamified environments, share their achievements, and learn from one another. Peer-to-peer learning and collaboration will become integral aspects of the learning process.
- ***Adaptive Content Creation with AI Assistance:*** Educators can leverage AI-driven content creation tools to develop adaptive learning materials. These tools can generate content that aligns with each student's individualized learning path, ensuring the material remains challenging yet relevant throughout their journey.
- ***Breaking Down Subject Silos through Cross-disciplinary Gamification:*** IoT-enabled gamification has the potential to break down traditional subject barriers. Incorporating elements of gamified learning experiences from multiple disciplines encourages cross-disciplinary thinking and problem-solving abilities.
- ***Gamification and Sustainability:*** The combination of gamification and sustainability can be leveraged in education through IoT-enabled devices. Students can use these devices to monitor energy consumption, track resource usage, and actively participate in sustainability challenges.
- ***Gamification Research Development:*** The research and development of IoT-enabled gamification is expected to grow. Researchers will delve into the impact of gamification on learning outcomes, ethical concerns, and privacy implications. Additionally, continuous gamification design and technology advancements will drive progress in this field.

As IoT technology and gamification evolve, educators, institutions, and developers can explore and harness these emerging trends to create compelling learning experiences. By staying updated with these developments and embracing innovation, integrating IoT-enabled gamification into education can bring transformative educational practices and outcomes.

10.9 Recommendations and Best Practices

Planning and executing the process thoughtfully is crucial to successfully implementing IoT-enabled gamification in education. Below are some recommendations and best practices for educators, institutions, and developers to ensure integration.

- ***Clearly define your learning objectives:*** Start by outlining the knowledge or skills you want students to acquire or enhance through the gamified experience. These objectives will serve as a guide for selecting IoT devices, game mechanics, and assessment strategies.
- ***Align gamification with curriculum:*** Ensure that gamification elements align with your curriculum and educational goals. The goal should be to enhance the learning process rather than distract from it. The integration of gamification should seamlessly blend with the subject matter.
- ***Thoughtfully choose IoT devices:*** Select IoT technologies and sensors that enrich the gamified learning experience while aligning with your learning objectives. Consider factors such as accessibility, affordability, and ease of use. These IoT devices must be reliable and suitable for their intended purpose.
- ***Prioritize user experience design:*** User experience design plays a vital role. Ensure the gamified experience is user-friendly and accessible to all students. Combine real-world IoT device data with the game's narrative to create an immersive environment. Offer constructive feedback to guide students throughout their journey.
- ***Safeguarding data privacy and Security:*** Implement measures to protect data privacy and security. Comply with data privacy regulations and obtain informed consent from students and their guardians—encrypt data when transmitting and storing it. Regularly update and patch IoT devices to address any vulnerabilities.
- ***Foster inclusivity:*** Create gamified experiences that cater to various learning preferences and abilities. Avoid emphasizing competition and consider the needs of all students. Personalize the learning experience to suit each learner individually.
- ***Monitor and adapt continuously:*** Track student progress and gather feedback to adjust the gamified experience accordingly. Use data analytics to identify student behavior patterns and trends, allowing you to make real-time adjustments. Provide real-time feedback to guide students.
- ***Evaluate and refine:*** Assess the effectiveness of the IoT-enabled gamification approach. Analyze data on student outcomes and engagement. Utilize this information to make decisions that continuously improve the impact of gamification on learning.
- ***Invest in development:*** Provide educators with training opportunities to effectively utilize IoT devices and incorporate gamification elements into their teaching practices. Ongoing support is crucial for implementation.
- ***Ethical game design:*** When designing gamification mechanics, ethical considerations are considered. Ensure that points, leaderboards, and rewards promote competition and cooperation rather than fostering harmful competition or exclusion.
- ***Collaborate and Share Insights:*** Educators and institutions can collaborate as researchers in IoT-enabled gamification to make education more engaging, interactive, and data-driven. We can collectively advance the field by sharing insights, experiences, and best practices.

Implementing IoT-enabled gamification in education using these recommendations not only ensures positive and enriching learning experiences but also has the potential to revolutionize education itself. The ultimate result will be improved learning outcomes and increased student motivation.

10.10 Conclusion

The fusion of Internet of Things (IoT) technology with gamification offers a promising future for advancement, providing interactive and stimulating learning opportunities for students. This section explores the use of assessment tools, practical examples, challenges, and ethical considerations to showcase the benefits and complexities of combining IoT and gamification in education. By utilizing real-time data insights, personalized learning pathways, and engaging environments, teachers can tailor learning experiences to help students boost engagement levels and enhance performance. Despite facing hurdles and ethical dilemmas, the outlook for integrating IoT-enabled gamification into education looks promising. Adopting emerging technologies like AI, machine learning, augmented reality (AR), virtual reality (VR) experiences, and predictive learning analytics has significant potential to improve the effectiveness and inclusivity of gamified educational settings. However, successful implementation relies on planning, user-centric design approaches, robust data security measures, and continuous evaluation. In summary, by embracing recommended strategies fostering collaboration efforts and emphasizing game design principles, educators, institutions, and developers can unleash the transformative capabilities of IoT-powered gamification. Through innovation initiatives and adaptability measures, IoT-based gamification has the potential to revolutionize education practices, inspire learning journeys, and empower students to excel in today's digital landscape.

References

Abiodun, M., Bamidele, A. J., Adeniyi, E., Ogundokun, R., & Misra, S. (2023). Analytics of IoT based system for monitoring students' progress in educational environment. In *New frontiers in cloud computing and Internet of Things* (pp. 1–29). Springer.

ANTT Robotics Ltd. (2024). *Revolutionizing education with IoT and gamification in math and science*. LinkedIn. https://www.linkedin.com/pulse/revolutionizing-education-iot-gamification-math-science-ovcvc/

Babalola, O. (2021). Internet of Things (IoT): Data security and privacy concerns under the General Data Protection Regulation (GDPR). In *10th International Conference on Natural Language Processing (NLP 2021)* (pp. 309–320). https://doi.org/10.5121/csit.2021.112324

Haleem, A., Javaid, M., Asim, M., & Suman, R. (2022). Understanding the role of digital technologies in education: A review. *Sustainable Operations and Computers, 3*(May), 275–285. https://doi.org/10.1016/j.susoc.2022.05.004

Huseman, T. (2023). *Challenges of gamification in education and how to overcome them?* Acadecraft. https://www.acadecraft.com/blog/gamification-education-challenges/

IFACET. (2023). *IoT devices and sensors: Types, functions, and use cases*. IIT Kanpur. https://ifacet.iitk.ac.in/knowledge-hub/internet-of-things/iot-devices-and-sensors-types-functions-and-use-cases/

Inspiroz. (2022). *Gamification in education: What Is gamification and why is it trending in schools?* LinkedIn. https://www.linkedin.com/pulse/gamification-education-what-why-trending-schools-inspiroz/

Jonathan. (2022). *Gamification in education*. Globsyn Business School. https://www.globsyn.edu.in/blog/gamification-in-education

Kumar, A. (2023). *IoT in education: A future of smart and sustainable learning*. LinkedIn. https://www.linkedin.com/pulse/iot-education-future-smart-sustainable-learning-ankit-kumar/

Pappas, G., Siegel, J., Vogiatzakis, I. N., & Politopoulos, K. (2022, June). Gamification and the Internet of Things in education. In *Handbook of intelligent techniques in educational process* (pp. 317–339). Springer International Publishing. https://doi.org/10.1007/978-3-031-04662-9

Ramesh, A., & Sadashiv, G. (2019). Essentials of gamification in education: A game-based learning. In *Smart innovation, systems and technologies* (pp. 1–7). https://doi.org/10.1007/978-981-13-5977-4_81

Savonin, M. (2022). *Gamification in education: Benefits, risks, examples*. Keenethics. https://keenethics.com/blog/simulation-gamification-of-education

Smart Sparrow. (2023). *Let's talk about adaptive learning*. Smart Sparrow. https://www.smartsparrow.com/what-is-adaptive-learning/

Smithsonian Science Education Center. (2023). *5 benefits of gamification*. Smithsonian Science Education Center. https://ssec.si.edu/stemvisions-blog/5-benefits-gamification

Wang, M., & Nunes, M. B. (2020). A design research approach for IoT gamification of museum visiting experiences. In *European Conference on Research Methodology for Business and Management Studies* (pp. 1–3). https://doi.org/10.34190/ERM.20.048

Xiao, R., Wu, Z., & Hamari, J. (2022). Internet-of-gamification: A review of literature on IoT-enabled gamification for user engagement. *International Journal of Human–Computer Interaction, 38*(12), 1113–1137. https://doi.org/10.1080/10447318.2021.1990517

Chapter 11
Secure IoT-Based Classroom

Abstract This detailed chapter explores how Internet of Things (IoT) technology is used in educational settings, focusing on topics like security, best practices for implementation, real-life examples, and future trends. It highlights the role of ensuring the security of IoT systems in classrooms to reduce potential risks, such as safeguarding data privacy, maintaining device integrity, strengthening network resilience, and verifying user identity. By discussing protocols such as MQTT, CoAP, HTTP/HTTPS, and AMQP, the chapter provides specific advice on planning strategies, evaluating risks in acquiring devices, setting them up correctly, and maintaining them. Case studies demonstrate implementations of IoT in classrooms by emphasizing teamwork approaches and privacy protection measures, educating users about security issues, conducting security audits following regulations, choosing vendors carefully, and encrypting data effectively. Additionally, it predicts developments and challenges in using IoT for education purposes like personalized learning experiences integrating reality into lessons promoting STEM subjects, facilitating remote learning opportunities addressing security issues, managing complex data systems dealing with scalability problems, and managing budgets efficiently. The chapter offers suggestions for overcoming these challenges by recommending strategies for managing data continuously, monitoring security measures, prioritizing privacy-focused design principles, adapting teaching methods to individual needs, promoting sustainability initiatives, and providing opportunities for educators to enhance their skills. This chapter provides a manual for educators looking to establish cutting-edge IoT-integrated classrooms, anticipating the ever-changing realm of educational technology.

Keywords Internet of Things (IoT) technology · Security · Implementation best practices · Personalized learning experiences · Remote learning opportunities · Privacy protection measures · Sustainability initiatives

M. Kurni, Srinivasa K. G., *The Internet of Educational Things*,
https://doi.org/10.1007/978-3-031-67387-0_11

11.1 Security Challenges in IoT-Based Classrooms

The Internet of Things (IoT) has brought advancements in various fields, including education. Nevertheless, incorporating IoT in educational settings brings security challenges and risks that must be thoroughly addressed. This section will explore IoT's security challenges and risks in educational environments.

Data Privacy and Confidentiality

One of the concerns when using IoT technology in classrooms is ensuring the privacy and security of confidential data. Educational institutions handle sensitive information such as student records, assessments, and teacher communications. However, some challenges and risks need to be addressed (Tawalbeh et al., 2020):

- ***Data Interception:*** IoT devices transmit data through networks, which can be intercepted if not properly secured. This could allow unauthorized access to information.
- ***Data Leakage:*** Insufficient security measures may lead to the exposure or sharing of confidential information with unauthorized individuals.
- ***Compliance Issues:*** Failing to protect student and faculty data may result in noncompliance with data protection regulations, potentially leading to legal consequences.

Educational institutions must address these concerns and implement security measures for safeguarding data transmitted through IoT devices.

Device Security

IoT devices are available in smartboards, tablets, wearable gadgets, and environmental sensors. It is crucial to prioritize the security of these devices to prevent any access or misuse. Some key security challenges and risks associated with device security include (Balbix, 2024; Trend Micro Incorporated, 2021; Hope, 2023):

- ***Weak Authentication:*** IoT devices might have inadequate or default authentication methods, making them vulnerable to exploitation.
- ***Firmware and Software Vulnerabilities:*** Numerous IoT devices rely on firmware and software that could potentially contain vulnerabilities. Attackers can take advantage of these weaknesses.
- ***Unauthorized Device Access:*** If not secured, unauthorized individuals could gain physical access to or tamper with IoT devices in the classroom.

Educational institutions must address these concerns and implement security measures for their IoT devices.

Network Security

The connectivity infrastructure that links IoT devices within an institution plays a crucial role in maintaining a secure ecosystem. There are challenges and risks associated with network security in this context (Rainbow Secure, 2023; Williams et al., 2022):

- ***Network Vulnerabilities:*** Educational institutions often have intricate network setups, which can expose vulnerabilities if not correctly configured and secured.
- ***Denial of Service (DoS) Attacks:*** IoT networks can be vulnerable to DoS attacks, disrupting service availability.
- ***Unauthenticated Devices:*** Compromised IoT devices can enter the network, potentially providing entry points for attackers.

User Authentication and Authorization

Ensuring authorized individuals can access and manage devices in the classroom is a critical security concern. There are challenges and risks to consider in this context (Chalishazar, 2023; Yousefnezhad et al., 2020):

- ***Weak Passwords:*** Users might select easily guessed or weak passwords, which could make it easier for unauthorized individuals to gain access.
- ***Insufficient User Access Control:*** Students and faculty members can unintentionally have access to specific IoT devices without proper user access control mechanisms.
- ***Lack of User Awareness:*** Users should be educated about potential security risks so that they do not unknowingly compromise the overall security of the IoT system.

Addressing these security challenges and risks is vital for establishing a secure classroom environment incorporating IoT technology.

11.2 Building a Secure IoT Infrastructure

Building a secure infrastructure in an educational setting is crucial for safeguarding the privacy and safety of students, faculty, and the institution's data. This section will explore the components (as shown in Fig. 11.1) of establishing a secure IoT infrastructure for a classroom environment.

Network Design and Segmentation Creating a secure IoT environment relies heavily on having a well-designed network. When designing the network infrastructure for your IoT-based classroom, it is important to consider the following aspects (Gyamfi & Jurcut, 2022; Elrawy et al., 2018):

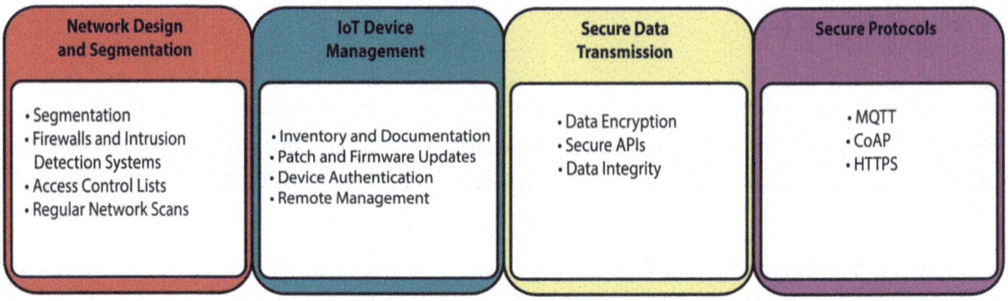

Fig. 11.1 Components of establishing a secure IoT infrastructure for a classroom environment

- ***Segmentation:*** Divide your network into segments to separate IoT devices from systems and sensitive data. This division helps contain any security breaches and restrict access.
- ***Firewalls and Intrusion Detection Systems (IDS):*** Implementing firewalls enables you to monitor network traffic and identify unusual or potentially malicious activities. These security measures defend against threats.
- ***Access Control Lists (ACLs):*** Utilize ACLs to regulate traffic between sections of your network. This ensures that authorized devices and users can communicate with the IoT devices.
- ***Regular Network Scans:*** Conduct routine network scans to identify vulnerabilities and weaknesses. By addressing these security gaps, you can maintain a defense against threats.

IoT Device Management Managing Internet of Things (IoT) devices is essential to maintaining a secure environment. Here are some important factors to consider when it comes to effective device management (Intuz, 2023; Takyar, 2024; AVSystem, 2020a):

- ***Inventory and Documentation:*** Keeping an inventory of all IoT devices and documenting their specifications, locations, and known vulnerabilities is crucial.
- ***Patch and Firmware Updates:*** To address vulnerabilities, regularly update the firmware and software of IoT devices. Develop a strategy for managing patches to ensure updates.
- ***Device Authentication:*** Implement device authentication mechanisms, such as secure login credentials and certificates.
- ***Remote Management:*** Enable remote management capabilities for IoT devices, simplifying the maintenance and security updates process without requiring physical access.

Secure Data Transmission Securing data while it is transmitted is crucial to prevent access and interception. To ensure the transmission of data within your infrastructure, you can consider the following measures (Rotenberg, 2023b; Global Cybersecurity Association, 2023):

- ***Data Encryption:*** Employ encryption techniques such as TLS (Transport Layer Security) to protect the data during transit. This helps prevent individuals from gaining access to information.
- ***Secure APIs:*** Use secure Application Programming Interfaces (APIs) for communication between devices and applications. Implement authorization and authentication mechanisms to ensure that only authorized entities can interact with the APIs.
- ***Data Integrity:*** Implement mechanisms that allow you to verify the integrity of transmitted data. This ensures that no tampering has occurred during its journey.

Implementing these steps can enhance the security of your data as it is transmitted within your infrastructure.

Secure Protocols To establish a secure IoT infrastructure, it is crucial to choose communication protocols carefully. Take into account the following protocols (Gerodimos et al., 2023; Sonee, 2020):

- ***MQTT (Message Queuing Telemetry Transport):*** MQTT is an efficient protocol commonly used in IoT. It can be made secure by implementing TLS/SSL encryption.
- ***CoAP (Constrained Application Protocol):*** CoAP is designed for devices with limited resources and can be secured using DTLS (Datagram Transport Layer Security).
- ***HTTPS:*** HTTPS (Hypertext Transfer Protocol Secure) ensures data encryption—secure communication between IoT devices and servers for web-based interactions.

By incorporating these measures, such as network design, device management, data transmission, and protocol security, you can establish a secure infrastructure in your classroom. These steps are essential for creating an environment where IoT devices can enhance education without compromising security.

11.3 Data Security and Privacy

Ensuring the security and privacy of data in an IoT-powered classroom is essential. Educational institutions are entrusted with sensitive information, and protecting this data from unauthorized access and breaches is crucial. This section will explore recommended strategies for safeguarding data in an IoT classroom.

Data Encryption Data encryption plays a crucial role in ensuring data security. It involves encoding data so that authorized individuals can decode and access it. When it comes to an IoT-based classroom, data encryption can be applied at various levels (IBM, 2024; Shahzad & Zia, 2022):

- ***End-to-end encryption:*** Encrypt data from the point of origin (IoT device) to its destination (server or storage) and vice versa. This prevents unauthorized access or eavesdropping during the transmission process.
- ***Encryption of Data at Rest:*** Implement encryption techniques for the data stored on IoT devices or servers. This ensures unauthorized individuals cannot access the stored data even if physical theft occurs.
- ***Key Management:*** Properly managing encryption keys is crucial to prevent unauthorized access. It is essential to employ practices for storage and regular rotation, which enhances the overall security of data encryption.

Implementing these measures can ensure that sensitive information remains protected and accessible by those authorized within an IoT-based classroom environment.

Compliance with Data Protection Regulations Educational establishments must often adhere to data protection laws, such as the Family Educational Rights and Privacy Act (FERPA) in the United States or the General Data Protection Regulation (GDPR) in the European Union. It is crucial to comply with these regulations to safeguard the privacy and security of student and faculty data. Here are some essential points to consider (Ashbel, 2020; New America, 2020):

- ***Understanding Regulations:*** Familiarize yourself with the data protection regulations that apply to your institution. Different regions and countries may have their own requirements.
- ***Data Classification:*** Classify data based on sensitivity and handle it accordingly. For instance, personal student information should be treated with higher security measures than public information.
- ***Consent and Transparency:*** When collecting data, obtain informed consent from individuals and maintain transparency about its usage. People should know what data is being collected and for what purposes.

User Data Privacy Best Practices Ensuring user data privacy in an IoT-based classroom is a legal requirement and a matter of trust and ethics. To achieve this, here are some recommended guidelines (Inbuilt Data, 2023; Hearon et al., 2021):

- ***Data Minimization:*** Collecting and retaining the data for educational purposes is essential. Avoid unnecessary data collection to minimize the risk of breaches.
- ***Anonymization:*** Anonymize the collected data to remove identifiable information whenever feasible. This practice ensures that even if someone gains access to the data, they cannot link it back to individuals.
- ***User Control:*** Grant users control over their data, allowing them to delete it or opt out of data collection whenever possible. By giving individuals control over their information, transparency, and trust are enhanced.
- ***Data Retention Policies:*** Implement policies that outline how long the collected data will be stored and when it will be securely deleted. Adhering to these policies helps reduce exposure to sensitive information.

By following these data security and privacy practices, educational institutions can establish a more responsible environment in IoT-based classrooms.

11.4 Physical Security Measures

Physical security safeguards devices and data in an IoT-based classroom. Focusing on securing the infrastructure is equally important as protecting information in the digital realm. In the following section, we will delve into measures that educational institutions can adopt to enhance the security of their IoT-based classrooms.

Device Physical Security Various physical security measures are implemented to ensure the safety of IoT devices and prevent theft, tampering, or unauthorized access. These devices encompass whiteboards, sensors, cameras, and other hardware (Rotenberg, 2023a; Elgan, 2024).

- ***Locked Cabinets:*** It is advisable to install locked cabinets or enclosures equipped with locks for IoT devices that contain data or configuration settings. This way, access can be restricted solely to authorized personnel.
- ***Cable Locks:*** Cable locks can secure devices at risk of theft. These locks can be fastened to fixed objects or structures to deter removal.
- ***Surveillance Cameras:*** Deploying classroom surveillance cameras prevents theft and unauthorized access. Additionally, these cameras can provide evidence in the event of security incidents.

Access Control Access control mechanisms are implemented to limit IoT device access, ensuring that only authorized individuals can interact with or manage these devices (Singh & Singh, 2023; Ragothaman et al., 2023)

- ***Electronic Key Cards:*** Utilize an electronic key card system to regulate access to the IoT classroom. These key cards can be deactivated as required.
- ***Biometric Access Control:*** Enhance security by implementing biometric authentication methods like fingerprint or retina scans. These methods are difficult to forge and bolster access control.
- ***Visitor Logs:*** Record visitors who enter the IoT classroom in a logbook. This log will document who entered and at what time.

Surveillance and Monitoring Surveillance and monitoring are vital in identifying and responding to security incidents or breaches in time (Neumetric, 2023).

- ***Security Cameras:*** To ensure the safety of the classroom, security cameras should be installed outside the premises. This will enable monitoring of activities and help identify any potential security threats.
- ***Intrusion Detection Systems (IDS):*** Implementing IDS can significantly enhance security by detecting unauthorized access or tampering with IoT devices. In some cases, immediate alerts can be sent to the security personnel.

- ***Motion Sensors:*** Motion sensors can detect movement within the classroom during operational hours. This proactive approach can trigger alarms or notifications if unauthorized individuals are present.

By incorporating these security measures, educational institutions can safeguard their IoT devices and infrastructure from physical threats and unauthorized access. Physical security must work hand in hand with digital security measures, creating a holistic approach to ensure a secure IoT-based classroom environment.

11.5 Authentication and Authorization

Authentication and authorization are vital in maintaining security within an IoT-powered classroom. These measures guarantee that authorized individuals can access and manage IoT devices, thus ensuring the integrity of the educational setting. This section will explore facets of authentication and authorization in an IoT classroom context.

User Authentication Methods User verification is vital in granting access to IoT infrastructure and devices. In educational settings, there are commonly used methods for authenticating users (Boehm, 2020; Mamdouh et al., 2021):

- ***Username and Password:*** This traditional approach requires individuals to enter a username and password to gain entry. Enforcing password policies, such as complexity and regular changes, is essential.
- ***Two-Factor Authentication (2FA):*** To add a layer of security, 2FA requires users to provide two authentication factors. These usually involve something they know (like a password) or possess (such as a one-time code sent to their device).
- ***Biometric Authentication:*** By utilizing data like fingerprints, facial recognition, or retinal scans, security is heightened as it becomes challenging for these features to be forged or replicated.

These various authentication methods enhance the security of user verification in educational environments.

Role-Based Access Control (RBAC) RBAC, which stands for Role-Based Access Control, is a method used to regulate and manage access to IoT devices based on the roles and responsibilities of users. Its primary goal is to ensure that each user is granted appropriate access and control over the devices they interact with. Here are the key roles within RBAC (Zhang, 2023; The ThingsBoard Authors, 2024):

- ***Administrator:*** Administrators hold the highest level of access and control. They are responsible for configuring, managing, and monitoring IoT devices and the underlying infrastructure.
- ***Teacher:*** Teachers can control classroom IoT devices and utilize various teaching tools. However, their privileges may not extend to administrative privileges.

- ***Student:*** Students possess access rights, typically allowing them to view content and interact with devices as authorized by their teacher.

By implementing RBAC, organizations can establish a system where users can only perform actions that align with their defined roles. This helps mitigate the risk of unauthorized access or unwanted changes to systems.

Single Sign-On (SSO) Solutions Single Sign (SSO) solutions simplify the user experience by allowing individuals to use one set of login credentials to access applications and devices. The key advantages of SSO are (OneLogin, 2024; Chakray, 2024):

- ***User Convenience:*** SSO eliminates the hassle of remembering usernames and passwords, making accessing the classroom easier for students and staff.
- ***Centralized Control:*** IT administrators can efficiently manage access and permissions from a centralized location, which enhances both security and ease of management.
- ***Enhanced Security:*** SSO solutions can incorporate multifactor authentication (MFA), providing an additional layer of protection.

Ensuring user authentication and strict control over access based on roles is crucial for maintaining an IoT-based classroom. These measures safeguard against access and potential security breaches.

11.6 Threats and Vulnerabilities

In a classroom that utilizes IoT technology, it is essential to recognize and address risks and weaknesses to ensure a safe environment. Educational institutions increasingly integrate IoT into their classrooms to improve learning, but this expansion also presents obstacles. This section aims to delve into the challenges and vulnerabilities found in IoT-based classrooms and effective strategies for managing and reducing them.

Common IoT-Related Threats Educational institutions that utilize IoT devices can encounter security concerns, which may include the following (Mykola & Anastasiia, 2021; Jennings, 2019):

- ***Unauthorized Access:*** Attackers may try to gain unauthorized access to IoT devices, systems, or data.
- ***Data Breaches:*** Vulnerabilities in IoT systems or devices can expose sensitive information like student and staff data.
- ***Denial of Service (DoS) Attacks:*** Attackers may overload the network with traffic, causing disruptions and rendering IoT devices inaccessible.
- ***Device Compromises:*** IoT devices are prone to compromise, allowing attackers to take control of their functionality.

- ***Physical Attacks:*** Security incidents involving breaches could result in the theft or tampering of IoT devices within educational settings.

Vulnerability Assessment Identifying and assessing security weaknesses in the IoT-based classroom is part of a vulnerability assessment. This process typically involves the following steps (Lal et al., 2023; Fernández-Caramés & Fraga-Lamas, 2020):

- ***Discovery:*** The first step is to identify all IoT devices, network configurations, and systems in the classroom.
- ***Assessment:*** Each device and system is thoroughly evaluated to identify known vulnerabilities, such as outdated software or weak configurations.
- ***Risk Ranking:*** Prioritizing the identified vulnerabilities based on their impact and likelihood.
- ***Remediation:*** Develop a comprehensive plan to address and mitigate vulnerabilities, including applying patches, adjusting configurations, or replacing devices.

These steps are essential for ensuring the security of the IoT-based classroom environment.

Threat Mitigation Strategies To safeguard IoT-based classrooms against threats and vulnerabilities, it is crucial to consider the following strategies (Guest, 2022; Altulaihan et al., 2022):

- ***Updates and Patch Management:*** It is essential to keep the firmware and software of IoT devices updated to address known vulnerabilities. Implementing a patch management strategy ensures timely updates.
- ***Network Segmentation:*** By dividing the network into segments, it becomes possible to isolate IoT devices from critical systems, thus minimizing potential attack surfaces.
- ***Intrusion Detection Systems (IDS):*** Implementing IDS allows monitoring network traffic, detecting potentially malicious activities, and responding to security incidents.
- ***Physical Security Measures:*** Security measures are essential in preventing access or tampering with IoT devices.
- ***User Training:*** Educating users, including students and staff, about security practices can significantly reduce the risk of being victims of social engineering attacks.
- ***Data Encryption:*** Encryption during transit and at rest is crucial to protecting data from eavesdropping and unauthorized access.
- ***Access Control:*** Implementing robust access control mechanisms such as role-based access control (RBAC) helps restrict who can interact with IoT devices and their actions.

By identifying vulnerabilities, addressing them promptly, and implementing these security measures, educational institutions can significantly minimize the risk of security incidents occurring in IoT-based classrooms. Regular monitoring and keeping up with updates are crucial for ensuring a secure environment and safeguarding information.

11.7 Secure IoT Protocols

Communication protocols are essential for safeguarding data in an IoT classroom that relies on technology. In an IoT-based environment, devices share information over networks. It is essential to safeguard these interactions from potential risks and unauthorized access. This section will delve into protocols and emphasize the significance of employing secure options.

Overview of IoT Protocols Devices utilize various communication protocols to exchange data and information. These protocols differ in efficiency, security, and suitability for use cases. Some employed IoT protocols include (Gerodimos et al., 2023; Sonee, 2020):

- ***MQTT (Message Queuing Telemetry Transport):*** This protocol is lightweight and efficient, making it ideal for high latency or unreliable networks. However, security considerations such as TLS/SSL encryption must be prioritized when using MQTT effectively.
- ***CoAP (Constrained Application Protocol):*** CoAP is designed to offer a solution to resource-constrained IoT devices. It relies on the Datagram Transport Layer Security (DTLS) protocol, a version of the Transport Layer Security (TLS) protocol, to ensure security.
- ***HTTP/HTTPS:*** The standard Hypertext Transfer Protocol (HTTP) is widely used for web-based communication. HTTPS (HTTP Secure) enhances security by incorporating SSL/TLS encryption.
- ***AMQP (Advanced Message Queuing Protocol):*** AMQP is a messaging protocol that proves helpful in systems where reliability and messaging play crucial roles. Ensuring authentication and data encryption are considerations when implementing AMQP securely.

Choosing Secure Protocols Choosing communication protocols for your IoT-based classroom is crucial when protecting data transmission and device interactions. Here are some essential factors to consider (AVSystem, 2020b; Gupta, 2023; Babun et al., 2021):

- ***Data Encryption:*** To keep your data secure, ensure that the protocol you select supports data encryption, such as TLS/SSL or DTLS.
- ***Authentication:*** Opt for protocols with authentication mechanisms. This will help verify the identities of both devices and users.
- ***Data Integrity:*** The chosen protocol should include mechanisms that ensure the integrity of your data. This way, you can be confident that the transmitted data has not been tampered with.

- ***Resource Constraints:*** Consider the limitations of your IoT devices regarding computing power and memory resources. Some lightweight protocols are specifically designed to work with these devices.
- ***Reliability and Message Queuing:*** Depending on your specific use case, you might need protocols that support reliable message delivery and queuing functions. This becomes particularly important in situations where any data loss is unacceptable.

Consider these factors when selecting communication protocols for an IoT environment in a classroom setting.

Protocols for Data Encryption Encryption plays a vital role in ensuring the security of communication. It offers protection against eavesdropping and unauthorized access to data. When deciding on a protocol for encrypting data, it is essential to consider the following options (Mrabet et al., 2020; Obaidat et al., 2020):

- ***TLS (Transport Layer Security):*** TLS is widely used to secure network communications. It provides encryption to ensure data integrity and authentication.
- ***DTLS (Datagram Transport Layer Security):*** DTLS is designed explicitly for datagram protocols like CoAP. It offers security features such as TLS. It is better suited for networks that may experience unreliability or packet loss.
- ***IPsec (Internet Protocol Security):*** IPsec encrypts data at the network layer and establishes end-to-end security. It is commonly employed when devices communicate over the Internet.

Choosing the suitable IoT protocol depends on your IoT-based classroom's unique requirements and limitations. Considering these protocol options and their respective security features, you can establish a communication framework that safeguards your data and devices from potential threats and vulnerabilities.

11.8 Implementing a Secure IoT-Based Classroom

Building a classroom that utilizes IoT technology necessitates preparation, thorough execution, and continual maintenance. This section will guide you through establishing a secure IoT-enabled classroom. By adhering to these recommendations (as shown in Fig. 11.2), you can guarantee the security and reliability of your educational setting.

Planning and Risk Assessment Planning and assessing risks is crucial to successfully implementing an IoT-based classroom. Here are the essential steps to consider during the planning and risk assessment phase (Kandasamy et al., 2020):

- ***Establish Goals:*** Clearly define the goals and objectives you aim to accomplish using IoT technology.

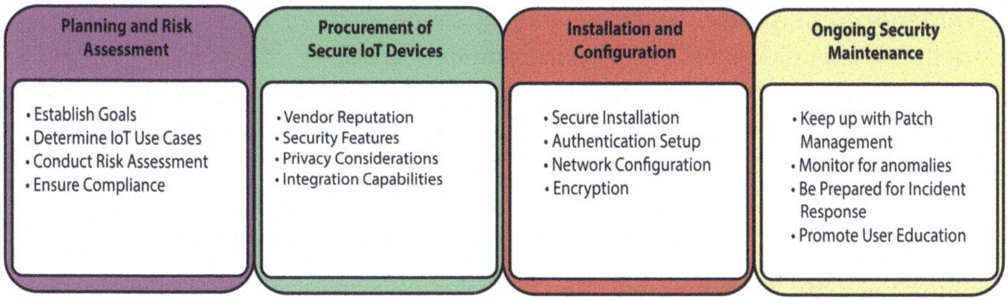

Fig. 11.2 Essentials for implementing a secure IoT-based classroom

- ***Determine IoT Use Cases:*** Identify and outline scenarios where IoT can be applied within the classroom. This will aid in selecting suitable devices and applications.
- ***Conduct Risk Assessment:*** Evaluate security threats and vulnerabilities associated with your IoT devices and infrastructure to understand the risks involved.
- ***Ensure Compliance:*** Familiarize yourself with your institution's data protection and privacy regulations and verify that your implementation meets these requirements.

These steps will prepare you to implement an IoT-based classroom and mitigate potential risks.

Procurement of Secure IoT Devices Ensuring the security of your classroom relies heavily on selecting secure IoT devices. When procuring IoT devices, it is essential to consider the following factors (Telecommunication Engineering Centre, 2023; Palo Alto Networks, 2024):

- ***Vendor Reputation:*** Choosing vendors with a track record of providing secure devices and ongoing support is recommended.
- ***Security Features:*** Evaluate the security features the devices offer, such as data encryption, authentication mechanisms, and firmware update capabilities.
- ***Privacy Considerations:*** Verify that the devices respect user privacy and adhere to data protection regulations. Take a look at privacy policies and terms of service.
- ***Integration Capabilities:*** Assess how well the devices seamlessly integrate with your network and existing systems.

Considering these factors, you can decide when selecting IoT devices for your classroom while prioritizing security.

Installation and Configuration Properly installing and setting up IoT devices is extremely important for ensuring security and functionality. Here are some steps you can follow (Connected Platforms, 2024; Ballejos, 2024):

- ***Secure Installation:*** Take measures to physically secure the devices so they are not easily accessible to individuals. This can include using locking cabinets or other physical security measures.

- ***Authentication Setup:*** Configure authentication methods for users and devices, such as login credentials or biometric authentication.
- ***Network Configuration:*** Ensure the devices are configured to connect securely to your network. Implement network segmentation, which separates IoT devices from sensitive systems.
- ***Encryption:*** Enable data encryption on the devices and their connected network. This will help protect data while it is being transmitted and at rest.

Ongoing Security Maintenance Ensuring the security of your IoT-enabled classroom is a vital task. Updating and adjusting your security measures to address emerging risks is essential. Here are some key steps to maintain security (A-Team Global, 2023; Yaacoub et al., 2023):

- ***Keep up with Patch Management:*** Check for firmware and software updates and have a strategy to apply patches promptly.
- ***Monitor for anomalies:*** Utilize intrusion detection systems (IDS) to monitor network traffic and detect any suspicious activity.
- ***Be Prepared for Incident Response:*** Develop a plan that outlines how to respond effectively to a security incident.
- ***Promote User Education:*** Regularly educate students, teachers, and staff about practices for security and privacy.

By following these steps, educational institutions can establish a secure IoT-based classroom that enriches the learning environment, protects data, and guards against potential security threats.

11.9 Case Studies and Best Practices

Gaining insights from real-life examples is a way to understand how IoT-based classrooms can be successfully implemented and the best practices that lead to effectiveness. This section will delve into case studies (see Table 11.1) of institutions that have embraced IoT technology and highlight the practices that can guide your IoT deployment.

Best Practices in IoT-Based Classrooms Based on the analysis of these real-world examples and their successful implementations, here are recommended guidelines for ensuring the security of IoT-based classrooms.

- ***Collaboration:*** Foster collaboration among educators, IT professionals, and administrators to design, implement, and manage the IoT environment effectively.
- ***Privacy as a Priority:*** Make privacy a fundamental aspect by default using technologies and practices that enhance data protection.
- ***User Education:*** Continuously educate students, teachers, and staff on security and privacy practices in IoT-enabled classrooms.

Table 11.1 Case studies on IoT implementations in education

Case study	Challenges	Solutions	Best practices
XYZ University's Smart Classroom	Elevating student engagement and enhancing learning outcomes. Safeguarding sensitive data belonging to students and faculty. Ensuring the seamless and reliable performance of IoT devices.	Leveraging smartboards and interactive displays to create a captivating learning environment. Implementing robust IoT protocols that encompass data encryption and access control measures. Conducting security audits and vulnerability assessments for protection.	Consistently update and patch devices to address any security vulnerabilities. Safeguarding access to IoT devices through locked cabinets and controlled entry methods. Equipping teachers and students with proper training on the secure utilization of IoT devices and systems.
Smart School District's Remote Learning Initiative	They aimed to enable learning for students located in various areas. Ensuring data privacy and security for students and teachers is a high priority. Ensuring network connectivity for IoT devices used in remote learning.	To address these challenges, they can implement learning platforms based on IoT technology focusing on secure communication. They can utilize cloud-based systems with data encryption measures in place. Additionally, they can provide support for connectivity to students residing in underserved areas.	Updates and patches can be applied to remote learning platforms and IoT devices. Secure video conferencing platforms with end-to-end encryption will be employed for meetings. Network performance will be constantly monitored, ensuring the resolution of any connectivity issues.

- ***Regular Security Audits:*** Conduct assessments to identify and address vulnerabilities and ensure robust security measures.
- ***Incident Response Plan:*** Develop a plan to respond effectively to any security incidents that may arise.
- ***Compliance with Regulations:*** Ensure adherence to data protection regulations and privacy laws in all aspects of classroom IoT implementation.
- ***Vendor Selection Criteria:*** Prioritize vendors with a proven track record of security measures when procuring devices.
- ***Data Encryption:*** Implement end-to-end encryption protocols to safeguard data during transmission and storage.

By embracing these best practices from case studies, educational institutions can confidently establish secure IoT-based classrooms that enhance learning experiences and prioritize protecting sensitive information.

11.10 Future Trends and Challenges in IoT-Based Education

As technology keeps advancing, the field of education also progresses. Classrooms equipped with IoT technology are expected to impact shaping the future of education. However, along with these advancements, new challenges and opportunities arise. This section will delve into future trends and potential challenges in IoT-based classrooms.

Trends in IoT-Based Education

- ***Personalized Learning:*** Internet of Things (IoT) devices and systems have the potential to gather data on students' performance, enabling adaptable learning experiences. AI-powered platforms can analyze this data to offer customized content and support.
- ***Virtual and Augmented Reality:*** By integrating IoT with reality technologies, we can create immersive learning environments that allow students to delve into subjects in 3D and interact with virtual objects.
- ***IoT in STEM Education:*** Classrooms equipped with IoT technology provide an ideal setting for Science, Technology, Engineering, and Mathematics (STEM) education. Students can utilize sensors, robotics, and data analytics to develop STEM skills.
- ***IoT and Remote Learning:*** As remote and hybrid learning models evolve, IoT technology will facilitate remote learning. It ensures connectivity while providing students with experiences.

Challenges in IoT-Based Education

- ***Security and Privacy:*** The rise of IoT devices in various educational settings poses a significant challenge in safeguarding the privacy and security of student and faculty information.
- ***Data Management:*** The abundance of data generated by IoT devices presents a significant task for managing and analyzing it for valuable educational insights.
- ***Infrastructure Scalability:*** Educational institutions must ensure that their network infrastructure can efficiently handle the growing number of IoT devices without compromising performance or security.
- ***Cost and Budgeting:*** Implementing and maintaining technology can incur huge expenses. Educational institutions must allocate funds for device acquisition and ongoing security and maintenance costs.

Best Practices for the Future To tackle the obstacles and leverage the trends in education powered by the Internet of Things (IoT), educational institutions can adopt the following recommended approaches.

- ***Data Management:*** Develop robust policies and strategies to handle the increasing amount of data IoT devices generate.
- ***Continuous Security Monitoring:*** Establish security monitoring and threat detection systems to safeguard IoT environments.
- ***Data Privacy Considerations:*** Prioritize data privacy by complying with data protection regulations, adhering to practices, and integrating privacy as an aspect of IoT system design.
- ***Adaptive Learning Models:*** Embrace learning models that utilize IoT device data to offer personalized educational experiences.
- ***Sustainability Focus:*** Consider the environmental impact of IoT devices and strive for sustainable and energy-efficient solutions.
- ***Professional Growth Opportunities:*** Provide development opportunities for educators to effectively integrate IoT technology into their teaching methods.

The future of education driven by IoT holds potential, offering improved learning experiences and tailored education. Educational institutions can successfully navigate this exciting landscape by addressing challenges and adopting these practices.

11.11 Conclusion

As educational institutions continue to embrace Internet of Things (IoT) technology to enrich learning experiences, securing and maintaining the integrity of these equipped classrooms is crucial. This section thoroughly explores the elements of establishing IoT-based classrooms, including protocols, recommended practices, real-life examples, and future directions. By preferring secure communication protocols, like MQTT, CoAP, and HTTPS, those involved in education can ensure the safety of data transmission and device interactions. The significance of data encryption, authentication processes, data integrity assurance, and dealing with resource limitations has been highlighted to guide protocol selection. Moreover, a detailed framework has been outlined for strategizing, evaluating risks, acquiring devices, setting up installations, configuring systems, and supporting setups in educational environments. Practical cases have showcased implementations that offer lessons on collaboration strategies, privacy protection measures, security evaluations, and adherence to regulations. Looking forward to IoT-driven education presents possibilities, including personalized learning experiences, virtual reality applications, STEM integration opportunities, and enhanced remote learning capabilities expected to revolutionize the education sector. Security issues, complexities in managing data scalability, and financial constraints must be tackled. To tackle these obstacles and make the most of their chances, educational institutions are advised to follow robust data handling approaches, ongoing security checks, privacy-focused design principles, adaptable learning models, sustainability efforts, and professional growth opportunities for teachers. In summary, this chapter acts as a manual for educational stakeholders aiming to introduce creative IoT-equipped classrooms. By adopting the principles discussed here, educational institutions can establish settings that enhance learning journeys, emphasize data protection, and equip students for the digital era.

References

Altulaihan, E., Almaiah, M. A., & Aljughaiman, A. (2022). Cybersecurity threats, countermeasures and mitigation techniques on the IoT: Future research directions. *Electronics, 11*(3330), 1–41.

Ashbel, A. (2020). *A beginner's guide to data privacy laws and compliance in the education industry*. NetApp, Inc. https://bluexp.netapp.com/blog/ccs-blg-data-privacy-laws-and-compliance-in-the-education-industry

A-Team Global. (2023). *Main IoT Security Issues and Solutions*. A-Team Global. https://a-team.global/blog/main-iot-security-issues-and-solutions/

AVSystem. (2020a). *IoT device management: definition and fundamentals*. AVSystem. https://www.avsystem.com/blog/iot/iot-device-management/

AVSystem. (2020b). *IoT standards and protocols guide — Protocols of the Internet of Things*. AVSystem. https://www.avsystem.com/blog/iot/iot-protocols-and-standards/

Babun, L., Denney, K., Celik, Z. B., Mcdaniel, P., & Uluagac, A. S. (2021). A survey on IoT platforms: Communication, security, and privacy perspectives. *Computer Networks, 192*(11), 1–52.

Balbix, I. (2024). *IoT security challenges and problems*. Balbix Inc. https://www.balbix.com/insights/addressing-iot-security-challenges/

Ballejos, L. (2024). *How to secure IoT devices: 5 best practices*. NinjaOne. https://www.ninjaone.com/blog/how-to-secure-iot-devices-5-best-practices/

Boehm, E. (2020). *The top IoT authentication methods and options*. Keyfactor. https://www.keyfactor.com/blog/the-top-iot-authentication-methods-and-options/

Chakray. (2024). *What is Single Sign On (SSO)? Definition, characteristics and advantages*. Chakray. https://www.chakray.com/what-is-single-sign-on-sso-definition-characteristics-and-advantages/

Chalishazar, T. (2023). *11 biggest security challenges & solutions for IoT*. Peerbits. https://www.peerbits.com/blog/biggest-iot-security-challenges.html

Connected Platforms. (2024). *Securing IoT devices – 7 important steps*. Connected Platforms. https://connectedplatforms.com.au/securing-your-iot-devices/

Elgan, M. (2024). *Physical IoT Security: How to secure the physical layer in IoT*. Verizon. https://www.verizon.com/business/resources/articles/s/how-to-secure-the-physical-layer-in-iot/

Elrawy, M. F., Awad, A. I., & Hamed, H. F. A. (2018). Intrusion detection systems for IoT-based smart environments: A survey. *Journal of Cloud Computing: Advances, Systems and Applications, 7*(21), 1–20.

Fernández-Caramés, T. M., & Fraga-Lamas, P. (2020). Teaching and learning IoT cybersecurity and vulnerability assessment with Shodan through practical use cases. *Sensors, 20*(3048), 1–25. https://doi.org/10.3390/s20113048

Gerodimos, A., Maglaras, L., Amine, M., Ayres, N., & Kantzavelou, I. (2023). IoT: Communication protocols and security threats. *Internet of Things and Cyber-Physical Systems, 3*(January), 1–13. https://doi.org/10.1016/j.iotcps.2022.12.003

Global Cybersecurity Association. (2023). *How does cybersecurity work on IoT devices?* LinkedIn. https://www.linkedin.com/pulse/how-does-cybersecurity-work-iot-devices/

Guest, T. (2022). *Top IoT security risks and vulnerabilities and how to mitigate them*. BeyondTrust. https://www.beyondtrust.com/blog/entry/top-iot-security-vulnerabilities

Gupta, M. (2023). *IoT protocols: A comprehensive guide to communication protocols in IoT*. Zenatix Solutions. https://www.zenatix.com/iot-protocols-a-comprehensive-guide-to-communication-protocols-in-iot/

Gyamfi, E., & Jurcut, A. (2022). Intrusion detection in Internet of Things systems: A review on design approaches leveraging multi-access edge computing, machine learning, and dtasets. *Sensors, 22*(3744), 1–33.

Hearon, K. O., Mckee, M., Hossain, N., & Canbaz, M. A. (2021). *IoT privacy and security in teaching institutions: Inside the classroom and beyond*. American Association of Engineering Education. July, 1–8.

Hope, E. (2023). *Internet of Things security challenges and solutions*. LinkedIn. https://www.linkedin.com/pulse/internet-things-security-challenges-solutions-hope-edet-stm1f/

IBM. (2024). *What is encryption?* IBM. https://www.ibm.com/topics/encryption

Inbuilt Data. (2023). *Data ethics in the digital age: Navigating the ethical waters of data in business | data ethics vs. business ethics*. LinkedIn. https://www.linkedin.com/pulse/data-ethics-digital-age-navigating-ethical-waters-business/

Intuz. (2023). *IoT device management: Importance, challenges, solutions*. Intuz. https://www.intuz.com/guide-on-iot-device-management

Jennings, J. (2019). *How to minimize IoT risks on education networks*. Edscoop. https://edscoop.com/how-to-minimize-iot-risks-on-education-networks/

Kandasamy, K., Srinivas, S., Achuthan, K., & Rangan, V. P. (2020). IoT cyber risk: A holistic analysis of cyber risk assessment frameworks, risk vectors, and risk ranking process. *EURASIP Journal on Information Security, 2020*(8), 1–18.

Lal, B., Ravichandran, S., Kavin, R., Kumar, N. A., Bordoloi, D., & Kumar, R. G. (2023). IOT-based cyber security identification model through machine learning technique. *Measurement: Sensors, 27*(May), 100791. https://doi.org/10.1016/j.measen.2023.100791

Mamdouh, M., Awad, A. I., Khalaf, A. A. M., & Hamed, H. F. A. (2021). Authentication and identity management of IoHT devices: Achievements, challenges, and future directions. *Computers & Security, 111*, 1–24. https://doi.org/10.1016/j.cose.2021.102491

Mrabet, H., Belguith, S., Alhomoud, A., & Jemai, A. (2020). A survey of IoT security based on a layered. *Sensors, 20*(3625), 1–19. https://doi.org/10.3390/s20133625

Mykola, & Anastasiia. (2021). *Internet of Things in education industry: Applications, benefits & challenges*. Aimprosoft. https://www.aimprosoft.com/blog/internet-of-things-iot-in-education/

Neumetric. (2023). *Digital security monitoring: Enhancing cybersecurity through comprehensive surveillance*. Neumetric. https://www.neumetric.com/digital-security-monitoring/

New America. (2020). *Privacy considerations in higher education online learning: Applicable laws*. New America. https://www.newamerica.org/oti/reports/privacy-considerations-higher-education-online-learning/applicable-laws/

Obaidat, M. A., Obeidat, S., Holst, J., Al Hayajneh, A., & Brown, J. (2020). A comprehensive and systematic survey on the Internet of Things: Security and privacy challenges, security frameworks, enabling technologies, threats, vulnerabilities and countermeasures. *Computers, 9*(44), 1–43.

OneLogin. (2024). *How does single sign-on work?* OneLogin. https://www.onelogin.com/learn/how-single-sign-on-works

Palo Alto Networks. (2024). *How to secure IoT devices in the enterprise*. Palo Alto Networks. https://www.paloaltonetworks.com/cyberpedia/how-to-secure-iot-devices-in-the-enterprise

Ragothaman, K., Wang, Y., Rimal, B., & Lawrence, M. (2023). Access control for IoT: A survey of existing research, dynamic policies and future directions. *Sensors, 23*(1805), 1–24.

RainbowSecure. (2023). *Striking a balance between security risks and benefits of IoT devices*. LinkedIn. https://www.linkedin.com/pulse/striking-balance-between-security-risks-benefits-iot-devices/

Rotenberg, D. (2023a). *Physical security of IoT devices*. LinkedIn. https://www.linkedin.com/pulse/physical-security-iot-devices-david-rotenberg/

Rotenberg, D. (2023b). *Safeguarding IoT: The crucial need to encrypt data at rest and in transit.* LinkedIn. https://www.linkedin.com/pulse/safeguarding-iot-crucial-need-encrypt-data-rest-david-rotenberg/

Shahzad, K., & Zia, T. (2022). A review of functional encryption in IoT applications. *Sensors, 22*(7567), 1–50.

Singh, I., & Singh, B. (2023, December). Access management of IoT devices using access control mechanism and decentralized authentication: A review. *Measurement: Sensors, 25*, 1–8. https://doi.org/10.1016/j.measen.2022.100591

Sonee, S. (2020). *Top IoT communication protocols*. HashStudioz Technologies. https://hashstudioz.com/blog/top-iot-communication-protocols/

Takyar, A. (2024). *What is IOT device management and how it works?* LeewayHertz. https://www.leewayhertz.com/iot-device-management/

Tawalbeh, L., Muheidat, F., Tawalbeh, M., & Quwaider, M. (2020). IoT privacy and security: Challenges and solutions. *Applied Sciences — Open Access Journal, 10*(4102), 1–17.

Telecommunication Engineering Centre. (2023). *Security by design for IoT device manufacturers.*

The ThingsBoard Authors. (2024). *Advanced Role-Based Access Control (RBAC) for IoT devices and applications*. ThingsBoard. https://thingsboard.io/docs/pe/user-guide/rbac/

TrendMicroIncorporated.(2021).*IoTsecurityissues,threats,anddefenses*.TrendMicroIncorporated. https://www.trendmicro.com/vinfo/us/security/news/internet-of-things/iot-security-101-threats-issues-and-defenses

Williams, P., Kaylan, I., Daoud, H., & Bayoumi, M. (2022). A survey on security in Internet of Things with a focus on the impact of emerging technologies. *Internet of Things, 19*, 100564. https://doi.org/10.1016/j.iot.2022.100564

Yaacoub, J. A., Noura, H. N., Salman, O., & Chehab, A. (2023). Ethical hacking for IoT: Security issues, challenges, solutions and recommendations. *Internet of Things and Cyber-Physical Systems, 3*(December 2022), 280–308. https://doi.org/10.1016/j.iotcps.2023.04.002

Yousefnezhad, N., Malhi, A., & Främling, K. (2020). Security in product lifecycle of IoT devices: A survey. *Journal of Network and Computer Applications, 171*(August), 102779. https://doi.org/10.1016/j.jnca.2020.102779

Zhang, E. (2023). *What is Role-Based Access Control (RBAC)? Examples, benefits, and more*. Fortra. https://www.digitalguardian.com/blog/what-role-based-access-control-rbac-examples-benefits-and-more

Chapter 12
Critical Thinking Using IoT for Learning

Abstract Incorporating the Internet of Things (IoT) in educational environments offers a transformative opportunity to improve students' critical thinking skills. This chapter delves into how IoT technology aids in problem-solving, decision-making, collaborative learning, and data analysis within education. By utilizing real-time data and interactive scenarios, students are actively involved in hands-on exploration, addressing issues such as managing energy usage in buildings and optimizing city traffic flow. Simulated decision-making settings and industry-related challenges enhance students' decision-making ability, while discussions on ethical considerations enrich their problem-solving methods. Collaborative IoT projects promote critical thinking through project-based learning, interdisciplinary cooperation, and teamwork. Furthermore, collaborative teamwork is fostered through data sharing and participation in open-source initiatives that encourage a culture of continuous learning and critical thinking. The chapter underscores the significance of data analysis and visualization in offering real-time feedback, customizing learning paths, and facilitating hypothesis testing to connect theoretical knowledge with practical implementation. Looking forward, it explores advantages like improved learning and global collaboration networks alongside obstacles such as ethical dilemmas and technological gaps. Teachers, decision-makers, and involved parties are urged to focus on professional growth, ethical standards, teamwork, technological support, and research to maximize the advantages of IoT technology in enhancing critical thinking abilities in education.

Keywords Internet of Things (IoT) · Critical thinking skills · Problem-solving · Collaborative learning · Data analysis · Hands-on exploration · Project-based learning

M. Kurni, Srinivasa K. G., *The Internet of Educational Things*,
https://doi.org/10.1007/978-3-031-67387-0_12

12.1 Introduction

The field of education is currently experiencing a transformation due to technological advancements. In this fast-paced era, educators face the challenge of providing students with knowledge and information and equipping them with the skills to navigate a complex and interconnected world. Against this backdrop, incorporating the Internet of Things (IoT) into educational practices emerges as a tool that can revolutionize students' development of critical thinking abilities.

Traditional education models often prioritize memorization rather than fostering critical thinking skills. As we find ourselves at the intersection of pedagogy and technology, there is an increasing recognition that nurturing critical thinking is crucial for producing graduates who can adapt, innovate, and make meaningful contributions to society.

12.2 Understanding Critical Thinking

Critical thinking goes beyond being a skill; it is a way of thinking that encourages individuals to question assumptions, analyze information, and make informed decisions. Critical thinking is crucial for success in today's world of information overload and rapid technological advancements. It helps students distinguish between reliable information and misinformation, fosters creativity, and gives them the confidence to tackle complex problems.

Enhancing critical thinking in education is about achieving academic success and preparing students for a future where adaptability and problem-solving skills are essential. As we witness the Fourth Industrial Revolution unfold with automation, artificial intelligence, and the Internet of Things (IoT), the ability to think critically becomes an advantage.

What Do You Mean by Critical Thinking? Critical thinking is a cognitive process encompassing, assessing, and integrating information, ideas, and arguments to make logical decisions or judgments. It is an ability that allows individuals to delve deeper into understanding by analyzing concepts, issues, or situations beyond the surface level (Criticalthinking.org, 2019; University of Louisville, 2024; Monash University, 2024).

Here are some key aspects of critical thinking (Kharbach, 2023; Bednarz, 2013; University of Tennessee at Chattanooga, 2024):

- ***Analysis:*** Critical thinkers break down complex information or problems into more manageable components. They carefully examine a subject's elements, relationships, and underlying assumptions to gain a thorough understanding.
- ***Evaluation:*** This involves appraising the quality, relevance, and credibility of information, arguments, or claims. Critical thinkers consider the reliability of

evidence sources and potential biases to determine the trustworthiness and validity of the information they encounter.
- ***Synthesis:*** After analyzing and evaluating information thoroughly, critical thinkers synthesize their findings to generate insights or ideas. They establish connections between pieces of information to form a well-structured perspective.
- ***Problem Solving:*** Critical thinking is closely intertwined with problem-solving. It entails identifying issues or challenges, brainstorming solutions, and selecting an effective course of action based on rationality and informed assessment.
- ***Decision Making:*** Critical thinkers base their decisions on gathered and evaluated information. They prioritize making decisions based on reasoning rather than intuition or emotional reactions.
- ***Effective communication:*** Effective communication is also an essential aspect of critical thinking that involves expressing thoughts and conclusions clearly and persuasively. It entails engaging in constructive dialogue and debate.

Critical thinking is a skill that can be applied in areas of life such as academics, professional endeavors, personal decision-making, and everyday problem-solving. It encourages individuals to question assumptions, consider perspectives, and reach grounded conclusions. Education institutions and workplaces highly value this skill as it enables individuals to adapt to challenges, innovate, and make choices.

Definition and Importance of Critical Thinking Critical thinking is a cognitive process that involves examining, interpreting, and assessing information and arguments. It goes beyond acquiring knowledge; it entails engaging with information, questioning assumptions, and developing the ability to draw well-reasoned conclusions. Critical thinking is a skill that empowers individuals to delve deeper and think systematically about the world around them (Criticalthinking.org, 2019).

Critical thinking is often regarded as the hallmark of a well-rounded education, but it is more than just acquiring facts and concepts. Through critical thinking, students can transform information into meaningful knowledge. This skill can be applied across disciplines, allowing individuals to approach problems analytically. Critical thinking is a foundation for effective learning and problem-solving in education, fostering intellectual curiosity.

The Role of Critical Thinking in Education Critical thinking in education is critical as it empowers individuals to analyze, evaluate, and synthesize information effectively. Some key aspects (shown in Fig. 12.1) that highlight the significance of critical thinking in education are (Pires, 2023; Eribo & Kano, 2019; Jace, 2023).

- ***Problem Solving:*** Critical thinking equips individuals with the skills to identify, analyze, and solve problems. It involves breaking down complex issues into manageable parts, considering different perspectives, and developing creative solutions.
- ***Decision Making:*** Education aims to prepare individuals to make well-informed decisions. Critical thinking nurtures the ability to assess options, weigh evidence, and make judgments based on reasoning.

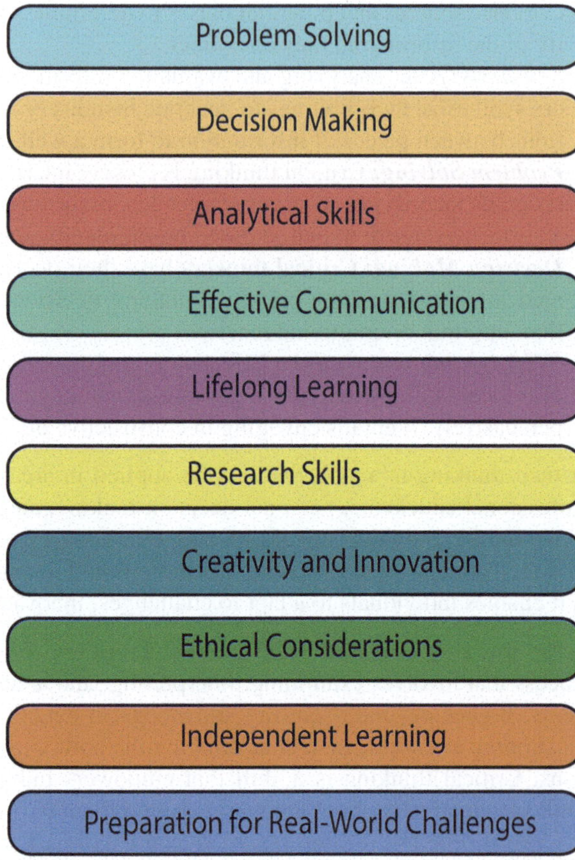

Fig. 12.1 The role of critical thinking in education

- ***Analytical Skills:*** Critical thinking enhances analytical abilities by allowing individuals to examine information objectively, identify patterns, and draw meaningful conclusions. It involves questioning assumptions and recognizing biases to arrive at accurate interpretations.
- ***Effective Communication:*** Education goes beyond acquiring knowledge and focuses on effectively conveying ideas. Critical thinking helps individuals express their thoughts clearly, express their opinions, and engage in constructive dialogue by considering diverse viewpoints.
- ***Lifelong Learning:*** Adaptability and continuous learning are crucial skills in an evolving world. Developing critical thinking skills cultivates a continuous learning mindset, motivating individuals to actively seek new knowledge, assess its relevance, and integrate it into their existing understanding.
- ***Research Skills:*** Critical thinking is closely intertwined with research skills. It involves gathering information, evaluating sources' credibility, and synthesizing data to construct coherent arguments or draw well-founded conclusions.

- ***Creativity and Innovation:*** Education should foster creativity and innovation. Critical thinking encourages individuals to think beyond norms, question ideas, and develop inventive solutions to address emerging challenges.
- ***Ethical Considerations:*** Critical thinking encompasses reasoning. It prompts individuals to assess the implications of decisions, actions, or viewpoints, fostering a sense of responsibility and ethical awareness.
- ***Independent Learning:*** Critical thinking promotes autonomous learning. It empowers individuals to take charge of their education, engage in self-directed learning endeavors, and explore subjects autonomously.
- ***Preparation for Real-World Challenges:*** Critical thinking skills are vital for navigating real-world complexities and uncertainties. An education that prioritizes critical thinking equips individuals with the tools to confront various aspects of life confidently.

Challenges in Developing Critical Thinking Skills Developing the ability to think critically can encounter obstacles within educational systems and broader societal contexts. Here are some common challenges associated with nurturing critical thinking skills (OpenLearn, 2024; Reddy & Nehru, 2021):

- ***Conventional Educational Approaches:*** Traditional educational methods often prioritize memorization and standardized testing over cultivating critical thinking. The focus on correct answers rather than the critical thinking process can impede the development of these skills.
- ***Class Sizes:*** In classrooms with several students per teacher, it becomes difficult for educators to provide personalized attention and feedback, which is crucial for fostering critical thinking skills. Interactive discussions and tailored guidance are often limited in large class settings.
- ***Assessment Methods:*** Assessments relying heavily on multiple-choice questions or memorization may not effectively gauge one's critical thinking abilities. The discrepancy between assessment methods and desired learning outcomes can hinder the promotion of these skills.
- ***Teacher Training:*** Some educators may lack training in incorporating instructional strategies that foster critical thinking into their teaching practices. Development opportunities focused on enhancing instruction in critical thinking may be limited.
- ***Contextual Variations:*** Different cultures may approach critical thinking from diverse perspectives. Educational systems may need to adjust their strategies to align with cultural norms as educators navigate the perspectives on critical thinking found in multicultural classrooms.
- ***Technology Dependency:*** One aspect to consider is reliance on technology. While technology can enhance learning experiences, providing guidance and avoiding becoming overly dependent on resources is essential. Over-reliance on access to information might discourage analytical skills and thorough exploration of subjects.

- ***Time Constraints:*** Time constraints also pose a challenge. The pressure to cover a curriculum within a timeframe can restrict opportunities for extended discussions, projects, and activities that foster critical thinking. Teachers sometimes feel compelled to prioritize content coverage over skill development.
- ***Resistance to Change:*** Resistance to change is another obstacle in implementing approaches that prioritize critical thinking. Institutional resistance and traditional mindsets among stakeholders such as administrators, parents, and policymakers may hinder the adoption of new methods that prioritize critical thinking.
- ***Student Motivation & Engagement:*** Students' motivation and engagement play a vital role in developing critical thinking skills; if students lack interest in the subject matter or fail to see its real-world relevance, their enthusiasm for inquiry may dwindle.
- ***Lack of Interdisciplinary Integration:*** Interdisciplinary integration can significantly benefit the development of critical thinking skills by incorporating perspectives from various fields of study. However, how education is organized, with its separation of subjects and lack of encouragement for exploration, can hinder the holistic development of critical thinking skills.

A collaborative approach involving teachers, school administrators, policymakers, and the wider community is crucial to tackle these obstacles. Implementing changes in curriculum design, enhancing teacher training programs, and adopting assessment methods that foster critical thinking are all steps in overcoming these challenges. Additionally, creating a culture that values critical thinking contributes to nurturing the necessary skills for lifelong learning.

12.3 Enhancing Critical Thinking with IoT

In the evolving world of education, the Internet of Things (IoT) brings about a shift, unveiling a transformative narrative focused on enhancing critical thinking abilities. This section takes us on a journey to explore the impact of combining IoT with education beyond conventional learning methods. The narrative explores how IoT enhances critical thinking through interactive learning platforms, wearable technologies, and smart simulations that actively engage students in real time.

The Significance of IoT in Enhancing Critical Thinking in Education The Internet of Things (IoT) can significantly enhance critical thinking skills in education. Here is how IoT contributes to developing critical thinking (ANTT Robotics Ltd, 2023). Figure 12.2 highlights how IoT boosts critical thinking in education, underscoring its importance in fostering students' problem-solving abilities.

- ***Real-world Application:*** In education, IoT is often used to connect classroom learning and real-life situations by incorporating IoT-enabled experiments and projects. This allows students to apply critical thinking skills to analyze, interpret, and draw conclusions from data.

Fig. 12.2 The significance of IoT in enhancing critical thinking in education

- ***Hands-on Learning Opportunities:*** IoT enables students to engage with physical devices, sensors, and actuators, providing experiential learning experiences. This hands-on approach encourages curiosity, investigation, and reflection on the outcomes of their interactions.
- ***Problem-Solving Complexity:*** IoT projects often present problems requiring critical thinking. Designing, implementing, and troubleshooting IoT systems involves analyzing various factors, considering alternatives, and making decisions—all essential skills for effective problem-solving and critical inquiry.
- ***Integration Across Disciplines:*** IoT projects typically involve knowledge from multiple disciplines, such as science, technology, engineering, and mathematics (STEM). The interdisciplinary nature of the Internet of Things (IoT) fosters critical thinking skills across domains, promoting an integrated problem-solving approach.
- ***Data Analysis and Interpretation:*** IoT generates vast amounts of data, allowing students to analyze it. Critical thinking comes into play as students assess the data quality, identify patterns, and draw conclusions. Interpreting data from IoT enhances their reasoning abilities.

- ***Collaboration and Communication Skills:*** Working on IoT projects often involves collaboration among students, encouraging communication, idea sharing, and collective problem-solving. Collaborating in an IoT context requires critical thinking to evaluate different perspectives and make informed decisions.
- ***Decision-Making Scenarios:*** IoT systems require real-time data-based decision-making. IoT project students must choose system configurations, interpret data, and resolve problems. This decision-making process nurtures critical thinking skills and the ability to weigh options.
- ***Inquiry-Based Learning:*** The nature of IoT lends itself well to inquiry-based learning approaches. Students can ask questions, design experiments, collect data, and draw conclusions—activities that align with the principles of critical thinking. Engaging in inquiry-based learning with IoT encourages curiosity and a deeper quest for understanding.
- ***Adaptability and Flexibility:*** When it comes to IoT systems, there is often a need to adapt to changing conditions and unexpected challenges. Students who engage in IoT projects learn the importance of adaptability and flexibility in their thinking. They become skilled at adjusting their strategies based on feedback and evolving situations, an aspect of critical thinking.
- ***Preparation for Future Technologies:*** With IoT playing a vital role in shaping industries, exposing students to IoT applications in education prepares them for the technology-driven future. Developing critical thinking skills within an IoT context equips students with the ability to navigate and contribute meaningfully to a rapidly evolving technological landscape.

IoT Tools and Technologies for Critical Thinking Several tools and technologies in the realm of IoT can be utilized to enhance critical thinking skills in education (see Table 12.1). These tools use the Internet of Things to create captivating learning experiences (ANTT Robotics Ltd, 2023). Here are a few examples;

Integrating tools and technologies into educational environments stimulates students to think critically when designing, implementing, and reflecting on IoT projects. This approach allows for hands-on learning experiences that extend beyond concepts, facilitating a more profound comprehension of critical thinking principles within a technological framework.

Case Studies of Successful IoT Implementations for Critical Thinking While there have not been specific case studies focused solely on integrating IoT into education for critical thinking, there have been instances where IoT implementations have successfully contributed to improving critical thinking skills. These examples (see Table 12.2) often involve experiential learning, problem-solving, and interdisciplinary approaches. Here are a couple of illustrations.

Although these examples do not explicitly highlight the impact on critical thinking skills, they underscore the potential of implementing IoT technologies to provide students with hands-on experiences that necessitate analytical thinking, problem-solving abilities, and effective decision-making. As incorporating IoT into education continues to evolve, focused case studies that emphasize developing critical thinking skills among students may arise.

Table 12.1 IoT tools and technologies for enhancing critical thinking

S. no.	Tools and technologies	Description	Application in critical thinking
1	Raspberry Pi and Arduino	Raspberry Pi and Arduino are known single-board computers and microcontrollers that can be utilized for building IoT projects.	Students can design and implement IoT projects using these platforms, encouraging critical thinking in problem-solving, programming, and hardware integration.
2	Micro: bit	MicroBit is a small programmable microcontroller specifically designed for educational purposes.	Through MicroBit, students can undertake IoT projects that promote critical thinking as they design, code, and troubleshoot their interactive devices.
3	IoT Development Kits	Various IoT development kits are available, such as the Intel IoT Developer Kit or the Microsoft Azure IoT DevKit.	These kits offer comprehensive tools for constructing IoT applications. Students can explore functionalities and experiment with sensors, developing critical thinking skills through hands-on projects.
4	Node-RED	Node-RED is a tool that lets you visually connect devices, APIs, and online services through programming.	Students can utilize Node-RED to build flow-based IoT applications, which allows them to think critically about how different components connect and interact.
5	ThingSpeak	ThingSpeak is a platform designed for the Internet of Things (IoT) that enables users to gather, analyze, and visualize data from their devices.	Students can leverage ThingSpeak to plan experiments, collect data, and analyze results. This fosters critical thinking skills by encouraging them to interpret data and draw meaningful conclusions.
6	Blockly for IoT	Blockly is a visual programming language that empowers users to create code by arranging visual blocks.	Blockly for IoT empowers students to develop code for their projects using a visual interface. This encourages critical thinking by promoting problem-solving abilities and algorithmic logic.
7	OpenHAB	OpenHAB is an open-source home automation platform created for home applications.	Students can utilize OpenHAB to develop home automation projects, encouraging critical thinking as they strategize, implement, and troubleshoot smart home solutions based on the Internet of Things (IoT).
8	LabVIEW	LabVIEW serves as a programming platform for system design and development.	Students can leverage LabVIEW to create data acquisition, analysis, and visualization applications. This enables them to enhance their critical thinking skills in design and instrumentation.

(continued)

Table 12.1 (continued)

S. no.	Tools and technologies	Description	Application in critical thinking
9	Smart Sensors and Actuators	Many sensors and actuators are available, including temperature, motion, and servo motors.	By incorporating these sensors into their projects, students are prompted to think when selecting appropriate sensors that interpret sensor data accurately and design responsive actions.
10	Cloud Platforms (e.g., AWS IoT, Azure IoT)	Cloud platforms such as AWS IoT and Azure IoT offer secure application infrastructure.	Students can explore these cloud platforms to gain insights into data storage mechanisms, security considerations, and scalability. This exploration helps them develop critical thinking abilities within the context of designing IoT system architectures.

12.4 Promoting Problem-Solving and Decision-Making

This section delves into the role of the Internet of Things (IoT) in developing problem-solving and decision-making skills in educational settings. The IoT brings dynamism to the learning environment by providing students with real-time data and interactive scenarios. This allows them to tackle issues such as managing smart building energy usage or optimizing traffic flow in smart cities. Through hands-on exploration facilitated by interactive devices and simulations, students engage with complex problems and immerse themselves in practical contexts that require critical thinking. The iterative process of collecting data through IoT devices helps refine problem-solving strategies, leading to nuanced understandings. Simulated decision-making environments and industry-relevant challenges also enhance students' decision-making ability, while ethical considerations add a layer of critical thinking to the process. Analyzing data from IoT devices promotes data literacy, encourages evidence-based decision-making, and fosters predictive analysis—all contributing to holistic development. This exploration highlights how the IoT enhances the educational experience by equipping students with cognitive tools for navigating complex real-world situations.

How IoT Supports Problem-Solving Skills? The field of IoT enhances education by offering a wide range of approaches that foster the development of adaptive and analytical problem-solving skills, which are crucial for navigating the complexities of the modern world (Bozanic, 2019).

- ***Engaging Scenarios:*** IoT introduces problem scenarios where students can interact with real-time data. This enables them to tackle problems like optimizing traffic flow in smart cities or managing energy consumption in smart buildings. This encourages critical thinking as they devise solutions.
- ***Hands-On Exploration:*** IoT facilitates hands-on exploration of problems through IoT devices and simulations. For example, students can use IoT sensors

Table 12.2 IoT projects in education and their impact on critical thinking

S. no.	Institution/ organization	Description	Application in critical thinking
1	"Smart Campus" Project at a University	A university can implement a "Smart Campus" initiative using IoT technology to enhance the learning environment.	Students will actively participate in designing and implementing various aspects of the Smart Campus, such as lighting, waste management, and energy efficiency. This hands-on experience requires them to think critically about problem-solving, data interpretation, and decision-making.
2	Incorporating IoT in Environmental Science Education	Educational institutions can integrate IoT into environmental science education using sensors to monitor environmental conditions.	Students will collect and analyze real-time data. This process encourages critical thinking as they interpret the data, identify patterns, and explore the impact of changes, fostering a deeper understanding of ecological principles.
3	Smart Agriculture Projects	Some educational programs focus on incorporating Internet of Things (IoT) applications in agriculture, providing students with opportunities to design and implement farming solutions.	Students are assigned tasks that involve optimizing resource utilization, implementing sensor-based monitoring systems, and developing automated solutions for processes. These tasks necessitate critical thinking skills in data analysis decision-making based on sensor inputs and addressing challenges encountered in practice.
4	STEM Education with IoT Kits	Various organizations offer STEM education kits with components related to the Internet of Things (IoT) specifically designed for schools and colleges.	Students will utilize these kits to construct IoT-based projects like weather stations or smart home systems. The interdisciplinary nature of these projects promotes critical thinking as students integrate knowledge from STEM disciplines to create functional and practical solutions.
5	Projects in Engineering Education	Engineering programs incorporate collaborative IoT projects where students collaborate in teams to design and implement real-world applications.	Students engage in problem-solving activities, system design tasks, and project management exercises. The collaborative aspect of these projects nurtures critical thinking skills, such as communication, teamwork proficiency, and adaptability, in tailoring solutions according to specific requirements.
6	Healthcare IoT Simulations	Medical schools can utilize IoT simulations to train aspiring healthcare professionals in patient monitoring and telemedicine.	Students will engage in critical thinking exercises within healthcare scenarios, interpret patient data obtained from IoT devices, make diagnostic decisions, and adjust treatment plans based on real-time information.

(continued)

Table 12.2 (continued)

S. no.	Institution/ organization	Description	Application in critical thinking
7	IoT in Computer Science Education	Computer science programs incorporate IoT projects where students develop applications for homes, wearable devices, or industrial automation.	Students must apply critical thinking skills when considering user experience, security implications, and system interactions within their applications. This approach encourages a problem-solving mindset.

to collect data and address ecological challenges. Students are encouraged to analyze potential solutions by immersing themselves in problem-solving contexts.

- ***Iterative Problem Solving:*** The iterative nature of IoT data collection allows students to refine their problem-solving strategies. They gain a nuanced understanding by analyzing data, adjusting, and observing real-time outcomes. This enhances their ability to think critically in evolving situations.

Real-World Decision-Making Scenarios The Internet of Things (IoT) facilitates the development of individuals who can make informed decisions and navigate complex real-world challenges (Kumar et al., 2019).

- ***Simulated Decision Environments:*** Through IoT, students can engage in simulated decision-making scenarios utilizing real-world data. For example, students may decide about resource allocation, traffic management, or environmental conservation in a simulated smart city setting. These scenarios encourage students to consider their choices and evaluate the consequences critically.
- ***Industry-Related Decision Challenges:*** By incorporating IoT into educational settings, students are exposed to decision challenges relevant to various industries. They can participate in decision-making exercises inspired by real-world situations by connecting with field professionals. This connection between education and industry enhances the practicality of decision-making exercises and prepares students for challenges they may encounter in the future.
- ***Ethical Considerations in Decision Making:*** The impact of IoT extends beyond technical skills and prompts discussion of ethical considerations. Students can explore the implications of data privacy, security, and societal impacts when making decisions. This ethical dimension adds critical thinking to their decision-making processes and encourages a holistic problem-solving approach.

Analyzing Data from IoT Devices for Informed Decision-Making The combination of IoT and data analysis is precious as it enables students to make evidence-based choices and promotes a holistic approach to critical thinking (Ai et al., 2023).

- ***Developing Data Literacy:*** The amount of data generated by IoT devices necessitates students to develop their data literacy skills. Analyzing and interpreting this data cultivates critical thinking by requiring an understanding of statistical concepts, patterns, and correlations. It empowers students to make informed decisions based on evidence.

- ***Making Evidence-Based Decisions:*** Real-time IoT device data availability promotes evidence-based decision-making among students. By learning to base their decisions on evidence, they can critically evaluate the reliability and relevance of the data they encounter. This approach instills a scientific mindset that contributes to the robust development of critical thinking skills.
- ***Predictive Analysis:*** IoT data often allows for predictive analysis, enabling students to anticipate future trends and outcomes. Engaging in predictive analysis fosters a critical thinking and analytical mindset, further enhancing students' ability to think critically about the implications of their decisions.

12.5 Collaborative Learning and IoT

In the changing field of education, the integration of the Internet of Things (IoT) is emerging as a catalyst for enhancing critical thinking skills and reshaping problem-solving and decision-making abilities. This section explores how IoT transforms approaches by presenting dynamic problem scenarios and encouraging hands-on exploration. Students get to tackle real-world challenges like managing energy consumption in smart buildings or optimizing smart city traffic flow, which helps them develop critical thinking skills. Additionally, IoT plays a vital role in decision-making by creating simulated environments and industry-related problems that require students to make choices based on real data. Discussions about ethical considerations related to data privacy and societal impact further enrich these decision-making conversations, fostering a holistic approach to problem-solving. Furthermore, analyzing data generated by IoT becomes crucial for making decisions and nurturing students' ability to understand and reason based on evidence.

Collaborative IoT Projects for Critical Thinking Collaboration in IoT projects catalyzes nurturing students' critical thinking abilities, preparing them to tackle the intricacies of real-world challenges (K.R. Mangalam University, 2023).

- ***Project-Based Learning:*** IoT opens up project-based learning avenues that encourage students to collaborate. Engaging in projects, such as designing and implementing IoT solutions for real-world problems, stimulates critical thinking by requiring students to integrate different viewpoints, analyze challenges, and propose innovative solutions.
- ***Interdisciplinary Collaboration:*** IoT projects often involve collaboration across disciplines, bringing together students with diverse expertise. This interdisciplinary approach fosters critical thinking, exposes students to problem-solving methods, and encourages them to synthesize knowledge from various fields to address complex challenges.
- ***Team-Based Problem Solving:*** Collaborative IoT projects inherently require teamwork. Students learn to navigate team dynamics, communicate effectively, and assign strengths-based tasks. These experiences contribute to developing critical thinking skills by highlighting the significance of problem-solving and leveraging diverse abilities.

Fostering Teamwork and Cooperation Fostering teamwork and cooperation in the context of IoT projects involves developing critical thinking skills that prepare students for real-world problem-solving (Teja, 2023).

- ***Building teams through challenges:*** Engaging in challenges where students collaborate to overcome technical hurdles or create innovative solutions promotes teamwork and cooperation. The shared responsibility of tackling complex problems encourages students to rely on each other's strengths and perspectives, fostering a collaborative mindset essential for critical thinking.
- ***Peer Learning and Support:*** Collaborative learning in IoT encourages peer-to-peer support. Students can share insights, troubleshoot challenges, and collectively enhance their understanding of complex concepts. This collaborative environment nurtures a culture of continuous learning and fosters critical inquiry.
- ***Developing communication skills:*** Working on IoT projects requires communication. Students must articulate their ideas, listen actively to others, and convey concepts. Emphasizing communication skills enhances critical thinking by challenging students to express and defend their ideas.

Sharing Data and Insights Through IoT Devices Collaborative data sharing through IoT devices has emerged as a strategy to nurture critical thinking skills, preparing students for the complexities of a data-driven world (Ai et al., 2023).

- ***Collective Data Analysis:*** The abundance of data generated by IoT devices presents an opportunity for collaborative learning, where students can collectively analyze and interpret this data. By sharing their insights and interpretations, students contribute to a shared pool of knowledge, fostering a data-driven approach to critical thinking.
- ***Building a Knowledge Community:*** IoT enables students to establish a knowledge community to share insights and discoveries. This collaborative environment extends beyond the confines of the classroom, allowing students to discuss IoT's implications in various fields and encourage them to reflect on shared experiences.
- ***Open-Source Projects:*** Participation in open-source IoT projects empowers students to become part of a global community. This collaborative effort exposes them to diverse perspectives and challenges, which promotes critical thinking by urging them to evaluate and refine their ideas within a broader context.

12.6 Data Analysis and Visualization

Step into the future of education, where the integration of the Internet of Things (IoT) brings about a change. In this era, a wealth of data generated by student interactions and collaborative projects becomes the foundation for enhancing critical thinking abilities. Through real-time feedback that shapes formative assessments and personalized learning paths tailored to needs, IoT creates an environment for students to explore and engage. Visualization tools transform data into understandable graphics, encouraging active participation, experimentation, and the creation of narratives through interactive dashboards. This educational journey goes beyond concepts by connecting academic knowledge with practical applications, fostering analytical skills, and instilling a scientific mindset. As students embark on this adventure, critical thinking transitions from being a skill to becoming a guiding principle in comprehending and navigating our interconnected world.

Utilizing IoT-Generated Data for Analysis Integrating the Internet of Things (IoT) into education brings about a wealth of data that can be used for real-time assessments, personalized teaching methods, and developing critical thinking skills by analyzing learning patterns and preferences (Skates, 2023).

- ***Data Analysis in Education:*** IoT implementation in education leads to the generation of high volumes of data. This data comprises information from sources such as students' interactions with IoT devices, environmental data collected from sensors, and collaborative project data. Analyzing this data gives educators and students insights into how learning happens, preferences, and areas that need improvement.
- ***Real-Time Feedback:*** The data generated by IoT enables educators to provide real-time feedback on student's performance, thereby supporting formative assessment strategies. Educators can track progress, identify areas where students struggle, and adjust their teaching methods accordingly. This approach, driven by data, enhances the effectiveness of formative assessments while encouraging students to reflect on their learning process.
- ***Personalized Learning Paths:*** By analyzing the IoT-generated data, personalized learning paths for each student can be created. Understanding how students engage with content and assessing the effectiveness of different instructional approaches allows educators to tailor learning experiences according to individual needs. This adaptive environment promotes critical thinking by challenging students and providing targeted support when necessary.

Data Visualization Tools and Techniques Incorporating data visualization tools and techniques into education has benefits. Firstly, it improves accessibility by presenting the information. Secondly, it fosters thinking through dashboards. Lastly, it helps students develop communication skills by allowing them to create narratives based on their interpretations of data generated by devices (Protopsaltis et al., 2020).

- ***Visualization for Accessibility:*** Visualizations enhance accessibility by presenting information in a format that makes it easier for students to understand complex concepts. This visual representation promotes critical thinking as students analyze and interpret the data within a clear framework.
- ***Interactive Dashboards:*** Interactive dashboards powered by IoT data allow students to engage with the information actively, encouraging hands-on exploration and experimentation. This approach fosters critical thinking skills as students identify patterns and draw conclusions from the datasets they navigate.

- ***Storytelling through Data:*** Data visualization enables students to construct narratives based on their interpretations of IoT-generated data. Students develop communication skills by presenting their findings through storytelling while further honing their critical thinking abilities by supporting their narratives with evidence.

The Role of Data-Driven Thinking in Education Engaging with data generated by the Internet of Things (IoT) in education has benefits. It helps students develop analytical skills, connects theoretical concepts with practical applications, and encourages hypothesis testing. These aspects foster a critical thinking mindset that can be applied across academic and professional contexts (Sharma et al., 2023).

- ***Developing Analytical Skills:*** Engaging with IoT-generated data enhances students' analytical skills. They learn to focus on details and identify information by collecting, organizing, and analyzing data. These analytical skills are crucial for critical thinking and transferable to other academic and professional areas.
- ***Connecting Theory to Practice:*** Data-driven thinking serves as a bridge between theoretical knowledge and real-world scenarios. By applying their understanding to analyze data, students strengthen the relevance of what they learn. This connection between theory and practice promotes critical thinking by encouraging students to evaluate the applicability and limitations of academic concepts.
- ***Encouraging Hypothesis Testing:*** IoT-generated data offers a valuable platform for hypothesis testing. Students can construct hypotheses based on their understanding of a phenomenon, analyze data, and draw conclusions based on evidence. This scientific approach nurtures critical thinking by instilling a mindset of inquiry focused on empirical investigation.

12.7 Potential Benefits and Challenges in the Future

The future of education about IoT applications shows potential benefits such as improved adaptive learning, global collaboration networks, and the integration of AR/VR. However, it also presents challenges like ethical concerns, technological disparities, and the need for pedagogical adjustments.

Potential Benefits The future of education is set to be revolutionized by cutting-edge IoT applications, which will transform learning experiences in several impactful ways:

- ***Enhanced Adaptive Learning:*** In the future, IoT applications can offer advanced adaptive learning experiences. Adaptive learning platforms can dynamically respond to students' progress using advanced analytics and AI technology. This continuous support and challenge help nurture critical thinking skills.
- ***Global Collaborative Learning Networks:*** IoT advancements may facilitate global collaborative learning networks connecting students and educators

worldwide. This interconnectedness exposes students to diverse perspectives and encourages the development of cultural critical thinking skills.

- ***Integration of Augmented Reality (AR) and Virtual Reality (VR):*** Combining AR and VR with IoT has the potential to create immersive educational experiences. Students could explore environments, conduct experiments, and engage in simulations that provide a unique context for applying critical thinking skills.

Potential Challenges As IoT technologies advance, several key challenges and considerations will shape their integration into education:

- ***Ethical Considerations Regarding Advanced Data Analytics:*** As data analytics advances, ethical implications surrounding student data privacy and responsible analytics usage will become increasingly important. Striking a balance between deriving insights and safeguarding individual privacy remains a challenge.
- ***Disparities:*** As advanced IoT applications are introduced, the gap between those with access to these technologies and those without access risks widening. Addressing this issue by ensuring access to technologies and preventing further exacerbation of existing educational inequalities is crucial.
- ***Evolving Teaching Methods:*** To fully utilize the benefits of advanced IoT technologies, educators must constantly adapt their teaching approaches. This requires development and a firm commitment to seamlessly integrating emerging technologies into the curriculum.

12.8 Call to Action and Recommendations

Moving forward, educators, policymakers, and stakeholders must take action to:

- ***Embrace Continuous Professional Development:*** Educators should actively participate in development programs to keep up with the latest IoT technologies and teaching best practices. This will ensure the integration of IoT into educational settings.
- ***Prioritize Ethical Considerations:*** Policymakers must prioritize establishing ethical guidelines for using IoT in education. Ensuring privacy, obtaining consent, and following data practices are essential to building trust in IoT-enabled learning environments.
- ***Promote Collaboration:*** Stakeholders should encourage projects that use IoT technologies. Students can benefit from diverse perspectives that enrich their critical thinking skills by fostering collaboration and global learning networks.
- ***Invest in Technological Infrastructure:*** Policymakers should allocate resources towards building technological infrastructure to address potential inequalities. Equal access to advanced technology is crucial in creating an inclusive educational environment.

- ***Support Research and Innovation:*** Ongoing research into the intersection of IoT and education is vital. Policymakers and educators should endorse initiatives exploring IoT applications to enhance critical thinking skills.

12.9 Conclusion

Implementing the Internet of Things (IoT) in education presents an opportunity to cultivate critical thinking abilities in students, equipping them with the complexities of today's world. Students are exposed to real-life challenges through hands-on experiences, simulated decision-making scenarios, and group projects, and they develop adaptive problem-solving approaches. Considering aspects of data privacy and societal impacts enhances their decision-making skills, encouraging a holistic problem-solving approach. Moreover, analyzing data generated by IoT devices empowers students to make evidence-based decisions and encourages a mindset that values data-driven insights. By visualizing data and linking concepts to uses, students enhance their analytical capabilities and learn how to convey their conclusions effectively. The potential advantages of integrating technology into education—such as improved learning methods and global collaboration networks—are significant. Nevertheless, obstacles like ethical concerns, technological discrepancies, and the need for teaching method adjustments need attention. Educators, policymakers, and stakeholders must embrace development opportunities, prioritize ethical standards, foster stakeholder cooperation, invest in technology infrastructure upgrades, uphold research efforts, and encourage innovation. In summary, by utilizing the potential of IoT technology and tackling the obstacles that come with it, education can significantly contribute to developing critical thinking skills crucial for navigating a connected and ever-changing world. With united efforts and dedication, we can guarantee that students will have the resources to address challenges and opportunities effectively.

References

Ai, I., Scenario, C., Alahi, E. E., Sukkuea, A., Tina, F. W., Nag, A., Kurdthongmee, W., Suwannarat, K., & Mukhopadhyay, S. C. (2023). Integration of IoT-enabled technologies and artificial advancements and future trends. *Sensors, 23*(5206), 1–36.

ANTTRoboticsLtd.(2023).*IoT,creativity,andcriticalthinkingskills–DoesIoThelp?*LinkedIn.https://www.linkedin.com/pulse/iot-creativity-critical-thinking-skills-does-help-anttroboticsltd/

Bednarz, T. F. (2013). *Seven components of critical thinking*. WordPress. https://majorium.wordpress.com/2013/11/26/seven-components-of-critical-thinking-2/

Bozanic, L. (2019). *IoT: The 21st century problem solver*. Medium. https://medium.com/@lana.bozanic/iot-the-21st-century-problem-solver-57979e4710cd

Criticalthinking.org. (2019). *Defining critical thinking*. Criticalthinking.Org. https://www.criticalthinking.org/pages/defining-critical-thinking/766

Eribo, N. M., & Kano, B. O. (2019). Education, critical thinking and national development. *Albertine Journal of Philosophy & Related Disciplines, 3*, 115–121.
Jace. (2023). *The importance of critical thinking in education*. Medium. https://medium.com/@spain24ledlight/the-importance-of-critical-thinking-in-education-393c34efca38
K.R. Mangalam University. (2023). *Tips to develop critical thinking skills*. K.R. Mangalam University. https://www.krmangalam.edu.in/tips-to-develop-critical-thinking-skills/
Kharbach, M. (2023). *The 8 elements of critical thinking*. Educators Techonology. https://www.educatorstechnology.com/2023/05/the-8-elements-of-critical-thinking.html
Kumar, S., Tiwari, P., & Zymbler, M. (2019). Internet of Things is a revolutionary approach for future technology enhancement: A review. *Journal of Big Data, 6*(111), 1–21. https://doi.org/10.1186/s40537-019-0268-2
Monash University. (2024). *What is critical thinking?* Monash University. https://www.monash.edu/student-academic-success/enhance-your-thinking/critical-thinking/what-is-critical-thinking
OpenLearn. (2024). *Barriers to critical thinking*. OpenLearn. https://www.open.edu/openlearn/mod/oucontent/view.php?id=64740&section=1
Pires, L. P. (2023). *The importance of critical thinking in education: Nurturing inquisitive minds*. LinkedIn. https://www.linkedin.com/pulse/importance-critical-thinking-education-nurturing-luis-palma-pires-fys1f/
Protopsaltis, A., Sarigiannidis, P. M., & Lytos, A. (2020). Data visualization in internet of things: Tools, methodologies, and challenges. In *15th International Conference on Availability, Reliability and Security, August, 1–11*. https://doi.org/10.1145/3407023.3409228
Reddy, P. J. K., & Nehru, R. S. S. (2021). Challenges in developing critical thinking skills in secondary school students. *Turkish Online Journal of Qualitative Inquiry, 12*(10), 45.
Sharma, A., Kapoor, D. S., Thakur, K., & Singh, K. J. (2023, August). Promoting deeper, meaningful learning in the contemporary educational landscape. In *Meaningful learning in the contemporary educational landscape* (pp. 112–152). https://doi.org/10.4018/978-1-6684-8208-7.ch005
Skates, A. L. (2023). *Five predictions for the future of learning in the age of AI*. Andreessen Horowitz. https://a16z.com/the-future-of-learning-education-knowledge-in-the-age-of-ai/
Teja, C. (2023). *The power of collaboration: Fostering teamwork and problem-solving skills in students*. LinkedIn. https://www.linkedin.com/pulse/power-collaboration-fostering-teamwork-skills-students-charan-teja/
University of Louisville. (2024). *What is critical thinking?* University of Louisville. https://louisville.edu/ideastoaction/about/criticalthinking/what#:~:text=Criticalthinkingistheintellectually,guidetobeliefandaction
University of Tennessee at Chattanooga. (2024). *Basic elements of critical thinking*. University of Tennessee at Chattanooga. https://www.utc.edu/academic-affairs/walker-center-for-teaching-and-learning/faculty-programs/faculty-fellow-programs/faculty-fellow-program-development/basic-elements-of-critical-thinking

Chapter 13
Ethics on the Use of IoT in Education

Abstract This chapter discusses the aspects surrounding using IoT (Internet of Things) devices in educational settings. It examines manufacturers' ethical guidelines when developing devices, highlighting various established standards, frameworks, and regulations like ISO/IEC standards, NIST Cybersecurity Framework, GDPR, etc. The chapter then examines the ethical implications of IoT, particularly on privacy, security, unintended consequences, social responsibility, and potential misuse. It subsequently addresses ethical concerns related to IoT in education, such as privacy and data security, informed consent, fairness and inclusivity, teacher independence, bias and prejudice, transparency, and accountability. In addition to exploring ethical issues in education, technology integration with IoT devices is presented with an emphasis on principles like student privacy protection and data security, as well as transparency, accountability, and sustainability. The chapter also provides suggestions for improving IoT deployment in education, including defined objectives, stakeholder engagement, and security privacy compliance, with regulations monitoring evaluation. Furthermore, key questions to consider when integrating tech into education are discussed, focusing on safeguarding privacy, obtaining informed consent, and ensuring fairness and transparency in making sound decisions. Finally, this chapter explores the significance of decision-making within educational settings. It emphasizes the role of ethics committees in assessing impacts, providing ethics training, and engaging with the community to establish policies safeguarding whistleblowers, conducting audits, striving for improvement, finding a balance between innovation and ethics, and ensuring legal compliance. This chapter examines the crucial principles and recommendations for integrating IoT responsibly in educational settings.

Keywords Internet of Things (IoT) · Privacy · Security · Data protection · Transparency · Accountability · Ethics

M. Kurni, Srinivasa K. G., *The Internet of Educational Things*,
https://doi.org/10.1007/978-3-031-67387-0_13

13.1 Ethical Standards Followed by the Manufacturers in Designing IoT Devices

Manufacturers and organizations will adhere to standards and guidelines when designing IoT devices. These standards typically align with ethical principles—some existing standards and frameworks (Allhoff & Henschke, 2018; Baldini & Botterman, 2018).

- ***ISO/IEC 27001:*** This widely recognized standard focuses on information security management systems. Manufacturers can follow these guidelines to ensure data and information security in IoT devices.
- ***ISO/IEC 27002:*** This standard provides a code of practice for managing information security covering various aspects for IoT device manufacturers.
- ***ISO/IEC 27018:*** This standard focuses on cloud privacy and offers guidance for safeguarding information (PII) in the cloud. As many IoT devices interact with cloud services, this standard is relevant.
- ***NIST Cybersecurity Framework:*** Developed by the National Institute of Standards and Technology (NIST), this framework guides managing and mitigating cybersecurity risks. Manufacturers can utilize this framework to evaluate and enhance the security of their IoT devices.
- ***IEEE P7000 Series:*** The IEEE has developed a series of standards and guidelines that address ethical considerations in the design of autonomous and intelligent systems, which often include IoT devices.
- ***EU General Data Protection Regulation (GDPR):*** Although not a requirement, the General Data Protection Regulation (GDPR) imposes strict regulations on data handling. Manufacturers dealing with data collection through Internet of Things (IoT) devices are expected to adhere to GDPR principles related to data protection and user consent.
- ***IoT Security Foundation (IoTSF):*** This organization offers resources, practice guides, and frameworks to support manufacturers and developers in ensuring the security of their IoT devices.
- ***IoT Privacy Forum:*** This forum specifically guides privacy concerns and IoT device data protection.
- ***Privacy by Design (PbD):*** PbD is a concept that promotes integrating privacy and data protection measures into the design and architecture of systems, including IoT devices.
- ***Open Connectivity Foundation (OCF):*** The OCF is an organization that provides IoT standards and certification programs for devices emphasizing interoperability, security, and privacy.
- ***UL 2900 Series:*** UL, a global safety science company, has developed a series of standards and cybersecurity certifications tailored for IoT devices and industrial control systems. These certifications can help manufacturers enhance the security of their products.
- ***ETSI EN 303645:*** This European standard focuses on cybersecurity measures for consumer-oriented IoT devices by highlighting baseline security requirements.

Manufacturers need to stay updated on the standards, guidelines, and best practices in the changing field of IoT. They should ensure their devices are designed and produced per ethical and security principles. It is also crucial for manufacturers to be aware of any requirements imposed by regional regulations on IoT device production. To stay compliant, manufacturers must keep themselves informed about the developments in this field and adjust their practices accordingly.

13.2 Ethical Implications of IoT

The Internet of Things (IoT) represents a change in how we interact with technology and our surroundings. With the increasing number of interconnected devices like home systems and wearable gadgets, IoT has become an essential part of our everyday lives. It offers us convenience, efficiency, and control over our environment. However, ethical concerns that require careful attention are raised as IoT progresses and expands. These concerns revolve around privacy, security, unforeseen consequences, social responsibility, etc. Hence, developers, manufacturers, and users must adopt a proactive approach to ensure IoT's ethical development and use (UNESCO, 2021; Talking, 2023).

- ***Privacy:*** One of the key ethical issues associated with IoT devices is safeguarding user privacy. The vast amount of data these devices collect includes sensitive information, raising concerns about misuse. While this data can be utilized for purposes such as targeted advertisements or personalized services, there are risks, such as identity theft or online harassment.

  To address these concerns effectively, IoT developers and manufacturers must prioritize user privacy by implementing security measures and privacy safeguards like encryption methods and authentication protocols. Additionally, limiting data collection/storage practices should be adopted while ensuring communication about data usage to users.

  Regulators and policymakers also have a role in establishing clear rules and regulations that govern data collection, storage, and utilization of IoT devices. This involves creating privacy policies and standards emphasizing transparency and informed consent from users regarding their data usage. It is vital to protect users against unauthorized access to their data and impose penalties on companies that violate these privacy regulations.

  Individual users should also prioritize safeguarding their privacy by being cautious when sharing information with IoT devices. Additionally, they should use unique passwords for their devices while regularly updating them with security patches and updates. By implementing these security measures, enforcing regulations, and promoting user awareness, we can ensure that potential privacy and security risks do not overshadow IoT technology's advantages.

- ***Unintended Consequences:*** Moreover, it is important to acknowledge that unintended consequences of IoT devices go beyond vulnerabilities. The widespread adoption of these devices raises concerns that must be addressed. As IoT devices become more prevalent, there is a risk of job displacement due to increased automation and artificial intelligence. Furthermore, certain groups may have access to or control this technology, exacerbating existing inequalities.

  To address these concerns effectively, it is imperative to develop ethical frameworks and guidelines considering the social and ethical implications of adopting IoT technology. Transparency and accountability play a vital role in ensuring development and deployment. This involves providing information about how data is collected, used, and accessed. Developers and manufacturers should also establish protocols for handling security incidents and vulnerabilities, promptly informing consumers and issuing security updates.
- ***Social Responsibility:*** We must prioritize ethical responsibility regarding IoT devices. By recognizing the critical ethical implications, we must ensure that these devices do not worsen existing social and economic inequalities. Accessibility and affordability should be guaranteed for all individuals regardless of their status. Promoting diversity inclusion in employment practices and engaging in community outreach and education initiatives to enhance awareness of IoT technology is essential.

  Environmental sustainability is another consideration for IoT devices. The production and disposal processes can impact resource depletion and release toxic chemicals. We must use materials and production methods to address this concern while minimizing waste generation emissions and ensuring disposal practices.
- ***Misuse and Abuse:*** A major ethical concern revolves around the misuse and abuse of devices. As the utilization of devices continues to grow, there is a concern that malicious individuals may exploit them for purposes like cyberattacks or acts of terrorism. It is crucial to establish guidelines and regulations for the development and implementation of IoT devices. This should encompass security and privacy standards to guarantee protection measures and protocols for detecting and responding to security incidents.

While IoT can transform our lives, we must not overlook its implications. These concerns encompass privacy, security, unforeseen consequences, social responsibility, and potential for misuse and abuse. To maximize the benefits of IoT while minimizing risks, it is necessary to establish ethical frameworks that prioritize transparency and accountability and ensure that IoT devices are developed and deployed in a socially conscious manner that considers environmental impact. Achieving this requires an effort among policymakers, industry leaders, and individuals who share the vision of using technology ethically and responsibly for the betterment of society.

13.3 Ethical Issues of IoT in Education

The Internet of Things (IoT) has the potential to bring about a transformation in the field of education by introducing tools and technologies that enhance the learning experience. However, like any technological advancement, IoT in education raises various ethical concerns that must be carefully addressed. Here are some important ethical considerations (see Fig. 13.1) related to the implementation of IoT in education (Weber, 2020; Tomás et al., 2020):

- ***Privacy and Data Security:*** Data collected from IoT devices used in educational settings may include sensitive student information, such as learning patterns, personal preferences, and even biometric data. Ensuring the security and privacy of this data is vital. Unauthorized access or breaches in data security can expose information, potentially putting students and educators at risk.
- ***Informed Consent:*** Students, parents, and educators must consent before IoT devices are deployed in educational environments. They should fully know how their data will be collected and monitored.
- ***Surveillance and Tracking:*** Using IoT devices to monitor student behavior can raise concerns about invading privacy. Balancing the goal of improving educational outcomes with respecting students' privacy can present a challenge.
- ***Discrimination and Bias:*** IoT systems may inadvertently perpetuate biases if not designed and tested correctly. Therefore, it is crucial to exercise caution during the development process to avoid discrimination or bias.

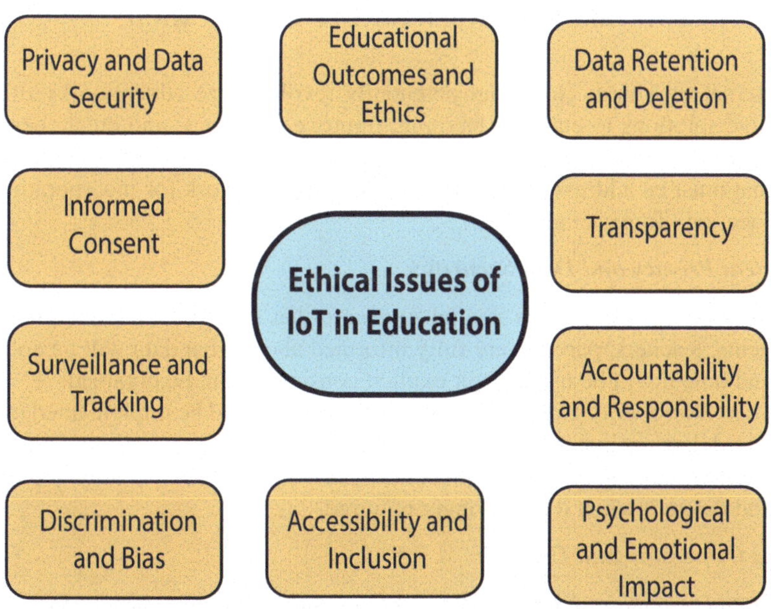

Fig. 13.1 Ethical issues of IoT in education

- ***Accessibility and Inclusion:*** Not all students can access IoT devices and technology. The digital divide can worsen inequalities because some students may lack the resources or connectivity for IoT-based learning.
- ***Psychological and Emotional Impact:*** Continuous monitoring and feedback from devices might cause students stress or anxiety, impacting their well-being. It is crucial to consider the effects of these technologies on learners.
- ***Accountability and Responsibility:*** Determining who should collect data and ensure its appropriate use can be challenging. Educational institutions, technology providers, and policymakers share some responsibility.
- ***Transparency:*** There should be transparency concerning the utilization of IoT in education. Stakeholders such as students, teachers, and parents should be well-informed about how data is gathered, stored, and utilized.
- ***Data Retention and Deletion:*** Policies must be established to govern data retention and deletion to prevent the storage of long-term educational data.
- ***Educational Outcomes and Ethics:*** Implementing IoT for improvement must be carefully balanced with considerations. Achieving optimal learning outcomes should never be at the expense of ethical principles.

Institutions, technology providers, policymakers, and stakeholders must collaborate to tackle these concerns about IoT in education. By establishing clear guidelines, ensuring consent, and consistently evaluating IoT technologies, we can address these concerns while harnessing the advantages of improved learning experiences.

13.4 The Ethical Framework for IoT in Education

The Internet of Things (IoT) can potentially revolutionize education by offering innovative solutions to enhance learning, improve efficiency, and create personalized experiences. However, implementing IoT in education also raises ethical concerns that must be addressed. Below is an ethical framework for incorporating IoT into education (Tomás et al., 2020):

- ***Student Privacy and Data Security:***
  - *Informed Consent:* It is crucial to ensure that all individuals involved (students, teachers, parents) are fully informed about what data will be collected and how it will be used. Their explicit consent should be obtained.
  - *Data Encryption:* Robust encryption methods should be implemented to safeguard data against unauthorized access.
  - *Data Minimization:* Only collect the necessary data for educational purposes and delete it when it is no longer required.
- ***Data Ownership and Control:***
  - *Data Ownership:* Clearly define who owns the data generated by IoT devices in educational settings and establish guidelines for maintaining control over it.

  - *Data Portability:* Students and their families should be able to access and transfer their data when they switch educational institutions.

- ***Transparency and Accountability:***

  - *Algorithmic Transparency:* It is essential to be open and transparent about how algorithms are used in making decisions like personalized learning recommendations.
  - *Accountability:* Educational institutions should establish lines of responsibility to ensure data security and ethical practices are maintained.

- ***Data Anonymization:*** Efforts should be made to anonymize student data as much as possible to protect identities while gaining valuable insights.
- ***Equity and Accessibility:*** Ensure that the benefits of IoT (Internet of Things) in education are accessible to all students regardless of their demographic background. Avoid any reinforcement of existing biases and disparities within the system.
- ***Cybersecurity:*** Implementing cybersecurity measures is crucial to safeguard devices from being compromised and misused for malicious purposes that could harm students or educational institutions.
- ***Compliance with Laws and Regulations:*** Staying current with laws and regulations like the Family Educational Rights and Privacy Act (FERPA) in the United States is essential. Educational institutions need to comply with these regulations.
- ***Ethical Use of Student Data:*** Student data should only be utilized for educational purposes. It should not be exploited for noneducational interests without explicit consent.
- ***Ethical Research Practices:*** Research IoT in education while adhering to standards and guidelines, especially involving students.
- ***Ethical Design and Development:*** Incorporate considerations into developing educational IoT devices and systems.
- ***Continuous improvement:*** Regularly assess the implications of implementing IoT in education and adjust policies and practices to address emerging challenges.
- ***Ethical Education and Training:*** Offer training and resources to educators, administrators, and students so that they can comprehend the aspects of IoT in education and learn how to safeguard their rights.
- ***Community Involvement:*** Engage parents, students, teachers, and the community as a whole in decision-making processes regarding the use of IoT in education. It is important to ensure that their opinions are heard.
- ***Ethical Considerations in EdTech Partnerships:*** Collaborate with EdTech companies that uphold principles and share a commitment to using IoT responsibly in education.
- ***Ethical Decision Making:*** Promote ethical decision-making within institutions by establishing mechanisms for addressing ethical dilemmas.

This framework serves as a guide for implementing IoT in education ethically while prioritizing the well-being and rights of students and all stakeholders involved in the educational process.

13.5 Recommendations to Enhance IoT Implementation in Education

Integrating IoT (Internet of Things) into education can bring many advantages. These include improved learning outcomes, increased administrative efficiency, and enhanced student engagement. To ensure the implementation of IoT in education, it is important to consider the following recommendations (LinkedIn, 2023; Melnik, 2023; Nagar, 2023):

- ***Defined Goals and Objectives:*** Establish specific aims for incorporating IoT in education, such as enhancing student performance, improving campus security, or reducing energy consumption. Having well-defined objectives will guide the implementation process.
- ***Involvement of Stakeholders:*** Engage educators, students, administrators, and IT staff in the planning and decision-making stages. Understanding their needs and expectations is vital for integrating technologies.
- ***Reliable Network Infrastructure:*** Ensure a reliable network infrastructure that supports high-speed data transmission for IoT devices. Consider investing in technologies like Wi-Fi 6 or 5G where appropriate.
- ***Emphasis on Security and Privacy:*** Prioritize cybersecurity measures and data privacy. Implement security protocols to safeguard IoT devices and the generated data. Train staff members and students regarding cybersecurity practices.
- ***Compliance with Regulations:*** Stay informed about data protection regulations such as GDPR or COPPA, especially when implementing IoT solutions involving student data. Adhering to these regulations is essential for maintaining privacy.
- ***IoT Device Management:*** Develop a strategy for tracking, monitoring, and updating IoT devices. This ensures that the devices are secure and perform optimally.
- ***Integration with Existing Systems:*** Ensure IoT solutions seamlessly integrate with educational technology systems such as learning management systems (LMS) and student information systems (SIS).
- ***Scalability and Future-Proofing:*** Design IoT implementations that are scalable and adaptable to future needs. Consider how the system can accommodate several devices and changing educational requirements.
- ***Data Analytics and Insights:*** Use IoT data to gain insights into student performance, campus operations, and resource utilization—leverage data analytics to inform decision-making processes and enhance educational outcomes.

- ***Student Engagement and Personalization:*** Harness IoT's power to create student learning experiences. Adaptive learning platforms can dynamically adjust content based on individual student progress.
- ***Resource Optimization:*** Implement IoT solutions for resource utilization, such as energy management systems to reduce utility costs or occupancy sensors to optimize classroom space usage.
- ***Teacher Training:*** Provide training and professional development opportunities for educators to effectively utilize IoT devices and leverage data in their teaching practices.
- ***Continuous Monitoring and Evaluation:*** Continuously monitor the performance of IoT systems. Evaluate their impact on education through ongoing assessment processes.
- ***Accessibility and Inclusivity:*** To ensure IoT solutions in education are accessible to all students, including those with disabilities, adjustments based on data and feedback are important. Additionally, it is crucial to consider the needs of diverse student populations.
- ***Community Engagement:*** Engaging parents, local communities, and other stakeholders in implementing IoT can foster support and transparency.
- ***Pilot Programs:*** Before implementing solutions, it is advisable to start with small-scale pilot programs. By testing these solutions on a full scale, any necessary improvements can be made based on feedback and evaluation of the results.
- ***Partnerships:*** Collaborating with technology providers, educational organizations, and experts in IoT can provide access to resources, expertise, and best practices. These partnerships can significantly enhance the implementation process.
- ***Sustainability:*** Sustainability should be considered when implementing IoT in education settings. Choosing energy-efficient devices and adopting sustainable practices that minimize environmental impact are essential.

A well-planned approach that considers each institution's specific needs and goals is essential to successfully implementing IoT in education settings. By incorporating these recommendations into their strategies, educational organizations can leverage the power of IoT to improve teaching methods and enhance learning experiences for students while ensuring security and privacy for both students and staff.

13.6 Elements to Consider and Questions to Ask

When incorporating IoT technology into education, adhering to ethical principles and prioritizing the well-being of students, teachers, and the educational community is crucial. This involves respecting privacy, equity, and other fundamental values. To address the ethical considerations related to implementation in education, it is essential to take into account the following aspects and pose relevant questions (LinkedIn, 2023; Digiteum, 2020) (Table 13.1):

Table 13.1 Ethical considerations for implementing technology in education, including key aspects and relevant questions

S. No.	Ethical aspect	Element	Questions
1	Privacy and data security	Ensuring the safeguarding of data, such as student and teacher information, to prevent unauthorized access or misuse.	How do we collect, store, and secure student and teacher data? Who has access to this data, and for what purposes? Are there apparent policies regarding data retention and deletion?
2	Informed consent	Ensure that students and their parents or guardians are fully informed about data collection and allow them to provide consent.	Are students, parents, and guardians aware of the IoT devices that collect data in the classroom? Is there a transparent process to obtain consent from all parties involved?
3	Equity and inclusivity	Enabling access to IoT technology for every student regardless of their socioeconomic status or abilities.	What measures are being implemented to bridge the divide and ensure access to IoT resources for all students? Have you considered the needs of students with disabilities or different learning styles?
4	Teacher autonomy	Ensuring that teachers have the freedom and power to make their decisions in the classroom.	Can teachers control when and how IoT devices are used in their teaching? Is there a balance between automation and the expertise of teachers?
5	Bias and discrimination	Ensuring fairness in the analysis of data and the process of making decisions.	How do you ensure that algorithms and methods used for data analysis are unbiased? Are IoT systems designed in a way that they do not promote perpetuating stereotypes or discriminate against groups of students?
6	Transparency and accountability	Maintain transparency in how IoT technology is used and establish clear lines of accountability.	Are technology-related policies and practices shared with all stakeholders? What mechanisms are in place to hold individuals or institutions accountable for misuse or breaches of data?

(continued)

Table 13.1 (continued)

S. No.	Ethical aspect	Element	Questions
7	Sustainability and environmental responsibility	Taking into account the consequences of IoT devices and embracing eco-friendly solutions.	Have you evaluated the impact of the IoT devices you plan to implement? What procedures should be followed for disposing and recycling IoT equipment?
8	Engagement of stakeholders	Involving students, parents, teachers, and the community in decision-making processes.	Do discussions about IoT in education include all stakeholders, such as students, parents, teachers, and the community? How do you collect feedback and address concerns raised by stakeholders?
9	Continuous monitoring and evaluation	Regularly evaluate how IoT technology affects student learning, engagement, and data privacy protection.	Which metrics do you use to assess the effectiveness of IoT implementations in education? How do you improve implementations based on feedback and lessons learned?
10	Ethical design and development	Promoting the development of Internet of Things (IoT) devices and applications while emphasizing the importance of an ethical foundation.	Are developers and manufacturers of IoT devices following ethical guidelines? Do educational institutions prioritize the well-being of students and educators during the design process?

Considering these factors and asking these questions can assist institutions in navigating the ethical aspects of IoT in education. It enables them to make informed decisions that prioritize the interests of students and educators.

13.7 Ethics on the Use of IoT for E-learning

Regarding using the Internet of Things (IoT) for e-learning, some ethical considerations should guide its implementation and usage. Here are some important ethical principles (see Fig. 13.2) to keep in mind (Tomás et al., 2020; Madni et al., 2022):

- ***Privacy Protection:*** The utmost respect for e-learners' privacy is crucial. E-learning platforms and IoT devices should only collect necessary data. Ensure that personal information is securely stored. Users must be informed about how their data is collected and consent with knowledge.
- ***Informed Consent:*** Both e-learners and educators should understand what data is being collected and how it will be used, and they should have the option to

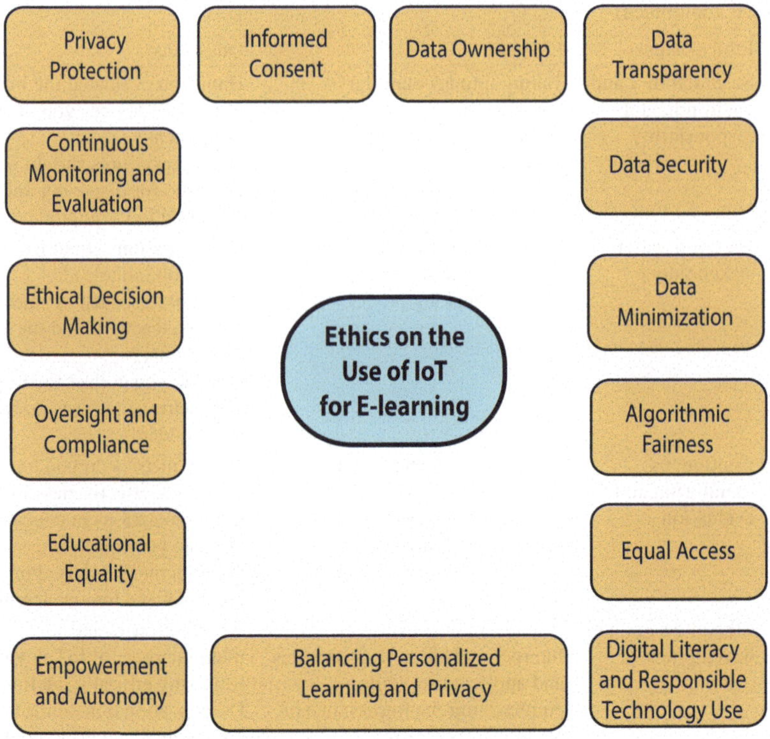

Fig. 13.2 Ethics on the use of IoT for E-learning

choose whether or not they want their data to be collected. An informed consent process is essential for ensuring the use of IoT in e-learning.

- ***Data Ownership:*** It is important to establish who owns the data generated by IoT devices in e-learning settings. E-learners, educators, and institutions may have different interests regarding this data, so addressing these differences is necessary to prevent conflicts.
- ***Data Transparency:*** E-learners should have access to their data and understand how it will be utilized. Transparent practices around data empower e-learners by allowing them to take control of their information.
- ***Data Security:*** Implementing security measures is crucial to protect against unauthorized breaches or unauthorized access to information. Failing to secure information can lead to violations.
- ***Data Minimization:*** Only collect necessary data for educational purposes to avoid unnecessary or irrelevant information and protect the privacy of e-learners.
- *Algorithmic Fairness:* Remain vigilant about biases in algorithms utilized in e-learning to prevent discrimination and ensure equal opportunities for all e-learners.

- ***Equal Access:*** Guarantee that all e-learners have equal access to IoT-enhanced e-learning resources, preventing any digital divide that could create student disparities.
- ***Digital Literacy and Responsible Technology Use:*** Promote digital literacy and encourage responsible digital citizenship among e-learners. Educate them about their rights, responsibilities, and ethical utilization of technology.
- ***Balancing Personalized Learning and Privacy:*** Striking a balance between learning and privacy is a task. Avoid data collection or profiling that may compromise the privacy of e-learners.
- ***Empowerment and Autonomy:*** Utilize IoT to empower e-learners and educators by providing insights and data that enhance the learning experience. Encourage informed decision-making regarding their learning paths.
- ***Educational Equality:*** Ensure that adopting IoT does not worsen existing inequalities.
- ***Oversight and Compliance:*** Adopting regulations and standards regarding data privacy and security in e-learning is important. Engaging with authorities and policymakers will help ensure that all necessary compliance measures are met.
- ***Ethical Decision Making:*** Ethical guidelines must be developed and followed throughout the decision-making process in e-learning with IoT. It is crucial to consider the implications of technology adoption at every planning and implementation stage.
- ***Continuous Monitoring and Evaluation:*** Regularly assessing the impact of IoT in e-learning is vital. This allows for adjustments to be made promptly if any emerging ethical issues arise.

Institutions, technology providers, policymakers, and educators must collaborate to use IoT in e-learning. By prioritizing respect for learner privacy, promoting fairness, and ensuring equal access for all learners, we can harness the benefits of IoT while upholding the ethical principles of e-learning.

13.8 Ethical Decision-Making in Educational Institutions

To ensure ethical practices in using IoT in education, educational institutions need to engage in ethical decision-making. This involves establishing internal guidelines and principles that promote the usage of IoT devices within the educational context. Here are some important factors to consider when making ethical decisions.

- ***Ethics Committee:*** Educational institutions should create an ethics committee comprising representatives from stakeholders such as educators, parents, students, and administrators. This committee will review and approve the deployment of IoT devices in educational settings.
- ***Impact Assessment:*** It is crucial to assess solutions' ethical implications. Consider both adverse effects when evaluating how the use of IoT devices may impact students, teachers, and other stakeholders.

- ***Ethics Training:*** Educators and administrators should receive ongoing training on using IoT in education. This training should cover aspects like safeguarding privacy, ensuring data security, and promoting technology usage among staff members.
- ***Community Engagement:*** To foster inclusivity and transparency, involve the community (including parents and guardians) in decision-making processes related to implementing IoT in education. Seek their feedback, address concerns, and ensure everyone feels part of the conversation.
- ***Ethical Policies:*** It is important to develop and communicate ethical policies that specifically address the use of IoT devices in educational settings. These policies should cover data privacy, security, transparency, and the responsible handling of student information.
- ***Whistleblower Protection:*** Establishing mechanisms to protect individuals who raise concerns or report misconduct related to the use of IoT in education is crucial to creating a culture of accountability and transparency within institutions.
- ***Regular Audits:*** Implementation of audits and assessments are necessary to ensure compliance with ethical guidelines. These audits should review data handling practices and security measures and analyze their impact on students and educators.
- ***Continuous Improvement:*** To stay current with emerging challenges, technological advancements, and stakeholder feedback, it is important to establish a culture of improvement by revisiting and updating ethical guidelines.
- ***Balancing Innovation and Ethics:*** While fostering innovation in education through IoT is important, it should never come at the expense of sacrificing ethical considerations. Striving for a balance between these two aspects ensures that we maintain our commitment to ethical principles.
- ***Legal Compliance:*** It is essential that all IoT implementations in education fully comply with national and international laws and regulations. To ensure the use of IoT devices in educational settings, educational institutions must prioritize adherence to data protection laws and privacy standards.
- ***Consent Mechanisms:*** Educational institutions should develop effective mechanisms to obtain consent from students, parents, and educators before implementing IoT devices. Individuals must understand the purpose and potential impact of data collection.
- ***Ethical Dilemma Resolution:*** Establishing a process to address ethical dilemmas that may arise while using IoT in education is essential. This could involve seeking guidance from an ethics committee or relevant authorities.

By incorporating these elements into their decision-making processes, educational institutions can foster a culture of responsibility. This will ensure that the integration of IoT in education aligns with the interests of students, educators, and the broader community.

13.9 Conclusion

Using IoT devices in educational environments offers many chances to enhance learning, streamline administrative tasks, and encourage innovation. Nevertheless, these advantages also bring about issues that must be addressed to ensure technology's responsible and ethical application in education. In this chapter, we have delved into integrating IoT in education. From the guidelines adhered to by manufacturers to the consequences of IoT, such as privacy concerns, security issues, unintended outcomes, and social obligations, we have examined the diverse ethical considerations within this domain. Specifically, we have underscored the significance of safeguarding student privacy and data security, gaining consent, advocating for fairness and inclusivity, upholding teacher independence, addressing bias and discrimination concerns, and ensuring transparency and accountability measures are in place. Additionally, we have offered a framework and recommendations for steering the ethical deployment of IoT in education by emphasizing stakeholder engagement and implementing security protocols that comply with regulations while maintaining ongoing monitoring and evaluation processes. Moreover, we have outlined factors for consideration and suggested questions when introducing IoT technology into educational settings. This underscores the importance of safeguarding privacy rights, respecting consent, promoting equity, maintaining transparency, and fostering decision-making. We have also stressed educational institutions' role in promoting a culture of accountability, morality, and adherence to rules, including establishing ethics boards evaluating impacts, ethics training to engage with the community, ethical guidelines, conducting audits, and striving for enhancement. To sum up, ensuring the responsible use of IoT in education necessitates a concerted effort by all parties involved, such as manufacturers, teachers, school leaders, policymakers, students, parents, and the wider society. By following ethical standards, advocating for transparency, and prioritizing the welfare of everyone involved, we can use IoT technology's capabilities while maintaining core values and moral principles in education. Through teamwork and making choices, we can establish a learning environment that fully utilizes technology's potential to empower students and educators to succeed in this digital era.

References

Allhoff, F., & Henschke, A. (2018). Internet of Things the Internet of things: Foundational ethical issues. *Internet of Things, 1–2*, 55–66. https://doi.org/10.1016/j.iot.2018.08.005

Baldini, G., & Botterman, M. (2018). Ethical design in the Internet of Things. *Science and Engineering Ethics, 24*(3), 905–925. https://doi.org/10.1007/s11948-016-9754-5

Digiteum. (2020). *How IoT is used in education: IoT applications in education*. Digiteum. https://www.digiteum.com/iot-applications-education/

LinkedIn. (2023). *IoT in the education industry: Embracing the new way of learning*. LinkedIn. https://www.linkedin.com/pulse/iot-education-industry-embracing-new-way-learning-intuz-1f/

Madni, S. H., Hussain, J. A., Husnain, H. A., Masum, M. H., Mustafa, S., Shuja, J., Maray, M., & Hosseini, S. (2022, July). Factors influencing the adoption of IoT for E-learning in higher educational institutes in developing countries. *Frontiers in Psychology, 13*, 1–22. https://doi.org/10.3389/fpsyg.2022.915596

Melnik, Y. (2023). *IoT in education: Main solutions IoT brings to education*. Edly. https://edly.io/blog/iot-in-education-main-solutions-iot-brings-to-education/

Nagar, T. (2023). *Top 6 things you should know about IoT in the education industry*. ELearning Industry. https://elearningindustry.com/top-things-you-should-know-about-iot-in-the-education-industry

Talking, I. T. (2023). *What are the ethical implications of IoT?* Talking IoT. https://talkingiot.io/what-are-the-ethical-implications-of-iot/

Tomás, C. C., Reis, D., & Teixeira, A. M. (2020). Ethical challenges in the use of Iot in education: On the path to personalization. In *European Distance and E-Learning Network (EDEN) Proceedings* (pp. 21–23). https://doi.org/10.38069/edenconf-2020-rw0024

UNESCO. (2021). *The ethical implications of the Internet of things (IOT)*.

Weber, A. (2020). The ethics of Internet of Things (IoT in Educational Contexts). In *INTED2020 Proceedings*, 4546-51. https://doi.org/10.21125/inted.2020.1265.

Appendix A: Simulation in Education

A.1 What Is Simulation?

Simulation is a method applied in various fields to replicate real-world processes or systems using computer programs or physical setups. It involves creating a simplified representation of systems or situations to study, analyze, and predict their behavior without interaction with the actual system (Dorries, 2023; Simul8 Corporation, 2024). Simulations have applications in research, engineering design, training, and decision-making.

Essential aspects of simulation include (Infopro Learning, 2022):

- ***Abstraction:*** Simulations simplify real-world systems by focusing on the aspects, variables, and parameters while disregarding unnecessary details.
- ***Modeling:*** Simulation models are based on mathematical equations, algorithms, or rules describing the system's behavior. These models define how system components interact and change over time.
- ***Experimentation:*** Simulations enable users to conduct virtual experiments and observe how the system responds under certain conditions or scenarios. This aids in comprehending the system's dynamics and making informed decisions.
- ***Control:*** Simulations often provide options to control various parameters and inputs to observe their impact on the system. This facilitates hypothesis testing and optimization of system performance.
- ***Visualization:*** Simulations offer users visual representations of systems utilizing tools like graphs, charts, animations, and other aids to help interpret and comprehend the results.

Simulation finds applications in fields such as (Gupta, 2023; HurixDigital, 2023):

- ***Engineering:*** Simulations assist in product design, testing, and optimization. For instance, engineers may employ computer-aided design (CAD) simulations to assess buildings' integrity or analyze aircraft's aerodynamics.

M. Kurni, Srinivasa K. G., *The Internet of Educational Things*,
https://doi.org/10.1007/978-3-031-67387-0

- ***Healthcare:*** Medical simulations contribute to training healthcare professionals to simulate surgeries and investigate the effects of treatment approaches.
- ***Economics:*** Economists use simulations to model financial markets, forecast economic trends, and evaluate policy change impacts.
- ***Transportation:*** Simulation is utilized in traffic modeling, airline scheduling optimization, and railway network analysis.
- ***Military:*** Military simulations serve as training exercises for personnel development, war games, strategy formulation, and tactics evaluation.
- ***Computer Science:*** Simulations test software functionality, model computer network behavior, or study algorithmic performance with various data structures.
- ***Environmental Science:*** Simulating climate models allows studying issues related to ecosystem dynamics or natural disaster scenarios.
- ***Education:*** Simulations often provide interactive and hands-on learning opportunities, enabling students to delve into complex systems.

Simulations prove invaluable tools for comprehending, predicting, and making choices about processes and systems, mainly when conducting costly, time-consuming, or unfeasible real-world experiments. They empower users to gain insights, test hypotheses, and enhance the performance of diverse systems and processes.

A.2 What Is Simulation-Based Education?

Simulation-based education (SBE) is an instructional method that utilizes simulations to facilitate learning and skills development across fields and disciplines. SBE exposes learners to realistic scenarios or situations that closely replicate real-world aspects. These scenarios can be presented in computer simulations, physical models, role-playing exercises, or virtual environments. The primary objective of simulation-based education is to create a safe and controlled environment where learners can practice, apply, and reinforce their knowledge and skills.

Key characteristics of simulation-based education include (Frasson & Blanchard, 2012; Roy, 2023):

- ***Realism:*** Simulations strive to recreate real-world contexts as closely as possible. This enables learners to encounter scenarios and challenges they may encounter in their academic domains.
- ***Active Learning:*** SBE encourages participation and engagement by allowing learners to assume roles, make decisions, and solve problems in the simulated environment.
- ***Experiential Learning:*** Learners gain hands-on experience by interacting with the simulated scenario. This type of learning can be more effective for skill development and retention than other learning methods.
- ***Risk-Free Environment:*** SBE provides a space for learners to make mistakes and learn from them without facing any real-world consequences. This is

especially crucial in industries like healthcare and aviation, where mistakes can have serious consequences.
- ***Feedback and Assessment:*** Feedback and assessment are aspects of simulation-based education (SBE). They provide learners with feedback, allowing instructors and educators to evaluate performance and provide guidance for improvement.

Simulation-based education finds applications in a range of fields, including (Movchan, 2024; Romanyuk & Maksymiak, 2022):

- ***Healthcare:*** Medical and nursing education often incorporates simulators and virtual scenarios to train healthcare professionals in clinical skills, decision-making, and patient care.
- ***Military and Defense:*** The military utilizes SBE to train soldiers, test strategies, and practice operations.
- ***Aviation:*** Pilots and aviation personnel utilize flight simulators to gain experience and practice emergency procedures.
- ***Business and Management:*** Business simulations allow participants to make strategic decisions while understanding the potential consequences. This is beneficial for management training programs.
- ***Education:*** Educational simulations and serious games teach subjects interactively.
- ***Engineering and Technology:*** Engineers can enhance their skills by practicing design, troubleshooting, and maintenance tasks within simulated environments.
- ***Emergency Services:*** First responders such as firefighters or paramedics use simulations as part of their training regimen to prepare for emergency scenarios.
- ***Social Sciences:*** Role-playing simulations in social science disciplines are often used to delve into the dynamics of society and relationships.

Simulation-based education has become increasingly popular because it allows learners to gain practical experience and apply their knowledge in real-life settings. This approach complements classroom instruction and is particularly valuable in professions and fields where hands-on experience is essential for success.

A.3 Why Teach with Simulations?

Teaching through the use of simulations offers a multitude of advantages for both educators and learners across fields. Here are several compelling reasons to integrate simulations into the teaching and learning process (SERC, 2024; UNSW Teaching, 2023):

- ***Experiencing Learning:*** Simulations provide a hands-on learning setting where students actively participate in and interact with the subject matter. This can help them better understand and retain concepts and skills.

- ***Applying Knowledge to Real-World Scenarios:*** Simulations enable learners to apply theoretical knowledge to real-life situations. They bridge the gap between theory and practice, helping students recognize the relevance of their learning.
- ***Safe Learning Environment:*** Simulations allow learners to make mistakes, experiment, and learn from errors without facing real-world consequences. This is especially valuable in fields where errors can have hazardous outcomes.
- ***Complex and Dynamic Situations:*** Simulations can replicate intricate, constantly changing scenarios that are challenging to recreate within classrooms. This aids learners in developing problem-solving abilities and adaptability.
- ***Interactivity:*** Simulations can be more stimulating than passive forms of learning because they are interactive and engage students, enhancing motivation and active participation.
- ***Immediate Feedback:*** Many simulations offer learners immediate feedback, enabling them to assess their performance and make real-time corrections. This feedback is valuable for improving skills and enhancing performance.
- ***Skill Development:*** Simulations are effective tools for practicing and refining specific skills. They are widely used in healthcare, aviation, and engineering to train and evaluate skill proficiency.
- ***Multidisciplinary Learning:*** Simulations often involve problem-solving across disciplines, fostering teamwork and providing a comprehensive understanding of complex issues.
- ***Resource Efficiency:*** Simulations can be a cost-effective and environmentally friendly alternative to real-world experiments or activities. They can be used repeatedly and tailored to learning objectives.
- ***Access to Diverse Scenarios:*** Simulations allow access to various scenarios and environments that may not be readily available in other settings. This is particularly beneficial in limited settings.
- ***Personalization:*** Simulations can be customized to accommodate individual learning styles and paces, empowering learners to progress at their rate while focusing on areas that require additional practice.
- ***Assessment and Evaluation:*** Instructors can use simulations to assess performance, providing qualitative student competence and comprehension measures.
- ***Research and Exploration:*** Simulations offer opportunities for scientific exploration, hypothesis testing, and gathering data. Researchers can utilize simulations to create models and study complex systems.
- ***Lifelong Learning:*** Professionals can benefit from simulations in their learning journey as they seek to update their skills or acquire new ones throughout their careers.
- ***Ethical and Cultural Sensitivity:*** Simulations also provide a controlled and respectful environment for exploring and discussing culturally relevant topics.

While simulations are a teaching tool, educators must design and integrate them carefully into the curriculum. This involves establishing learning objectives, providing guidance during the simulation, and conducting debriefing sessions afterward. These practices help students reflect on their experiences and solidify their learning.

When implemented effectively, simulations greatly enhance the educational experience by preparing learners for the challenges they will encounter in their fields.

A.4 Types of Simulation-Based Learning

Simulation-based learning encompasses a variety of approaches and technologies (shown in Fig. A.1) that aim to provide hands-on learning experiences and foster skill development. These approaches can be classified into simulation types with unique characteristics and applications. Here are some encountered forms of simulation-based learning (Romanyuk & Maksymiak, 2022)

- ***Virtual Simulations:*** These computer-generated simulations create a digital environment where learners can interact with objects, characters, or systems. Examples include virtual laboratories, immersive field trips, and educational video games.
- ***Computer Simulations:*** These simulations utilize computer programs to model and replicate real-world processes or systems. They are used to study complex phenomena in science, engineering, and economics.
- ***Role-playing simulations:*** In these simulations, participants assume roles and engage in scenarios or role-play exercises. They are frequently employed in social sciences, communication studies, and conflict resolution training.
- ***Business Simulations:*** In business simulation, participants are placed in a simulated corporate setting that allows them to make strategic decisions, manage resources effectively, and experience the complexities of running a business.
- ***Medical Simulations:*** Medical simulations play a vital role in healthcare education by providing training opportunities for healthcare professionals. This includes simulators for patients (high-fidelity mannequins), procedures training programs, and virtual surgical operations training.

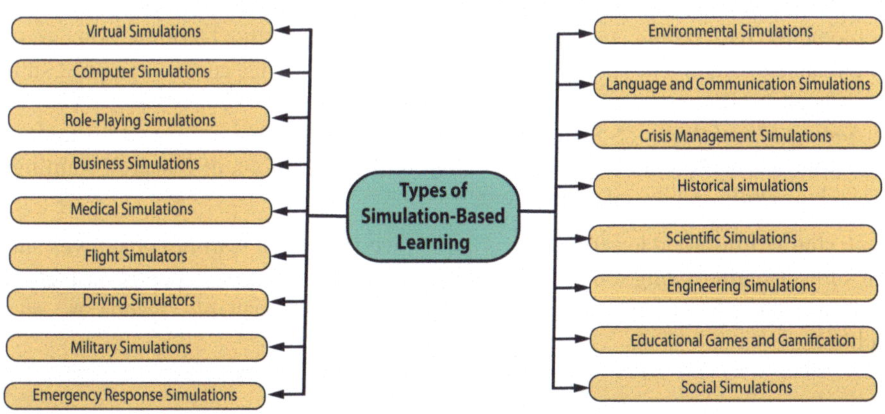

Fig. A.1 Types of simulation-based learning

- ***Flight Simulators:*** These specialized simulations are utilized in pilot training to create a realistic setting for practicing aviation skills, including aircraft control and emergency protocols.
- ***Driving Simulators:*** Driving simulations are employed in driver education and training to teach driving practices, enhance hazard perception abilities, and evaluate driver performance.
- ***Military Simulations:*** The military utilizes simulations for training, such as wargaming and tactical decision-making. These simulation programs can range from soldier training to large-scale war games.
- ***Emergency Response Simulations:*** First responders like firefighters, paramedics, and police officers undergo these simulations to learn how to handle emergencies effectively, including disaster management and crisis response strategies.
- ***Environmental Simulations:*** Environmental science employs simulations to model ecological systems that predict climate change scenarios and simulate disasters for research purposes and educational materials.
- ***Language and Communication Simulations:*** Language learning simulations create environments where students can use real-world scenarios and interactions to improve their language skills.
- ***Crisis Management Simulations:*** These simulations prepare individuals and organizations for cybersecurity breaches, public relations crises, or disaster response events.
- ***Historical simulations:*** Historical simulations aim to recreate past events and allow students to explore and comprehend historical contexts, decisions, and their consequences.
- ***Scientific Simulations:*** Scientific simulations involve modeling chemical or biological phenomena to help students understand scientific principles and conduct virtual experiments.
- ***Engineering Simulations:*** Engineers employ simulations to design, test, and analyze systems and structures before they are physically constructed. Finite element analysis and fluid dynamics simulations are commonly utilized in this field.
- ***Educational Games and Gamification:*** These simulations incorporate game elements like points, competition, and rewards into the learning process to enhance engagement and interactivity. Educational games cover a range of subjects and skills.
- ***Social Simulations:*** Social simulations simulate interactions and behaviors within societies and communities. They find applications in research training, such as exploring social phenomena.

Each simulation-based learning type is customized based on learning objectives and the subject matter being taught. The choice of simulation type depends on factors such as the educational context, desired outcomes, available resources, and technology.

A.5 Examples of Simulation-Based Learning

Simulation-based learning is widely utilized across domains and contexts to offer practical knowledge and hands-on experience. Here are a few instances of simulation-based learning in various fields (HurixDigital, 2023; e-Learning Infographics, 2019):

- ***Medical Education:***
  - *Patient Simulators:* These are mannequins that replicate human physiology. They serve as tools for training students, nurses, and healthcare professionals in clinical skills and procedures.
  - *Surgical Simulators:* Both virtual and physical simulators enable trainees to practice and refine their surgical techniques before surgeries on actual patients.
- ***Aviation Training:***
  - *Flight Simulators:* These highly realistic training devices provide aspiring pilots a safe environment to practice flight operations, emergency procedures, and navigation under controlled conditions.
- ***Business and Management:***
  - *Business Simulation Games:* Often employed in business schools, these simulations recreate real-world business environments. Students engage in decision-making, resource management, and competition within business settings.
- ***Engineering and Technology:***
  - *Finite Element Analysis (FEA) Simulations:* Engineers employ FEA software to simulate how structures and components respond to physical forces like stress or heat.
  - *Electronic Circuit Simulations:* Engineering students can use software tools to simulate the behavior of circuits. This allows them to design and troubleshoot circuits before creating prototypes.
- ***Military and Defense:***
  - *War Games:* Military personnel conduct war games and strategic exercises using simulations. These simulations aid in developing, testing, and refining tactics and strategies within a controlled environment.
- ***Firefighter Training:***
  - *Firefighter Simulators:* These simulators serve as training resources for firefighters. They provide scenarios for practicing responses to fire-related situations, including structure fires, wildfires, and hazardous materials incidents.

- ***Law Enforcement Training:***
  - *Use of Force Simulators:* Police officers use them to enhance decision-making abilities in force-use scenarios. They can also improve their judgment and reaction skills.
- ***Emergency Medical Services (EMS):***
  - *Emergency Medical Simulations:* EMS personnel can practice patient assessment, triage, and treatment skills in simulated medical emergencies, refining their abilities in a realistic setting.
- ***Environmental Science:***
  - *Climate Change Models:* Scientists use climate models and simulations to investigate the impacts of climate change, predict climate patterns, and devise strategies for mitigation and adaptation.
- ***Language Learning:***
  - *Language and Communication Simulations:* Language learning simulations allow language learners to engage in simulated conversations and scenarios, enabling them to practice their language skills in real-world contexts.
- ***History and Social Sciences:***
  - *Historical Simulations:* Historical simulations are valuable in studying history and the social sciences. They recreate past events, allowing students to role-play and make decisions that help deepen their understanding of historical contexts.
- ***Crisis Management and Public Relations:***
  - *Crisis Management Simulations:* Organizations and communication professionals use crisis management simulations widely. They help prepare individuals for crisis scenarios such as cybersecurity breaches or public relations crises, allowing them to develop strategies for response and recovery.
- ***Computer Science and Programming:***
  - *Coding and Algorithm Simulations:* Computer science and programming students can enhance their coding skills through algorithm simulations. These simulation environments allow students to practice coding techniques and algorithm development.
- ***Teaching and Education:***
  - *Educational Games and Gamification:* Teachers employ games and gamified activities in teaching and education. By incorporating these elements into lessons, educators make learning more engaging and interactive for students.

- ***Healthcare and Patient Safety:***
  - *Interprofessional Healthcare Simulations:* Healthcare professionals utilize healthcare simulations to enhance teamwork skills among students from healthcare disciplines. These simulations simulate scenarios where students collaborate on patient care, promoting effective communication within a multidisciplinary healthcare team.

Here are a few examples of how simulation-based learning is utilized in various fields. The use of simulation-based education is constant. Broadening its scope allows learners to acquire hands-on experience and develop skills within a controlled environment.

A.6 How Can Educational Institutions Incorporate Simulations?

Educational institutions have the opportunity to enhance the learning experience and equip students with skills and knowledge by incorporating simulations into their teaching methods. Here are some ways in which they can achieve this (Neendoor, 2023; Gupta, 2023):

- ***Integration within the Curriculum:***
  - Identify areas within the curriculum where simulations can augment learning outcomes.
  - Integrate simulations as a component of the course material, aligning them with specific learning objectives.
- ***Selection of Suitable Tools:***
  - Choose simulation tools or software based on the subject matter and educational level. This could range from basic online simulations to advanced software and hardware solutions.
  - Consider factors such as cost, accessibility, and the technology infrastructure available at the institution.
- ***Training and Support:*** Provide comprehensive training and support for educators utilizing simulations. They should understand how to employ these tools in their teaching methods.
- ***Access to Necessary Resources:***
  - Ensure students can access the required hardware and software for simulations on campus or remotely.

  - Establish guidelines and support systems for students to troubleshoot any issues they may encounter.

- ***Assessment and Feedback:***
  - Develop assessment criteria that align with the learning objectives of each simulation.
  - Gathering feedback from students and instructors is vital to continuously enhancing the quality and effectiveness of simulations.

- ***Interdisciplinary Approach:*** Promoting collaboration among institutions' departments can help explore simulations' diverse applications in various fields.
- ***Realistic Scenarios:***
  - Simulations must closely resemble real-world scenarios and challenges to provide students with experiences.
  - It is also essential to ensure that these scenarios remain up-to-date and relevant to the field of study.

- ***Simulation Pedagogy, Debriefing, and Reflection:*** Instructors should receive training in simulation pedagogy to effectively incorporate simulations into teaching. This involves understanding how to utilize simulations during class time and facilitating debriefing sessions where students can reflect on their experiences, discuss what they have learned, and connect it with theoretical concepts.
- ***Adaptive Simulations:*** Incorporating adaptive simulations can greatly benefit personalized learning experiences. These simulations can adjust their difficulty and complexity based on student skill levels.
- ***Collaborative Learning:*** Fostering learning through simulations encourages students to work as a team and develop strong communication skills. This approach promotes an environment where students can learn from one another.
- ***Feedback Loops:*** Including feedback loops in simulations enhances learning. These loops allow students to receive feedback on their decisions and actions, enabling them to learn from their mistakes.
- ***Real-time Data Analysis:*** Using data analytics and real-time tracking to monitor student progress during simulations is advisable. This way, educators can make adjustments and provide targeted support whenever necessary.
- ***Research and Evaluation:*** Encouraging faculty and staff to research the effectiveness of simulations in achieving goals is crucial. Such research can help refine the use of simulations over time, ensuring their continued improvement.
- ***Accessibility and Inclusivity:*** It is essential to ensure that all students, including those with disabilities, have access to simulations. Alternative means of engagement should be considered for students facing accessibility challenges.
- ***Continuous Improvement:*** For simulations to remain effective, it is essential to update and refine simulation scenarios, technology, and instructional methods based on student feedback and emerging trends.

By incorporating these strategies, educational institutions can offer students engaging learning experiences through simulations that equip them with skills for real-world challenges.

A.7 How IoT Enables Simulation to Enhance Learning

The Internet of Things (IoT) has the potential to significantly improve learning through simulation in domains including education, healthcare, and manufacturing. Simulation is a tool for hands-on learning and becomes even more effective when combined with IoT technologies. Here is how IoT enhances simulation to enrich the learning experience (Bayani, 2020). Figure A.2 illustrates the diverse applications of IoT in enabling simulation-based learning, showcasing its pivotal role in enhancing educational experiences.

- ***Real-time Data Gathering:*** IoT devices can gather real-time data from the physical world and transmit it to simulations. This data may include information about the environment, equipment status, and user interactions. For example, IoT-enabled sensors can monitor a patient's vital signs in a medical simulation and send that data to the simulation instantaneously.
- ***Immersive Experiences:*** We can create learning experiences by leveraging IoT capabilities. For instance, in a virtual reality (VR) or augmented reality (AR) simulation, IoT sensors can provide feedback or replicate environmental conditions to make the simulation more authentic and engaging. This enhances the learning experience by immersing learners in a sensory-rich environment.
- ***Remote Learning:*** IoT-enabled simulations enable learners to access them remotely with an internet connection. This means that participants can engage in

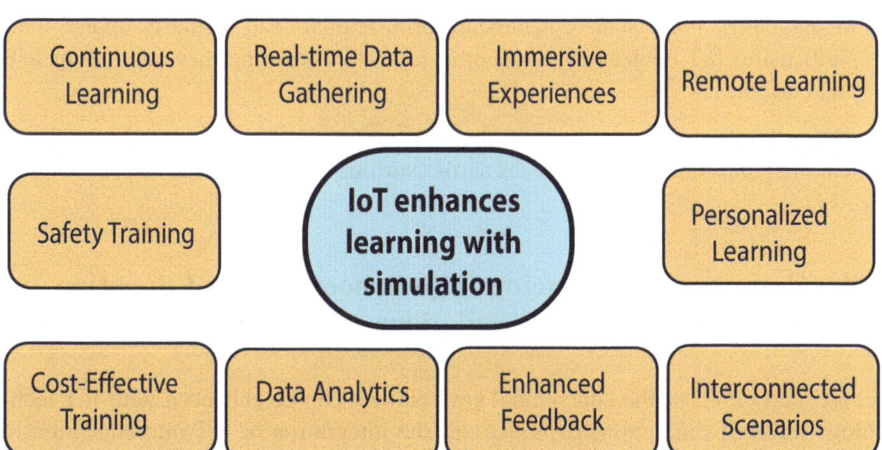

Fig. A.2 IoT's role in facilitating simulation-based learning

simulations without being physically present at a location. By harnessing the power of IoT technology within simulations, we open up possibilities for interactive and engaging learning across various fields. This holds value in the context of online learning as it allows education to be more easily accessible to a broader range of people.

- ***Personalized Learning:*** IoT devices can gather data on a learner's performance and dynamically adjust simulations to provide personalized feedback and challenges. This adaptive approach to learning helps individuals with varying skill levels and learning preferences improve their abilities effectively.
- ***Interconnected Scenarios:*** Through IoT, simulations and scenarios can be interconnected, resulting in interconnected learning experiences. For example, in an industrial setting, simulations can replicate different stages of a manufacturing process and demonstrate how they interact. This enables learners to gain an understanding of the production workflow.
- ***Enhanced Feedback:*** IoT sensors can provide detailed feedback on a learner's performance. In training, for instance, IoT sensors can assess the accuracy of medical procedures and offer immediate feedback to assist learners in enhancing their skills.
- ***Data Analytics:*** The vast amount of data IoT devices collect can be analyzed to identify patterns and trends. This data analysis empowers educators and trainers to refine simulations and curricula to improve learning outcomes.
- ***Cost-Effective Training:*** IoT-driven simulations can reduce the expenses associated with hands-on training. For example, aviation flight simulators with IoT devices can partially replace flight training by replicating real-world conditions.
- ***Safety Training:*** By incorporating IoT technology into simulations, learners can practice in safe environments for high-risk or dangerous situations like firefighting, disaster response, or handling hazardous materials. This allows them to gain experience without the risk of harm.
- ***Continuous Learning:*** IoT-enhanced simulations also enable learning and skill maintenance. For instance, healthcare professionals can regularly update their skills using IoT devices in the healthcare sector, ensuring they stay competent and current.

As IoT technologies continue to advance and evolve, they are expected to enhance educational and training experiences across various fields.

A.8 Case Study: Enhancing High School Physics Education with IoT-Enhanced Simulations

A case study on how the educational environment can be enhanced with IoT technology through simulations demonstrates the integration of IoT into education to create dynamic learning experiences. Here is an example to illustrate;

Background In a city driven by technology, a school aimed to enhance its physics education program by incorporating IoT-enhanced simulations. The goal was to give students an engaging, hands-on understanding of physical concepts.

Implementation

- ***Smart Physics Lab:*** The school can establish a "smart" physics laboratory with IoT sensors. These sensors collect real-time data on physical phenomena, including motion, light, sound, and temperature.
- ***Connected Experimentation:*** Through an online platform, students can access the smart lab's data, work remotely, and monitor IoT-connected equipment, allowing them to conduct experiments virtually. For instance, students can utilize IoT sensors to study the motion of a pendulum. They could adjust parameters like length or gravitational acceleration and observe real-time data generated by these changes.
- ***Dynamic Simulations:*** Collected IoT data from experiments can be utilized to create simulations. These simulations allow students to actively explore and manipulate real-world concepts. For example, in the pendulum experiment, students can adjust parameters and observe how they directly influence the pendulum's behavior in the simulation.
- ***Interdisciplinary Learning:*** One notable aspect was that these IoT-enhanced simulations facilitated learning by integrating physics concepts with data science and programming. Students can analyze and visualize the data they collected using coding and data analysis tools, gaining an understanding of the pendulum's motion.
- ***Project-Based Learning:*** Project-based learning can also be emphasized. Students will be assigned projects that involve designing and conducting experiments, analyzing data, and creating reports. Collaborative efforts can be encouraged in projects focusing on physics applications, like designing a bridge or a basic IoT device.
- ***Real-World Context:*** IoT sensors and simulations can be designed to provide a real-world context by connecting them to real-world scenarios. For instance, when studying a parachute system, students can examine how wind resistance and gravity impact its performance. This allows them to grasp how these fundamental concepts apply in practical situations.
- ***Assessment and Feedback:*** Teachers can utilize the data collected from these IoT-enhanced simulations for assessment purposes and to provide valuable feedback on student progress. This data-driven method can be effective in identifying areas where students require assistance.

Key Outcomes

- ***Increased Engagement:*** Students can exhibit enthusiasm for physics as the simulations, which are interactive and hands-on, make the subject more intriguing and accessible.
- ***Enhanced Comprehension:*** Students better understand physics concepts by engaging with real-world data and experimenting with various parameters.

- ***Improved Achievement:*** Incorporating IoT-enhanced simulations associated with academic performance in physics, resulting in better exam preparation and assignment completion.
- ***Skill Development:*** This approach helps students acquire data analysis, programming, and problem-solving skills highly applicable within STEM fields and beyond.
- ***Integrated Learning:*** The interdisciplinary approach enables students to recognize the interconnections between physics and other subjects, enriching their STEM education.

Integrating IoT technology into the learning environment can profoundly enhance STEM education. Students will gain practical exposure by incorporating IoT technology into their experience while thoroughly comprehending complex concepts. Furthermore, they can acquire skills that prepare them for careers within STEM fields. This approach will improve performance and instill a deep passion for STEM subjects.

A.9 What Will the Future of Simulation-Based Learning Be?

The future of simulation-based learning holds promise. It is expected to witness significant advancements and widespread adoption across various educational domains. Let us explore future simulation-based learning trends and possibilities (Kumar, 2023).

- ***Embracing Virtual Reality (VR) and Augmented Reality (AR):*** As VR and AR technologies improve and become more accessible, they will play a central role in simulation-based learning. These immersive technologies have the potential to create interactive educational experiences.
- ***Integration of Artificial Intelligence (AI) and Machine Learning:*** Incorporating AI-driven simulations can cater to learners' needs by offering experiences and feedback. AI can also enhance simulations by making them more dynamic and responsive.
- ***Cloud-Based Simulations:*** Storing and running simulations in the cloud allows for effortless access and collaboration. Students and educators can access simulations from anywhere via the Internet, making education more flexible.
- ***Development of Soft Skills through Simulation:*** In addition to technical and subject-specific skills, simulations will increasingly focus on nurturing soft skills such as critical thinking, problem-solving, effective communication, and emotional intelligence.
- ***Immersive Healthcare Training:*** Immersive training in the healthcare industry will advance by integrating patient simulators and virtual surgery, providing students and professionals with more realistic learning experiences.

- ***Simulated Laboratories:*** Science and engineering education will shift towards virtual labs and simulations as replacements or supplements to traditional laboratories. This transition will bring about cost savings and greater accessibility.
- ***Gamification Elements:*** Simulations will incorporate gamification elements to make learning captivating and enjoyable. Students can be motivated to excel in their journey by introducing points, leaderboards, and rewards.
- ***Cross-Disciplinary Simulations:*** Simulations will be utilized to teach subjects and address real-world challenges requiring skilled professionals. This approach aligns with the growing need for interdisciplinary expertise.
- ***Global Collaboration:*** Through simulations, students worldwide will have opportunities to collaborate on projects and scenarios, fostering global perspectives while developing cross-cultural communication skills.
- ***Simulations for Assessment:*** Simulations will not be limited to learning purposes; they will also help assess student competence by evaluating their skills through simulated scenarios.
- ***Experiential Learning in Online Education:*** The future of education is expected to witness advancements in innovation, accessibility, and the creation of more immersive and personalized educational experiences. As technology progresses, simulations will equip students with the skills and knowledge to tackle the opportunities and challenges of the twenty-first century.
- ***K-12 Education Integration:*** Simulations are poised to bridge the gap between face-to-face and online education by offering students experiences and skills within virtual environments. This integration is particularly relevant for K -12 education, where simulations will become increasingly prevalent, enabling students to explore various subjects.
- ***Data-Driven Feedback:*** Simulations will generate large amounts of data on student performance, providing educators with insights that can be used to offer targeted feedback and enhance the overall learning experience. This data-driven approach ensures that educational content can be refined based on needs.
- ***Ethical Dilemma Simulations:*** Another significant aspect is that simulations can tackle complex ethical dilemmas. By immersing students in scenarios within controlled environments, these ethical dilemma simulations foster thinking as individuals grapple with real-world moral challenges.
- ***Sustainability and Environmental Simulations:*** Moreover, simulations have potential regarding sustainability and environmental issues. They offer a tool for helping students understand and address these pressing concerns by encouraging them to develop eco solutions.

With increased innovation and accessibility, simulation-based learning will empower learners by providing tailored experiences that mirror real-world situations. As a result, students will be better equipped for success as they navigate the twenty-first century's changing landscape.

A.10 Conclusion

Simulation-based learning plays a vital role in education by providing hands-on, engaging learning experiences across various fields. As discussed in this chapter, simulations and simulation-based education promote active participation in practical skill development and safe experimentation. In engineering, healthcare, aviation, or emergency services, simulations offer learners opportunities to apply knowledge, refine skills, and prepare for real-world situations. Moreover, integrating IoT technologies can transform simulation-based learning by offering real-time data insights, personalized experiences, and improved interaction. The case study illustrates how IoT-enhanced simulations can revolutionize educational settings by boosting student engagement levels, understanding of concepts, and skill acquisition. Advancements in simulation-based learning promise a future; in reality, artificial intelligence (AI) and cloud computing are set to enhance experiences even further. As simulations progress, educational institutions must embrace innovation and collaboration while striving for improvement to leverage their benefits. Ultimately, simulation-based learning embodies the essence of modern education—it is interactive and customized to meet the diverse needs of learners. Through simulations and embracing technologies, teachers can equip students with the skills, knowledge, and flexibility needed to succeed in a constantly evolving society.

References

Bayani, M. (2020). The influence of IoT simulation in the learning process: A case study. In *2020 8th International Conference on Information and Education Technology* (pp. 24–27). https://doi.org/10.1145/3395245.3396427

Dorries, H. (2023). *What is simulation?* LinkedIn. https://www.linkedin.com/pulse/what-simulation-hans-dorries/

e-Learning Infographics. (2019). *4 examples of simulation-based learning*. E-Learning Infographics. https://elearninginfographics.com/4-examples-of-simulation-based-learning/

Frasson, C., & Blanchard, E. G. (2012). Simulation-based learning. In N. M. Seel (Ed.), *Encyclopedia of the sciences of learning* (pp. 1–6). Springer.

Gupta, D. (2023). *What is simulation training? (+benefits, examples)*. Whatfix. https://whatfix.com/blog/simulation-training/

HurixDigital. (2023). *Simulation training: 7 ways to leverage it across various industries*. HurixDigital. https://www.hurix.com/simulation-training-across-industry/

Infopro Learning. (2022). *Simulation-based learning: The future of learning & development*. Infopro Learning. https://www.infoprolearning.com/blog/simulation-based-learning-the-future-of-learning-development/

Kumar, S. (2023). *The power of simulations in education & future trends*. LinkedIn. https://www.linkedin.com/pulse/power-simulations-education-future-trends-sumeet-kumar/

Movchan, S. (2024). *Applications of simulation-based learning*. Raccoon Gang. https://raccoongang.com/blog/applications-simulation-based-learning/

Neendoor, S. (2023). *The role of simulations in higher education institutions and colleges*. HurixDigital. https://www.hurix.com/role-of-simulations-in-higher-education-institutions-

and-colleges/#:~:text=Withproperprogramming%2Ccomputer-supported,systemandhonetheir knowledge

Romanyuk, O., & Maksymiak, I. (2022). *Simulation-based learning in education – Benefits and examples*. Keenethics. https://keenethics.com/blog/simulation-based-learning-in-education-benefits-and-examples

Roy, D. (2023). *Simulation-based learning: A real world learning!* Mindler. https://www.mindler.com/blog/simulation-based-learning/

SERC. (2024). *Why teach with simulations?* SERC. https://serc.carleton.edu/sp/library/simulations/why.html

Simul8 Corporation. (2024). *What is simulation?* Simul8 Corporation. https://www.simul8.com/what-is-simulation

UNSW Teaching. (2023). *Simulations*. UNSW Teaching. https://www.teaching.unsw.edu.au/simulations#:~:text=Simulationspromotetheuseof,activitymoreenthusiasticallyandinteractively

Appendix B: Digital Twins for Education

B.1 What Is a Digital Twin?

A digital twin refers to a representation of a physical object or system. It is a digital counterpart replicating its real-world equivalent characteristics, behavior, and properties (IBM, 2023; McKinsey & Company, 2023). Various industries, such as manufacturing, engineering, healthcare, and more, utilize twins to gain understanding, monitor progress, and optimize physical assets and processes.

Listed below are some features and applications of digital twins (Happiest Minds, 2017; Telefónica, 2023):

- ***Representation of Physical Objects or Systems:*** Digital twins can represent various entities, including individual components, machinery, entire factories or infrastructure setups, and even complex systems like smart cities.
- ***Real-time Monitoring:*** They play a vital role in real-time monitoring by collecting data from sensors and other sources to provide an up-to-date view of the physical object or system's current state.
- ***Simulation and Analysis:*** Digital twins enable simulations and analysis of the behavior exhibited by the physical object or system. This helps predict performance outcomes, identify issues in advance, and test scenarios without impacting the object.
- ***Historical Data:*** They store data that allows users to track changes and improvements over time.
- ***Optimization:*** Digital twins optimize operations management, maintenance procedures, and overall performance efficiency. Take, for instance, the manufacturing sector, where a digital replica of a machine can schedule maintenance proactively, thereby reducing downtime.
- ***Remote Control:*** In some scenarios, digital twins control and manage physical assets. This allows operators to make adjustments and decisions from a distance.

M. Kurni, Srinivasa K. G., *The Internet of Educational Things*,
https://doi.org/10.1007/978-3-031-67387-0

- ***IoT and Sensors:*** Internet of Things (IoT) devices and sensors are frequently integrated into digital twin systems to provide continuous data inputs and updates.
- ***Interconnected Systems:*** In specific settings, multiple digital twins can be interconnected to model and optimize entire ecosystems or supply chains.

Digital twins are valuable in industries prioritizing efficiency, predictive maintenance, and real-time decision-making. They serve as a bridge between the physical and digital realms by offering insights and control that would otherwise be unattainable with a physical object alone.

B.2 How Can Digital Twins Be Applied to the Educational Domain?

Digital twins can also be used in education, providing solutions to enhance the teaching and learning experience. Here are a few ways in which digital twins can be applied in education (Shivashish, 2023; Tao & Xu, 2022):

- ***Personalized Learning Environments:*** We can create digital twins of students to track their progress, learning styles, and specific needs. By analyzing the data from these digital twins, educators can customize instruction and content for each student, enabling them to learn effectively.
- ***Virtual Laboratories and Simulations:*** Digital twins of scientific equipment or experiments can serve as virtual laboratories for students. Students can experiment, make mistakes, and learn without requiring physical equipment, which is particularly valuable for science and engineering education.
- ***Campus Management:*** Educational institutions can develop digital twins of their campuses to optimize facility management. This includes monitoring building conditions, energy consumption, and security measures. It helps reduce costs while enhancing the campus experience.
- ***Adaptive Curriculum Design:*** Digital twins of curricula or courses can adapt based on students learning progress. Students who interact with these twins' materials adjust the content and pace according to their needs.
- ***Predictive Analytics:*** Educational institutions can use digital twins to analyze data and identify students at risk of dropping out or falling behind. With intervention strategies in place, these students can receive support.
- ***Teacher Professional Development:*** Digital twins enable simulated classroom environments for teacher training and professional development. Educators can practice teaching techniques, classroom management skills, and student engagement strategies within a risk-free digital setting.
- ***Remote Learning and Virtual Field Trips:*** Digital twins allow students to take virtual field trips to historical sites, museums, or distant locations. This allows them to explore the world and delve into events from the comfort of their classrooms.

- ***Sensory and Assistive Technologies:*** Through digital twins, students with disabilities can access personalized educational experiences. These experiences may include tutors, accessibility tools, and tailored learning resources catering to their needs.
- ***Research and Data Analysis:*** In education settings, digital twins are models for simulating complex research scenarios ranging from scientific experiments to social simulations. Researchers benefit from these simulations by refining their methodologies and collecting data efficiently.
- ***Interactive Learning Environments:*** Digital twins create three-dimensional (3D) immersive educational environments that make challenging subjects more engaging and comprehensible.

Digital twins in education can help make data-based decisions, improve student engagement and learning results, and streamline facility management tasks. These uses can potentially make education more impactful, accessible, and efficient, thus benefiting both students and educators.

B.3 Benefits of Digital Twins in Education

Digital twins offer various benefits for educators and learners in education. Here are some key advantages associated with using digital twins in education (Turner, 2023; Yogesh, 2023):

- ***Increased Student Engagement:*** Digital twins create immersive learning environments using virtual reality (VR) and augmented reality (AR) technologies. This allows students to explore digital spaces, interact with objects, and engage with students captivatingly.
- ***Improved Learning Outcomes:*** Digital twins design engaging and compelling learning experiences by simulating real-world scenarios. Students can interact with the environment, grasp concepts, and develop skills efficiently.
- ***Enhanced Assessment:*** Digital twins enable precise assessment of student progress. Educators can gauge their understanding of concepts and accurately track their advancement.
- ***Immersive Learning:*** Digital twins provide a controlled environment for students to explore and experiment, enhancing comprehension and knowledge retention.
- ***Collaboration and Teamwork:*** Virtual simulations of student collaboration encourage teamwork, communication, and problem-solving in complex scenarios.
- ***Real-World Relevance:*** By simulating real-world scenarios, digital twins help students develop practical and critical thinking abilities that will be useful in their future careers.
- ***Personalized Learning:*** Digital twins revolutionize learning, ushering in an era where students can learn at their own pace and explore subjects deeply. They can

undertake projects that foster independent thinking, creativity, and problem-solving abilities. Digital twins adapt to each student's learning style and speed, allowing them to customize their journey based on their strengths and aspirations.

Educational institutions can create tailored and effective learning experiences by harnessing the potential of digital twins.

B.4 Types of Digital Twins for Education

Digital twins play a vital role in enhancing the educational experience by taking various forms. In the education sector, we can utilize a few types of digital twins with specific purposes (Rudra, 2022; Meenakumari, 2021):

- ***Student Digital Twins:*** These are representations of students that gather data on their learning styles, preferences, strengths, and weaknesses. By utilizing student digital twins, we can create personalized learning experiences, develop adaptive curriculum designs, and provide early intervention for students who may be struggling.
- ***Curriculum or Course Digital Twins:*** These digital twins model the content and structure of a course or curriculum. They adjust according to students' progress and include various learning materials such as lectures, assignments, and assessments. Curriculum digital twins allow for customized learning paths and continuous enhancement of course materials.
- ***Campus and Facilities Digital Twins:*** These digital twins replicate the physical campus and its facilities. They monitor building conditions, energy consumption, and security to manage resources while maintaining a conducive learning environment.
- ***Virtual Laboratories and Experiment Simulations:*** Digital twins of scientific equipment and experiments provide virtual laboratory environments for students to engage in hands-on learning without requiring physical resources. This is particularly advantageous in science and engineering education.
- ***Educational Content and Resource Digital Twins:*** These digital twins represent various educational materials, including textbooks, interactive modules, and multimedia content. They can adapt according to students' needs and learning progress, providing a personalized learning experience.
- ***Virtual field trips and historical site digital twins:*** These digital twins are virtual replicas that allow students to explore historical sites, museums, and other locations regardless of their physical location. This enables students to incorporate these places into their learning experiences.
- ***Teacher Training and Classroom Simulation Digital Twins:*** These digital twins create simulated classroom environments for aspiring educators. They provide a space for practicing teaching techniques, classroom management skills, and student engagement strategies.

- ***Learning analytics and predictive digital twins:*** These digital twins analyze data from educational systems to create predictive models. These models assist educators and institutions in identifying students who may be at risk academically, optimizing resource allocation, and making decisions based on data.
- ***Sensory and assistive digital twins:*** These are explicitly designed for students with disabilities. They provide tailored experiences that cater to these individuals' needs. They can offer tools like virtual tutors, accessibility aids, and personalized learning materials.
- ***Research and Laboratory Experiment Digital Twins:*** Digital twins have proven valuable in simulating and modeling experiments and research scenarios in education and research institutions. This enables researchers to refine their methods and optimize data collection.
- ***Interactive 3D and Immersive Learning Environments:*** Another practical application is creating 3D and immersive learning environments through digital twins. These environments make abstract or complex subjects more tangible and engaging for students.

The choice of type of digital twin depends on specific educational objectives and the needs of students, teachers, and administrators. By utilizing these digital twins, educational institutions can enhance the quality and effectiveness of their teaching and learning processes.

B.5 Applications of Digital Twins in Education

Digital twins have found various applications in the field of education. Here are some of the uses of digital twins within an educational context (Turner, 2023; Meenakumari, 2021):

- ***Virtual Classrooms:*** Digital twins allow for the creation of virtual classroom environments, giving students the flexibility to access resources, collaborate with their peers, and participate in activities regardless of location.
- ***Virtual Labs:*** Digital twins enable students to engage in laboratory experiences, enabling them to perform experiments and analyze data within a virtual setting. This enhances their learning opportunities.
- ***Personalized Learning:*** Digital twins facilitate personalized learning journeys for students. By utilizing digital twin technology, students can access customized resources that align with their preferences and needs, promoting more efficient progress in their studies.
- ***Assessment and Evaluation:*** Digital twins can help educators assess students' learning progress and track their development.
- ***Gamification:*** Digital twins can incorporate gamification elements into education. Educators can leverage this technology to introduce rewards and challenges that motivate students and create an enjoyable learning experience.

Utilizing digital twins in education has the potential to enhance learning experiences by making them more effective, engaging, and inclusive. It also enables educational institutions to become more data-oriented and better equipped to address each student's needs.

B.6 Best Practices for Developing and Utilizing Digital Twins

Following a set of best practices (shown in Fig. B.1) is essential to effectively implementing digital twins in education. Here are some key guidelines to consider (Turner, 2023):

- ***Identify Clear Objectives:***
  - Clearly define the goals and outcomes you aim to achieve using digital twins.
  - Make sure that digital twins align with your institution's educational strategy.
- ***Involve Educators and Stakeholders:***
  - Collaborate with educators, students, and other stakeholders when designing and implementing initiatives.
  - Seek input from educators who deeply understand students' learning needs and challenges.
- ***Select Appropriate Technology:***
  - Select appropriate hardware and software tools for creating and managing digital twins.
  - Ensure that the technology selected is user-friendly, reliable, and capable of supporting the intended educational applications.
- ***Date Privacy & Security:***
  - Prioritize data security by implementing security measures to protect student and institutional data.
  - Ensure compliance with data protection regulations and policies.

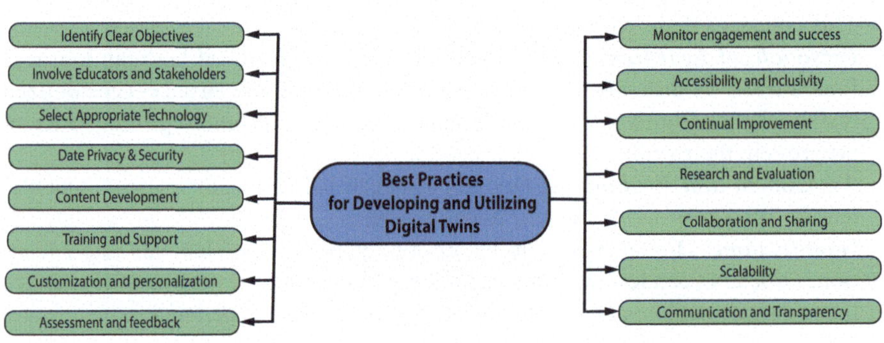

Fig. B.1 Best practices for developing and utilizing digital twins

- ***Content Development:***
  - Develop quality educational content that aligns with curriculum objectives.
  - Ensure the content is interactive, engaging, and suitable for the digital twin environment.
- ***Training and Support:***
  - Provide training and support for educators and students on how to use digital twins.
  - Establish a helpdesk or support resources to address any technical issues promptly.
- ***Customization and personalization:***
  - Utilize the capabilities of digital twins to tailor learning experiences according to each student's needs.
  - Create pathways that allow students to explore their interests within the curriculum.
- ***Assessment and feedback:***
  - Develop tools that assess student progress and performance within the digital twin environment.
  - Gather feedback from educators and students to continuously enhance the digital twin experiences.
- ***Monitor engagement and success:***
  - Implement monitoring and analytics systems that track student engagement and achievements.
  - Utilize data insights to inform decisions and make adjustments in the digital twin environment.
- ***Accessibility and Inclusivity:***
  - Ensure all students, including those with disabilities, can access digital twins.
  - Implement technologies that support diverse learning needs.
- ***Continual Improvement:***
  - Review and update digital twins' content and features to stay up-to-date with the best educational practices and emerging technologies.
  - Embrace innovation and adapt to evolving needs.
- ***Research and Evaluation:***
  - Engage in research to assess how digital twins impact student learning outcomes.
  - Utilize evidence-based insights to refine and optimize the use of digital twins in education.

- ***Collaboration and Sharing:***
  - Promote collaboration among educators to share their practices and lessons learned in utilizing digital twins.
  - Explore partnerships with other educational institutions or organizations to expand the utilization of digital twins in education.
- ***Scalability:***
  - Ensure that digital twin solutions are scalable enough to meet the growing needs of your institution.
  - Consider the long-term sustainability of your technology infrastructure.
- ***Communication and Transparency:***
  - Maintain communication with all stakeholders, informing them about the objectives and progress of your digital twin initiatives.
  - Be transparent about the benefits and potential challenges of adopting digital twins.

By implementing these recommended strategies, educational organizations can leverage the power of digital twins to deliver efficient and tailored learning experiences that benefit both students and educators.

B.7 Digital Twins in Education—Use Cases

The idea of digital twins in education is still relatively new. Some educational institutions have begun experimenting with this technology. Here are a few examples of adopters and potential case studies:

- ***Iowa State University—Virtual Laboratory:*** Iowa State University has developed a virtual chemistry laboratory that enables students to conduct experiments in a digital setting. This initiative proved valuable during COVID-19 when conducting in-person labs was not feasible. The virtual laboratory employs technology to simulate chemical reactions, offering students a safe and effective way to gain hands-on experience.
- ***University of Texas at Austin—Virtual Reality Learning:*** The University of Texas at Austin has been exploring the integration of digital twins and virtual reality (VR) within education. They have created VR environments for subjects such as physics and astronomy. Students can explore celestial bodies and engage with complex scientific concepts through interactive and captivating experiences.
- ***University of Maryland—Augmented Reality Campus Tours:*** The University of Maryland has developed an augmented reality (AR) application that provides campus experiences akin to digital twins. Prospective students can take tours using the app, which overlays information and interactive elements onto the

environment through AR technology. This enhances campus exploration, creating an experience for prospective students.

- ***Microsoft's HoloLens in Education:*** Microsoft's HoloLens mixed reality headset has found its way into education, where it is utilized to create digital twins and holographic experiences. For instance, medical schools have adopted the HoloLens to display 3D anatomical models for students' study purposes. This technology offers an interactive approach to learning subjects.
- ***Swansea University College of Engineering, United Kingdom:*** This institution has harnessed digital twins' power to enhance its students' learning experience in engineering disciplines. It has created virtual replicas of laboratory equipment, allowing students to conduct experiments in a digital environment. These digital twins enable students to practice and refine their skills before working with equipment, resulting in improved safety measures and cost reductions. Moreover, these virtual laboratories can be accessed remotely, enabling distance learning and providing flexibility for students.
- ***The University of Washington's Virtual Planetary Laboratory in the USA:*** The VPL has leveraged digital twins to create captivating and interactive learning experiences for astronomy and planetary science students. They have developed 3D models of planets and celestial bodies that can be explored using virtual reality (VR) and augmented reality (AR) environments. Students can interact with these digital twins, gaining knowledge about geology, atmospheres, etc.
- ***Harvard University—Virtual Labs:*** Harvard School of Engineering and Applied Sciences (SEAS) has been actively developing virtual labs using digital twin technology. These virtual labs aim to provide students with hands-on experiences in science and engineering when they cannot physically be present in a lab. This innovative approach addresses the challenges of learning in STEM fields.
- ***Online Learning Platforms with Adaptive Elements:*** Prominent online learning platforms like Khan Academy and Coursera incorporate learning elements that can be seen as digital twins. By collecting data on student progress, these platforms personalize the learning experience based on performance, resembling how a digital twin customizes the user's journey.
- ***Virtual Field Trips—Various Institutions:*** Several educational organizations are exploring using digital twins to create virtual field trips. These initiatives allow students to visit sites, museums, and other inaccessible locations virtually. The recent COVID-19 pandemic has accelerated the adoption of virtual experiences.
- ***VR Language Learning Platforms:*** Multiple companies and institutions have developed language learning platforms that leverage digital twin technology to create virtual environments for language acquisition. These platforms allow students to practice real-life conversations and cultural interactions in virtual environments.
- ***Simulations in Medical Education:*** Medical schools and institutions use digital twins to create realistic simulations for medical students. These simulations enable students to practice procedures, diagnose patients, and perform surgeries within a controlled digital space.

- ***EdTech Companies and Startups:*** EdTech companies and startups are exploring the potential of digital twin technology to enhance personalized learning experiences. Although specific case studies are not mentioned, these companies are developing platforms that utilize digital twins to customize content, pacing, and support according to each student's needs.

The implementation of digital twins in education is gaining traction, with pioneering institutions and organizations leading the way in harnessing this technology's potential to revolutionize teaching and learning. These early adopters have explored applications, including virtual laboratories, immersive experiences, personalized learning platforms, and augmented reality campus tours. These initiatives showcase the adaptability and versatility of digital twins in meeting the evolving demands of education.

As digital twins advance and find application in education, the possibilities for engaging and effective learning experiences expand. The increasing momentum we are witnessing highlights the significant impact of digital twins in education. It brings forth a future where personalized learning, skills development, and immersive exploration become more accessible and captivating than ever before.

B.8 Building a Digital Twin Virtual Reality Campus for Students—A High-Level Procedure

Developing a Virtual Reality Campus as a digital twin for students is a multifaceted endeavor that involves technical, logistical, and educational considerations. Below is an outline to help guide the creation of such a campus;

- ***Establishing Goals and Meeting Stakeholder Requirements:***
  - Identify the objectives that the virtual campus aims to achieve.
  - Gather insights from students, educators, administrators, and other stakeholders to understand their needs and expectations.
- ***Building Technical Infrastructure:***
  - Obtain or develop the virtual reality (VR) hardware and software infrastructure.
  - Select VR headsets, motion-tracking devices, and interactive tools.
  - Configure servers and cloud resources to host the virtual campus effectively.
- ***Creating the Digital Twin:***
  - Capture every detail, including buildings, classrooms, and landscaping, to generate a digital twin of the physical campus.
  - Utilize 3D modeling software, photogrammetry techniques, or laser scanning to ensure precision in creating this representation.
  - Incorporate interactive elements, like textures and animations.

- ***Designing the VR Environment:***
  - Conceptualize and develop a virtual reality environment where students can navigate effortlessly.
  - Create 3D models of classrooms, labs, libraries, and other campus facilities.
  - Incorporate interactive elements like whiteboards, desks, and equipment into the environment.
- ***Content Development:***
  - Develop materials that align with the curriculum and the digital twin of the campus.
  - Produce lectures, simulations, and virtual experiments for laboratory sessions.
  - Make sure that the content is engaging, interactive, and educational.
- ***User Interface (UI) and User Experience (UX):***
  - Design a user interface for students to navigate through the campus quickly.
  - Prioritize an experience where students can access resources effortlessly and interact with their peers seamlessly.
- ***Accessibility and Inclusivity:***
  - Ensure that the virtual campus caters to all students' needs, including those with disabilities or special requirements.
  - Implement technologies and customization options to accommodate learning needs effectively.
- ***Integration of Educational Tools***
  - Integrate tools and platforms that enhance the campus's functionality, such as Learning Management Systems (LMS) or collaboration software.
  - Guarantee connectivity for both students and educators.
- ***Testing and Quality Assurance:***
  - Thoroughly test the system to identify and fix any issues, bugs, or problems with usability.
  - Engage students and educators in testing to gather their feedback. Make necessary improvements.
- ***Educator Training:***
  - Provide training for educators on how to utilize the virtual campus.
  - Familiarize them with the tool's content delivery methods and navigate the virtual environment.
- ***Student Orientation:***
  - Conduct orientation sessions for students to help them get acquainted with the campus.
  - Offer guidance on using VR equipment and navigating through the environment.

- ***Data Privacy and Security:***
  - Implement measures to ensure data privacy and security, safeguarding student and institutional information.
  - Comply with regulations and policies regarding data protection.
- ***Support and Helpdesk:***
  - Establish a support system and helpdesk to address issues, assisting students and educators.
  - Offer resources such as troubleshooting guides and FAQs for access.
- ***Continuous Improvement:***
  - Regularly update the digital twin, VR environment, and educational content provided.
  - Gather feedback from users to make improvements.
- ***Evaluation and Assessment:***
  - Assess the influence of the campus on learning outcomes and student engagement.
  - Utilize data insights continuously. Optimize the campus.
- ***Scale and Expand:*** Strategize for the campus's scalability and expansion to accommodate a growing student population.
- ***Research and Innovation:*** Engage in research to discover ways of leveraging the potential of the virtual campus for innovative educational experiences.

Creating a Digital Twin Virtual Reality Campus necessitates collaboration between educational specialists, VR developers, and IT professionals. This guide outlines the stages of constructing a virtual campus that provides students with an immersive, captivating, and impactful educational environment.

B.9 How IoT Enables Digital Twins to Enhance Learning?

The combination of the Internet of Things (IoT) and digital twins has the potential to enhance learning experiences greatly. Here is how IoT supports digital twins in improving learning. Figure B.2 exemplifies the transformative impact of IoT-driven digital twins, illustrating their revolutionary role in reshaping the learning landscape.

- ***Integrating Real-World Data:*** IoT devices can gather real-time data from objects and settings such as temperature, humidity, and movement. This data is integrated into the digital twin, accurately representing the physical world. Students can interact with this real-world data in an environment that enriches their understanding of concepts.
- ***Practical Learning Simulations:*** IoT-enabled digital twins enable the creation of simulations for practical learning. For instance, in a science class, students can

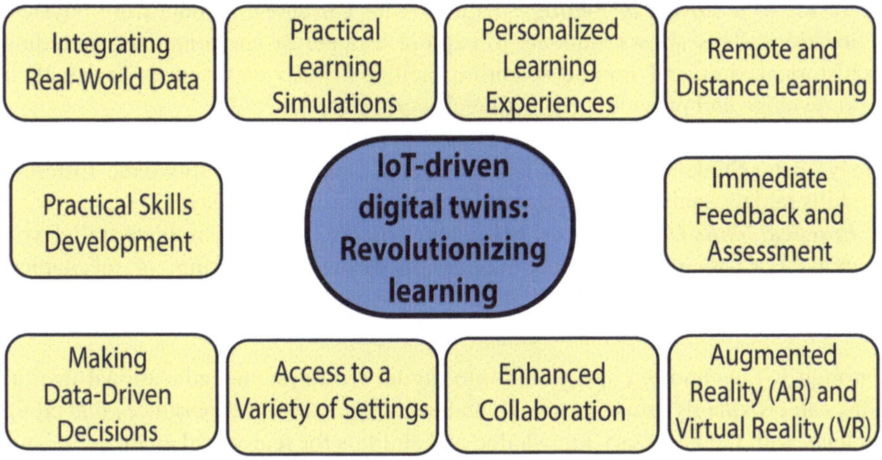

Fig. B.2 IoT-driven digital twins: revolutionizing learning

engage with a digital twin of a laboratory that replicates actual equipment and experiments. This allows students to practice and experiment without necessitating facilities, increasing accessibility and safety.

- ***Personalized Learning Experiences:*** IoT sensors can collect data on students' interactions with their digital twins. Machine learning algorithms analyze this data to customize the learning experience according to each student's pace and preferences. These combined technologies can transform education by providing opportunities for hands-on learning, personalized instruction, and access to real-world scenarios within safe virtual environments. The digital twin concept enables a personalized learning experience for students, offering tailored content and challenges to keep them engaged and motivated.
- ***Remote and Distance Learning:*** IoT-enabled digital twins play a crucial role in distance learning by providing access to practical experiences regardless of location. Students can interact with laboratory equipment remotely, conduct experiments, and collaborate with their peers, overcoming geographical limitations.
- ***Immediate Feedback and Assessment:*** One significant advantage is the feedback and assessment of IoT sensors within the digital twin environment. Students receive assessments on their actions and performance, allowing them to promptly correct mistakes and learn from their experiences.
- ***Augmented Reality (AR) and Virtual Reality (VR):*** Integrating augmented reality (AR) and virtual reality (VR) into digital Twins takes student experiences to different levels. For instance, in geology studies, students can explore a representation of a mountain while receiving real-time weather data or seismic information. This enhances their comprehensive understanding of geological processes.
- ***Enhanced Collaboration:*** IoT-enabled digital twins foster enhanced student collaboration. They can connect through digital twin environments to work on projects, experiments, or problem-solving exercises in various locations.

- ***Access to a Variety of Settings:*** Digital twins can integrate data from physical locations. This allows students to explore a range of environments, including historical sites and remote scientific facilities. Such experiences enrich their knowledge and provide them with real-world experiences.
- ***Making Data-Driven Decisions:*** Digital twins with IoT sensors generate extensive data. Students can learn how to analyze and interpret this data, fostering skills in data analytics, which are increasingly necessary today.
- ***Practical Skills Development:*** IoT-enabled digital twins can simulate skill development across various fields, such as medicine, engineering, or mechanics. Students can refine their skills in an environment without any associated risks, enhancing their competency levels.

Through IoT technology integrated into digital twin systems, educational institutions can provide dynamic, practical, and engaging learning experiences that equip students with the necessary knowledge and abilities for real-world challenges. This amalgamation holds the potential for transforming education, offering students learning environments tailored to their needs while incorporating rich datasets for enhanced understanding.

B.10 IoT Enables Digital Twins to Enhance Learning Experience at Monash University—Case Study

Monash University values providing students with opportunities to engage with emerging technologies increasingly prevalent in various industries. These technologies include simulation, digital twins, the Internet of Things (IoT), and Augmented reality (AR) (Monash University, 2023).

Enhancing Learning Experiences for Students

During the planning phase of the Monash Engineering Student Pilot Plant, faculty members at Monash University recognized an opportunity to incorporate PTC Industry 4.0 technology. The goal was to create an accessible learning experience for students enrolled in the Bachelor and Master of Engineering programs. This initiative aims to expose students to the operations of an industrial process, specifically focusing on water treatment.

The pilot plant will integrate Internet of Things (IoT) devices, an augmented reality (AR) component, and a digital twin into its infrastructure. These technologies will demonstrate their potential to expand user accessibility, improve existing processes, enhance operator training, and enable comprehensive process optimization planning.

The Monash Engineering Student Pilot Plant and its associated Industry 4.0 technologies aim to replicate world scenarios and effectively meet industry requirements. For example, a digital twin can increase production capacity without expanding a facility's footprint, thus improving cost efficiency. Moreover, digital twins play a role in education and training by allowing access to simulating processes and facilitating scenario-based learning activities.

Addressing Challenges with Technology Water treatment is an aspect of various industries involved in manufacturing processes. Monash University has selected water treatment as the point of their Student Pilot Plant because it is relevant to the industry. As a result, students who engage with the pilot plant during their studies will gain experience that they can directly apply to their careers.

Another obstacle arises from using equipment in university laboratories, which often face limitations regarding scale, remote accessibility for students, and simultaneous student accommodation. Incorporating digitalization technologies like remote access, simulation, and digital twins is essential to overcome these constraints and ensure a learning experience for all students.

The Student Pilot Plant also provides an avenue for advancements in industrial water treatment processes. Real-time optimization of water treatment processes is rare due to factors like profit margins or designs aimed at waste treatment to meet disposal and regulatory standards.

The adoption and integration of Industry 4.0 and digitalization technologies in water treatment have been limited. Although traditional water treatment plants already have SCADA/DCS systems for automated control and remote access, these systems mainly focus on regulatory control and heavily rely on operators' input and expertise.

Highlighting a Digital Twin Solution Digital twin technology application is anticipated to bring various prospects in education, training, and overall process enhancement. These possibilities encompass tasks such as streamlining optimization processes and lessening the need for operator expertise and specialized knowledge in decision-making.

The Monash Student Pilot Plant will be an example of implementing this digital twin technology. It will act as a tool for students and industry professionals, demonstrating process automation and operation while utilizing the digital twin to provide a working example for educational, instructional, and research purposes within the university. Moreover, it will showcase the practicality of a digital twin to potential industry partners in various processes and industries beyond just water treatment.

Data from IoT devices installed on the pilot plant, such as control valves and flow meters, will be transmitted to the digital twin for analysis and interpretation using AI and machine learning.

This analysis will provide insights from data, allowing for real-time process optimization. Furthermore, it will expand the possibilities of using data in simulations, enabling case studies and providing an understanding of intricate procedures.

The New Solution Dramatically Enhances the Learning Experience for Hundreds of Students Every Week For the university, this digital innovation can potentially remove limitations associated with laboratory equipment used in education. Integrating digital twins that combine IoT and augmented reality (AR) can significantly enrich the learning journey for several students every week. This bypasses the constraints imposed by physical resources. Additionally, it is expected to provide a user experience for student engineers replicating how they would engage with industrial processes through control systems and process simulations—for online or offline training, design, or optimization purposes.

B.11 Conclusion

Digital twins and IoT in education signal a paradigm shift in teaching methods, providing unique chances for tailored, immersive, and data-centric learning experiences. As schools adopt changes, the impact of digital twins on teaching and learning processes is becoming more evident. Through personalized learning spaces, virtual labs, and customized curricula, digital twins empower students to interact with educational material meaningfully. Moreover, the Monash University case study showcases how digital twins and IoT can enhance learning experiences in various educational settings. The Monash Engineering Student Pilot Plant demonstrates how Industry 4.0 technologies can simulate industrial processes, improve operations, and offer hands-on learning opportunities for students. As educational institutions maneuver through the challenges of digital transformation, it is crucial to focus on engaging stakeholders, developing infrastructure, creating content, ensuring accessibility, and continuously improving. Schools can fully harness these tools by adopting practices and utilizing digital twins and IoT technologies to encourage student innovation, collaboration, and skill development. In summary, digital twins and IoT-powered technologies could transform the field of education, enhancing accessibility, engagement, and effectiveness for both students and teachers. Embracing these advancements and promoting an environment of creativity can equip students to triumph in a rapidly growing digital world.

References

Happiest Minds. (2017). *Digital twins*. Happiest Minds. https://www.happiestminds.com/insights/digital-twins/

IBM. (2023). *What is a digital twin?* IBM. https://www.ibm.com/topics/what-is-a-digital-twin

McKinsey & Company. (2023). *What is digital-twin technology?* McKinsey & Company. https://www.mckinsey.com/featured-insights/mckinsey-explainers/what-is-digital-twin-technology#/

Meenakumari. (2021). Digital Twins in education – An insight. *Times of India*, 25–28. https://timesofindia.indiatimes.com/readersblog/education-insights/digital-twins-in-education-an-insight-38045/

Monash University. (2023). *IoT is enabling digital twins to enhance learning experience at Monash University*. https://www.ptc.com/en/case-studies/monash-university

Rudra, S. (2022). *What are digital twins and how can higher Ed use them?* EdTech. https://edtech-magazine.com/higher/article/2022/03/what-are-digital-twins-and-how-can-higher-ed-use-them

Shivashish. (2023). *Exploring the future of learning: How digital twins are revolutionizing education*. Muvi. https://www.muvi.com/blogs/digital-twins-education/

Tao, Z., & Xu, G. (2022). Digital twin technology in the field of education — Take the management of the HTC vive as an example. In *International Conference on Smart Learning Environments* (pp. 1–11).

Telefónica. (2023). *Digital twins: What are them and what do they consist of?* Telefónica. https://www.telefonica.com/en/communication-room/news/digital-twins-what-are-them-and-what-do-they-consist-of/

Turner, C. (2023). *Unleashing the potential of digital twins in education – A revolution in learning*. LinkedIn. https://www.linkedin.com/pulse/unleashing-potential-digital-twins-education-learning-turner/

Yogesh, C. (2023). *Digital twins in higher education: Revolutionizing experiential learning*. LinkedIn2. https://www.linkedin.com/pulse/digital-twins-higher-education-revolutionizing-learning-chauhan/

Index

M. Kurni, Srinivasa K.G., *The Internet of Educational Things*,
https://doi.org/10.1007/978-3-031-67387-0

nufacturer's authorised representative in the EU is Springer
istomer Service Centre GmbH, Europaplatz 3, 69115 Heidelberg,
f you have any concerns regarding our products, please
uctSafety@springernature.com

nd by CPI Group (UK) Ltd, Croydon, CR0 4YY
01/10/2026
02225906-0003